SACRED
BRITANNIA

Miranda Aldhouse-Green

SACRED
BRITANNIA

The Gods and Rituals
of Roman Britain

 Thames & Hudson

I dedicate this book to Alison, James and Francis,
and to the spirit of Milson

Frontispiece: Detail of a late Roman silver dish
from Mildenhall, Suffolk, with the face of Oceanus
in the central roundel.

First published in the United Kingdom in 2018
by Thames & Hudson Ltd, 181A High Holborn,
London WC1V 7QX

*Sacred Britannia: The Gods and Rituals of Roman
Britain* © 2018 Thames & Hudson Ltd, London

British Library Cataloguing-in-Publication Data
A catalogue record for this book is available
from the British Library

ISBN 978-0-500-25222-2

Printed and bound in Slovenia by
DZS-Grafik d.o.o.

To find out about all our publications,
please visit **www.thamesandhudson.com**.
There you can subscribe to our e-newsletter,
browse or download our current catalogue,
and buy any titles that are in print.

CONTENTS

Introducing a Sacred Isle

'Most of Britain is marshland…The barbarians usually swim in these swamps
or run along in them, submerged up to the waist. Of course, they are practically
naked and do not mind the mud because they are unfamiliar with the use of
clothing, and they adorn their waists and necks with iron…They also tattoo their
bodies with various patterns and pictures of all sorts of animals. Hence the reason
why they do not wear clothing, so as not to cover the pictures on their bodies.'

HERODIAN[1]

Herodian, a Roman civil servant of Greek origin, wrote his *History* nearly
two hundred years after Britain became part of the Roman Empire, and
so his observations of its inhabitants are unexpected. He presents Britain
as home to people so bizarre and uncouth as to be barely human, in spite
of the civilizing influence of Rome. We can detect in his writing the kind
of deliberate stereotyping of 'the other' that seeps into the discourse of
far-right nationalists who seek to demonize the foreign, the different
and the peripheral today. What truth was there in Herodian's account
of the Britons? He was far from alone in painting Britannia as alien and
beyond. The Augustan poet Horace made several references to 'untouched
Britons' and 'Britons at the end of the world',[2] although his comments
are the more understandable in so far as he was writing before Britain
became a Roman province. Part of Rome's suspicion of Britain derived
from its separation from the European land-mass by Ocean, the great river
perceived by Greeks and Romans as encircling the world, so putting the
island of Britain literally outside human habitation. When first Caesar
and later Claudius made the decision to conquer Britannia, their prestige
was greatly enhanced by their courage in taking their armies to overcome
Ocean and all its sea-monsters in order to bring the Never-Never land of
Britain under Roman rule. *Sacred Britannia* explores the religious character

of the isle in the period between Caesar's expeditions in 55/54 BC and the traditional 'end' of Roman Britain in the early 5th century AD, when the emperor Honorius allegedly sent instructions to the cities of Britain to organize their own defence against barbarian incursions from Germanic tribes, the Roman Empire itself being in crisis owing to persistent threats from the Goths.[3] We shall see how the incoming religious traditions of the invaders collided with local forms of worship, and explore the great diversity of ancient British religious beliefs that flourished against the kaleidoscopic background of mixed cultures and peoples that populated the Roman Empire, including its army and its governance, with all the tensions, anxieties, misrepresentations, hostilities, tolerances and acceptances that drove religion into so many different avenues and directions at the edge of the known world. But in order to be able to open doors into that far-off world of two thousand years ago, it is important sometimes to use modern keys. A persistent thread running through the book is the relevance of attitudes obtaining at that time to modern perceptions of 'us' and 'them', the familiar and the 'other'. In both the ancient and modern worlds, there is a wired-in tendency to distrust and, whether deliberately or not, to misunderstand other cultures, beliefs and ideologies. How different was Herodian from the successful Republican candidate for the 2016 US Presidency, Donald Trump, with his stated intention to build a wall between the US and Mexico? How easy it is to construct a scaffolding of scaremongering stories about those different from ourselves, in order to bolster our sense of identity and indulge our fears of change. Study of the past is fascinating in itself but it can be more than that if we can relate it to the world we currently inhabit; the resonances between past and present can be very loud.

Prongs of evidence

Two pathways, neither of them straight but both narrow, lead modern pilgrims back into the past: those of ancient literature and of archaeology. Both serve to enlighten the traveller, but also to trap the unwary. Iron Age Britons were non-literate, and so left no first-hand testimony about themselves, their sense of identity or how they thought about the material and spirit worlds. So we are forced to rely on the reports of authors from the Greco-Roman world, who wrote about the 'barbarians' to their north with varying degrees of ignorance and spin. Historians, both past and present, can never be wholly objective; they are inevitably products of their own culture and cannot entirely shed that baggage. And, particularly in the 1st centuries BC/AD, when Romans and Britons came head to head in conflict, the texts of those chronicling such events were bound to reflect their Roman bias. However, we must not underestimate the value of ancient literature, despite its flaws, for it populates the past with individuals and reveals far more than it obscures. In terms of religious beliefs, the texts introduce us to the Druids (see Chapter 1) and, occasionally, to named British deities, like the fearsome Andraste, goddess of war and victory, in whose sacred grove in London Boudica made blood sacrifices in AD 60, including the mutilation and skewering of well-born Roman women.[4]

Archaeological evidence, conversely, possesses an objectivity of a kind – material culture itself cannot lie – but it comes with its own set of challenges: principally those of incomplete survival and of interpretation. The discovery of pits full of gold and silver jewelry, like those found at Snettisham, Norfolk, buried in the 70s BC, might be variously explained as hoards interred for safe-keeping at a turbulent time, as the equivalent of the contents of a modern Hatton Garden vault, or as votive offerings to the gods. At the hillfort of Danebury, Hampshire, excavators uncovered several Iron Age roundhouses of 'normal' British Iron Age (the period between c. 750 BC and the Claudian invasion of AD 43) form inside a typical enclosure boundary, but in the centre of the site were unusual square structures. Were they granaries, assembly halls or, perhaps, shrines? How are we to detect religious intent behind such ambiguous remains? Once we enter the world of Roman Britain, things become somewhat clearer. For one thing, the Romans brought epigraphy: writing in stone that helps to reveal the function of structures, including those of a religious nature. Architecture, too, is easier to interpret, because building plans became more clearly specific to function: there is less confusion about whether or not a building was religious in purpose, for there was unequivocal temple-architecture. There is also a great proliferation of material culture in general and, for sacred activity, a new form of common religious expression – that of iconography, which was relatively sparse in the Iron Age. Does this vast change in sacred material culture, triggered by the Roman occupation, represent a chasmic shift in cosmologies and belief-systems, or simply a new way of expressing religious beliefs? In other words, was a new sacral system born in Britain under Rome or were the old, previously 'silent', local cults given a new voice? The Roman occupation of Britannia unquestionably brought with it 'new technologies of worship'[5] in epigraphy and iconography, but how deeply did these new modes of expression affect people's perceptions of the divine?

Julius Caesar's legacy

The hundred years between Caesar's expeditions, the first 'official' Roman activity in the island, and the invasion of the emperor Claudius that resulted in Britain's annexation to the Roman Empire in AD 43 represent a crucial period in Britannia's history, although often overlooked, being

Portrait of Julius Caesar.

considered a time of minimal interaction between Britain and Rome. Despite their brevity, Caesar's two sojourns in the island in 55 and 54 BC had a profound influence over the way the future province reacted to *romanitas* – the set of political and cultural principles that the Romans adhered to; allegiance to an imperial state with a standing army, codified laws and formal political ways of expressing religious devotion, including the worship of lifelike representations of the gods and the construction of temples with a highly formalized architecture – in the time of Claudius and beyond. When Claudius sent his legions to Britain under his general Aulus Plautius, the British tribes of southeast England were already familiar with Rome, partly on account of trade but also because some tribal leaders were turning covetous eyes towards the Empire as a means of enhancing their status at home. (The prevailing 'north–south' divide in modern Britain was as relevant on the cusp of the 1st millennium BC

Map of southern Britain showing
pre-Roman tribal boundaries.

as it is today.) Indeed, Caesar himself may have laid the foundations for these ambitions. He is sometimes credited as a 'king-maker', involved in creating or at least encouraging late Iron Age political hierarchies that resolved themselves, in the decades between his first contact and Claudius's conquest, into polities with firm leadership among such tribes as the Catuvellauni and the Atrebates, whose lands lay respectively north and south of the Thames. One product of these fiefdoms was the desire of some overlords to send their sons to the imperial court at Rome to be educated as Roman gentlemen. John Creighton[6] has argued convincingly for the hostage-practice, well known in other Roman provinces, such as Judaea, as pertinent to late Iron Age Britain. These youths, called *obsides* ('friendly hostages'), returned to Britain having adopted Roman dress and speaking and writing Latin and Greek, with a smattering of knowledge of Roman law and their heads full of the glamour and prosperity of the Roman world. During their stay in the capital, they would have rubbed shoulders not only with native Romans but with other *obsides* from the other side of the empire, places like Egypt, Judaea and the Near East, and inevitably absorbed some of their mores. Archaeology may provide some evidence for the existence of *obsides* in late Iron Age Britain and thus, indirectly, for Caesar's legacy. Sometime in the early/mid-1st century BC, a wealthy family belonging to the tribe of the Atrebates in southeast England acquired some special gold jewelry, perhaps made for a husband and wife, for the ornaments were paired: two necklets of different sizes, two pairs of brooches and two unfinished bracelets (see p. ii). These were not locally made, but the work of Greek goldsmiths. Signs of wear on the jewelry indicate that it was worn for a time before being ritually deposited on a hilltop, chosen for its commanding views and isolated situation, near Winchester in Hampshire. Fanciful, possibly, but could these precious and foreign gold objects have been brought back from abroad by someone who had been at the Roman imperial court and had perhaps commissioned special ornaments from a Greek workshop in Rome?[7] The apparently ritual nature of the jewelry's deposition chimes with synchronous activity in the Atrebatian kingdom, namely the building of a shrine on Hayling Island off the southwest coast of England in the later 1st century BC.[8] The shrine began its life as a rectangular timber hall, later replaced by a substantial circular stone building, within an enclosure. This structure was the focus for votive depositions of personal objects such as brooches and coins, some ritually broken, as if to sever their connection to the world of the living and enable them to be accepted by the spirits. The interpretation of this late Iron Age building as a sanctuary is buttressed by the temple of early Roman date that replaced it, for there is abundant evidence that special places, once sanctified, remained so even where political and religious situations changed. The Roman-period temples to Nodens at Lydney (see pp. 94–96) and to Mercury at Uley (see pp. 192–93), both in Gloucestershire, are cases in point. Lydney had been an Iron Age hillfort, and there is evidence for ritual practices at Uley stretching even as far back as the Bronze Age. It has been suggested that the Hayling Island religious complex was erected to honour a cult of the Atrebatian royal dynasty founded by Caesar's onetime friend Commius, who may well have been one of the kings created by Julius Caesar, the 'king-maker'.[9] Significantly, the architecture of the Roman shrine adhered to the circularity of the earlier building, despite the fact that Roman temples usually followed the Classical rectangular form. Around the time that the Roman temple was built at Hayling Island, in about AD 40, another royal Briton, Togidubnus, was active in religious affairs at Chichester in West Sussex. The origins of Togidubnus's entry onto the British political scene are uncertain. It is even possible that he came from Gaul.[10] Publius Cornelius Tacitus, a Roman senator and historian, referred to Togidubnus as a client-king and lauded his 'unswerving loyalty' to Rome, while at the same time sneering at his subservience, in his account of Publius Ostorius Scapula's governorship of the new province of Britannia. This was a turbulent period, characterized by British resentment of and rebellion against the new regime, and Togidubnus played a major role in keeping the peace. In recognition of his alliance, the emperor made over to him certain tracts of land in southeast England.

We have firm archaeological evidence for Togidubnus's presence in the form of an inscription from Chichester that records this client-king's dedication of a temple to the Roman deities Neptune and Minerva (with

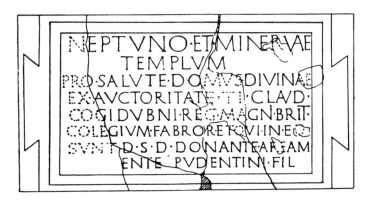

Reproduction of the Chichester inscription,
recording Togidubnus's dedication of a local
temple to Neptune and Minerva.
W. c. 125 cm (49¼ in.).

no mention of local gods). Intriguingly, the inscription reveals that
Tiberius Claudius Togidubnus (note his adoption of Roman imperial
names) styled himself 'Great King of the Britons', perhaps because of his
non-British origins. This title was foreign to the western Roman Empire
but was common in the east, in places like Egypt. Could Togidubnus have
been one of the British *obsides* sent to Rome to learn how to be a Roman
gentleman and, while there, might he have picked up this rather flamboyant and exotic title from his fellow guests? If so, the custom of sending
royal children to the imperial court to be educated survived Caesar for
a hundred years. The Chichester inscription is a testament to the power
of *romanitas* even in the half-fledged province of the mid-1st century AD,
and the personal histories of Britain's *obsides* may have been crucial to
the way that Britain reacted to the new order brought in under Claudius.

The past is a (very) foreign country

The foregoing discussion indicates how tricky it is to try to interpret
what went on in Britain's remote past. All of the types of evidence at our
disposal have strengths and weaknesses; all are capable of producing
various interpretations. Colouring every attempt to understand past lives,

especially those in a pre-literate context, is our own cultural background, which inevitably seasons how we view a two-thousand-year-old world. What I hope to present in the pages that follow is a story that engages modern readers in pursuit of an ancient world, while both acknowledging the problems associated with accessing ancient systems of thought and spiritual belief and facing honestly the tensions between past and present. Roman Britain was a cultural palimpsest in which, under the rule of Rome, what it meant to be British became just as complex and multi-layered as it is today. While the apparent 'direction' of ideological travel in the early post-conquest years was Romanocentric, there is plenty of evidence – much of it associated with belief systems – that displays the two-way traffic of cultural exchange between Britain and Rome.

A curious facet of this has only recently come to light, in excavations of Roman London. Wooden writing tablets discovered between 2010 and 2014 have revealed the conscious re-establishment of British identity by some inhabitants of this prosperous and very Roman port.[11] Some of the inscriptions indicate that people with totally Roman names chose to give their children names of Gallo-British origin. What drove their decision? Could it be something akin to the trend among certain middle-class English and monoglot parents in parts of Wales in the present day who make the deliberate choice to send their offspring to schools that teach entirely in the Welsh language? Perhaps these early Londoners, whether their heritage lay in Britain or in other Roman provinces, chose British names for their children to communicate and consolidate their own connection with Roman Britannia. Similar issues relate to the interplay between imported and indigenous cults; in religious terms, the period immediately before and after the Claudian invasion of AD 43 could be seen through the metaphor of a crucible in which different metals undergo change to form new alloys. To what extent did religion affect, or was affected by, the perceived identity of individuals? *Sacred Britannia* will endeavour to further our understanding of what it meant to be, and to feel, British in Roman Britain.

CHAPTER ONE

The Druids
Priesthood, power and politics

'But, we all owe a debt beyond measure to the Romans
because they destroyed these horrible activities in which
human sacrifice was thought to please the gods, and
eating the victim thought to be good for one's health.'

PLINY THE ELDER[1]

Pliny compiled his monumental *Naturalis Historia* in the 1st century AD.
He collected information from all over the then known world, mining
the writings of hundreds of previous authors, some of his resultant work
factually accurate, but much of it warped by an overactive imagination and
a certain credulousness. In this quotation, the author was referring to the
Druids, the high priests in charge of religion in Gaul and Britain in the
last few centuries BC and still highly influential at the time of the Claudian
invasion of Britannia in AD 43. Pliny was by no means alone in his literary
condemnation of the Druids as savage, barbarous and wildly uncivilized,
but his testimony takes intolerance to a whole new level: Pliny was unable
to resist the temptation to add a further layer of shock and disgust to his
comment about human sacrificial practices, laying the charge of cannibalism at the Druids' door. This has interesting parallels with similar charges
levelled at early Christians, whose Eucharistic rituals were interpreted by
some of their pagan contemporaries as involving the literal consumption
of a person's flesh and blood.[2]

The Druids' arena was Iron Age Britain and Gaul, particularly during
the 1st centuries BC and AD (though there is literary testimony for their
presence in Gaul as late as the 4th century AD), and they are crucially

important to the story of early Roman Britain because they represented an organized, well-educated religious opposition to the imposition of Roman rule on the island, one capable of causing very real problems to the invading army, and the new administration and governance introduced by Rome. The Druids thus played a significant role in the shaping of the new province of Britannia during its first decades. The seismic shift in British society caused by the new order threatened to take away the Druids' power base and, indeed, their *raison d'être*. So, in opposing *romanitas*, they were fighting for their very survival.

Human sacrifice

'The Gauls believe the power of the immortal gods can be appeased only if one human life is exchanged for another, and they have sacrifices of this kind regularly established by the community. Some of them have enormous images made of wickerwork, the limbs of which they fill with living men; these are set on fire and the men perish, enveloped in the flames. They believe that the gods prefer it if the people executed have been caught in the act of theft or armed robbery or some other crime, but when the supply of such victims runs out, they even go to the extent of sacrificing innocent men.' CAESAR[3]

The Romans took the moral high ground when it came to ritual murder, even though such practices only became illegal in Rome as late as 97 BC. Accusations of such barbarous rites as endemic within the Druid-ridden societies of Britain and Gaul could therefore be used as a convenient smoke-screen in order to justify the annihilation of a dangerously nationalistic priesthood. The reality of human sacrifice in late pre-Roman Britain is difficult to evaluate. Some of the human bodies buried in disused grain silos at Danebury, Hampshire, may well have been sacrificial victims. Heads, complete bodies and separated body parts were carefully interred here, and at least some of the skeletons show evidence of having been bound.[4] At Alveston, near Bristol, human remains bearing evidence of violence and dating to the late 1st century BC were found in a sinkhole, and may have been victims of ritual murder.[5] But the bias of foreign texts, coupled

The body of Lindow Man, a young adult male ritually killed and placed
in a peat-bog at Lindow Moss, Cheshire, in the mid-1st century AD.

with the ambiguity of archaeological testimony, presents a stiff challenge
to objective considerations. Of the various possible candidates for such
ritual killings, two Roman-period deaths are especially persuasive: those
of the bog-man from Lindow Moss in Cheshire, who died in the mid-1st
century AD,[6] and a young boy whose defleshed skull shows signs of wear
on the base, indication that it was mounted on a pole and displayed in
front of a shrine at Folly Lane in 2nd-century AD Verulamium. 'Lindow
Man' underwent a complicated and prolonged death that involved at least
three fatal injuries – blows to the head, strangulation and throat-slitting
– before he was pushed head-first, naked, into a remote marsh pool. It is
hard to interpret such a calculated series of acts as having any other than
a ritual purpose. The adolescent boy from the Roman city of Verulamium
– killed by a massive head-injury – may also have been a ritual victim
and, if so, proves that such practices were not entirely stamped out by the
Roman presence. The child's head was carefully stripped of its flesh, using
a thin, sharp-bladed knife, placed on display outside a temple and then
interred in a deep pit together with the body of a puppy and a whetstone,
used for sharpening tools.[7] This burial is itself interesting in as much as
the items accompanying it appear to reinforce both the boy's youth and

the manner of his head's defleshing, with a sharpened knife. Bearing in mind the Classical literary testimony linking the Druids with human sacrifice, it is possible – maybe even likely – that they were involved in these British ritual killings, even though their spheres of influence would have declined sharply following the Roman occupation.

Druids' footprints: material remnants of an ancient priesthood

> 'Hailing the moon in a native word that means "healing all things", the Druids prepare a ritual sacrifice and banquet beneath a tree and bring up two white bulls, whose horns are bound for the first time on this occasion. A priest arrayed in white vestments climbs the tree and with a golden sickle cuts down the mistletoe, which is caught in a white cloak.'
> PLINY THE ELDER[8]

If we believe the testimony of ancient authors such as Caesar and Pliny, the Druids were a hugely dominant force within Britain and Gaul before and during the process of bringing these western regions into the fold of the Roman Empire. If so, such a group might be expected to have left tangible traces of their ritual activities within later Iron Age material culture, even if they were to all intents and purposes emasculated under imperial rule. The reality is that, despite a wealth of archaeological material relating to cult matters, there is virtually nothing that can be linked unequivocally to the Druids. However, there is some persuasive circumstantial evidence both for Druidic presence in Britain and, even more so, in Gaul.

Anglesey: the sacred isle of Mona

> 'The groves devoted to Mona's barbarous superstitions he demolished. For it was the Druids' religion to drench their altars in the blood of prisoners and consult their gods by means of human entrails.' TACITUS[9]

The 'he' mentioned here is Suetonius Paulinus, Roman governor of Britain in AD 60, and the occasion to which Tacitus refers is Paulinus's strategic attack on Anglesey, a remote island off the northwest coast of Wales reputed to be the Druids' holy of holies. No archaeological evidence for such a sanctuary survives, which is not altogether surprising, given that Paulinus's army burned it to ashes. However, there is a site on Anglesey that was clearly of major religious importance during the later Iron Age: Llyn Cerrig Bach.

In 1942, the military airbase at RAF Valley in northwest Anglesey underwent construction work. As part of the operation, a peat-bog was excavated and a large amount of Iron Age metalwork came to light.[10] The material was deliberately deposited by the ancient island inhabitants on a dry islet within the swamp, and included high-status martial equipment, such as swords, spears and parts of shields, and horse-gear and chariot-fittings, including iron nave-hoops for the wheels. Some of the copper-alloy objects were decorated with La Tène designs.[11] These abstract and animal- and plant-based motifs, named after the site on the shore of Lake Neuchâtel in Switzerland where they were first recognized on hundreds of Iron Age metal objects in the late 19th century, are found across Britain and non-Mediterranean Europe dating between c. 500 BC and the early years of the Roman period. Recent research at Anglesey has identified a number of phases of deposition, between the 4th century BC and the early 2nd century AD, suggesting that people visited the site over a long period, perhaps as pilgrims.

The practice of deliberately placing valuable objects in watery places has long been recognized as a sacrificial rite widespread in Bronze Age and Iron Age Britain and Europe.[12] Bogs, pools, lakes and rivers were persistently chosen as foci for sacred activities, offerings often being made to the gods perceived as dwelling therein. Water seems to have been regarded as special, and charged with supernatural energy. The ancient Greek geographer Strabo, writing in the late 1st century BC and early 1st century AD, describes the practice of sinking great masses of gold and silver treasure into sacred lakes. He explains that nobody dared to profane these watery offering-places by trying to steal their contents.[13] At Llyn Cerrig Bach, the first phase of religious expression appears to be represented by animal sacrifice; unfortunately, during excavation only a very few animal bones were collected, and the majority of those thrown

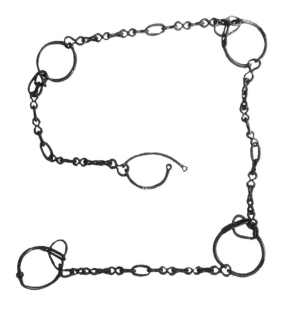

Late Iron Age iron slave-gang chain (top) and bent iron sword from a sacred lake at Llyn Cerrig Bach, Anglesey.

away without proper assessment or recording, but a pony, sheep, cattle and dogs were among the beasts whose remains were found at the site – though sadly no evidence survives as to how they met their deaths.[14] In any case, this practice was later replaced with the destruction and offering of prestigious metal goods.

The site of Llyn Cerrig Bach may have been purposely chosen because of its extreme remoteness from the rest of Britannia: Anglesey is off the northwest coast of Wales, and the sanctuary itself lies on the far north-west of the island. While there can be no direct connection between this rich deposition site and the Druids, it is nonetheless tempting to imagine a link with Tacitus's sacred Druidic grove. Islands may be considered special, 'thin'[15] places, where the divide between the realms of the sacred and the mundane can seem particularly narrow. Such 'thin' places were, and are, repeatedly sought out as loci of spiritual refuge. In about AD 600, the remote island of Skellig Michael 8 miles (13 km) out in the Atlantic on the southwest coast of Ireland, was home to a tiny early Christian monastic community, its drystone circular houses and oratory perched precariously on the precipitous barren rock.[16] I have been fortunate enough to visit Skellig Michael myself, and it is the epitome of both wild isolation and tranquillity. The sea is treacherous and landfall almost impossible unless the ocean is dead calm. Similarly 'thin' places exist today, for example in northern Greece, in the Meteora and Mount Athos, where Greek Orthodox monasteries are suspended in the air on near-vertical cliff faces and rock pinnacles.[17]

Many medieval Celtic myths refer to the Otherworld dwelling places of the spirits as being on islands, like the 'Isle of Apple Trees' described in the early Irish text *The Voyage of Bran*, synonymous with King Arthur's Avalon ('Apple Isle').[18] One of the things about Britain that fascinated the Romans was its separation by the sea, or the great river Ocean, from the 'known' world, a feature that led some even to doubt its very existence. In an emotive text, an unknown author of a festival oration created for a late Roman emperor described Julius Caesar's attitude to Britain when he first visited it in 55 BC: the Roman commander was amazed by its sea-girt remoteness and felt that he had 'found another world'.[19] If Britain itself was regarded an enigma, then Anglesey (and its Druids) must surely have seemed sufficiently off the scale of oddness to be surrounded by mystery and spirituality, a place to draw Roman pilgrims[20] and, at the same time, to be worth Suetonius Paulinus's while to desecrate and destroy.

'Druidic' regalia in Iron Age Britain

The single quotation marks bracketing 'Druidic' are well placed because there is no solid archaeological evidence for the presence of the Druids in Iron Age Britain. Although the material from Llyn Cerrig Bach is persuasive because of the Tacitean link between Anglesey and the Druids, even that association is by no means certain. However, Iron Age British sites have produced some spectacular artefacts associated with cult practices.[21] Among these, headdresses and 'divination' spoons are especially compelling. A headdress, superbly reconstructed by National Museum Wales, comes from a grave at Cerrig-y-Drudion, Denbighshire, in North Wales, dating to the 4th century BC (see pp. ii–iii).[22] Three centuries later at the opposite end of Britannia, a young man died and was given a ceremonial burial with a spectacular array of military equipment in the cemetery at Mill Hill, Deal, in Kent.[23] Two things mark him out as having a possibly sacred role in his community: on his head he wore a decorated bronze diadem, of a kind so far unique to Iron Age Britain and Europe but comparable to ritual crowns discovered at Romano-British temple sites,[24] rather than the helmet we might expect of a military man; and his body was interred not in the main part of the burial-ground but positioned on its outer edge, as if – perhaps – he was considered too charged with spiritual force to be with the other

Pair of bronze 'divination spoons' from
Castell Nadolig, Cardiganshire,
1st century AD. L. *c.* 11 cm (4¼ in.).

bodies, maybe even a shaman.[25] His burial, close to a Bronze Age barrow, may be significant: in putting his body there, were his mourners deliberately referencing the earlier burial, as if it were perceived important to connect him with the past, with a site of earlier reverence and perhaps even seen as close to his ancestors? If the man from Deal was a religious practitioner, his interment with a sword and shield might feasibly be interpreted as a mark of especial respect, somewhat akin to the 'full military honours' accorded some prominent people, not just soldiers, in today's world.

If the Deal man was a shaman working in Britain in the early 1st century BC, one of his principal tasks would have been to divine the will of the gods and the future of his community (see Chapter 6). To help him accomplish this role, the tools of his trade might have included the curious pairs of 'divination spoons' frequently found as grave-goods or ritually deposited in marshes within late Iron Age Britain. The precise function of these objects cannot be known for certain but, interestingly, just such a pair was found in another grave at Deal.[26] In most instances, the inner surface of one spoon was divided into four quadrants by intersecting incised lines, while that of the other spoon had a hole drilled through it. One theory is that the two spoons were placed together so that their flat surfaces were touching, then a liquid or powder blown through the hole. 'Reading' the resultant scatter of deposit on the quadrant-marked spoon could have been used to determine whether the omens were good or bad.[27]

Pride and prejudice: the chroniclers of British Druidism

'The system of divination is not even neglected among barbaric peoples, since in fact there are Druids in Gaul; I myself knew one of them, Divitiacus of the Aedui, your guest and eulogist, who declared that he was acquainted with the system of nature which the Greeks call natural philosophy and which he used to predict the future by both augury and inference.' CICERO[28]

In order to put the flesh on the bones of ancient Druids, we must turn to the (biased) reporting of their Roman contemporaries. There could hardly have been a more dyed-in-the-wool Roman than the urbane, sophisticated and well-connected Marcus Tullius Cicero, a prolific author, philosopher, politician, lawyer and orator. The above quote comes from a letter he wrote to his brother Quintus, a soldier, while hosting the Gallic Druid Divitiacus. The meeting with the Gallic Druid to which he refers took place in 60 BC, when Divitiacus visited Rome in order to petition the Senate for military aid in the repulsion of the German leader Ariovistus, who was threatening to invade Aeduan territory in Burgundy.[29] Cicero's description of this Druid is both admiring and patronizing: it betrays surprise and grudging respect for a 'barbarian'. Contrary to Cicero's expectations, the foreign religious leader had shown talent in a field deeply significant to Roman religious custom, namely the ability to predict the future by contact with the spirit world, which was possible only if the correct ritual practices were observed; maybe Divitiacus used equipment like the divination spoons found at Deal.

Julius Caesar was a contemporary of Cicero's, but far more familiar with contemporary Gaul, having served nearly ten years there as conqueror and governor. Quintus Cicero served under him and had probably written about him to his brother. Caesar himself appears to have had few prejudices against the Druids, despite their potential for undermining his authority and fomenting rebellion. Indeed, he wrote of them at some length in Book Six of the eight-volume *Commentarii de Bello Gallico*, describing their far-reaching influence in the fields of religion, politics, teaching and judicial matters.[30] Caesar and Divitiacus were allies, and even friends; Divitiacus was loyal to the Roman general, supporting his campaigns and keeping his army supplied with grain. However, the Aedui were split into pro- and anti-Roman factions, the former led by Divitiacus and the latter by his fervently nationalistic brother Dumnorix. The brothers shared political leadership of their divided tribe, and they seem also to have shared religious duties, for although Dumnorix's role as a priest (or Druid) is never explicitly stated by Caesar, it is implied by the freedom-fighter's reluctance to accompany Caesar to Britain for the general's second expedition to Britain in 54 BC. Dumnorix is quoted by Caesar as having produced two excuses for not wishing to travel away from Gaul: that he was frightened of sailing the ocean and that 'religious considerations prevented him'.[31] What Dumnorix failed to mention was his anti-Roman fervour, which made him too dangerous for Caesar to leave behind in Gaul while absent in Britain.

Island of magic: changing Roman attitudes

'Even today Britain is still spell-bound by magic, and performs its rites with so much ritual that she might almost seem to be the source of Persian ritual.' PLINY THE ELDER[32]

If high-profile Romans like Caesar and Cicero had respect for the Druids in the mid-1st century BC, opinion shifted sharply in the next century, when Pliny the Elder specifically records the desires of early Roman emperors to eradicate them. Caesar made a direct association between the Druids and Britannia, commenting that 'it is thought that the doctrine of the Druids was invented in Britain'.[33] A hundred years later, Pliny the Elder said precisely the opposite, claiming that Druidism spread from Gaul to Britain. In language charged with high drama, he wrote, 'why should I call to mind these matters of a profession which has now crossed the ocean and betaken itself to the void [Britannia] beyond our world?'[34] This comment is significant, for what Pliny was doing, in a sense, was equating the Druids and the Britons as (literally) beyond the pale of civilization. He compounds his diatribe against the Druids with his assertions that they practised human sacrifice and cannibalism.[35]

Attitudes demonstrated by other authors broadly contemporary with Pliny, such as Lucan and Tacitus, betray similar prejudices levelled at a priesthood and an island each inspiring Roman fear and hostility in equal measure. Lucan's tone is very similar to Pliny's, commenting darkly on the Druids' return to their 'barbarous rites' and 'wicked religion' when the opportunity arose, as the Roman focus was distracted by the civil war between Caesar and Pompey.[36] Although Lucan does not dwell specifically on the association between the Druids and human sacrifice in this particular passage, earlier in the same piece he does speak generically about ritual murder as practised by 'those Gauls who propitiate with human sacrifice the merciless gods Teutas, Esus and Taranis…'.[37] And it is difficult not to believe that by his phrase 'their wicked religion', he was referring to the sacrifice of human victims, for it is hard to imagine what else would have caused him such shock and revulsion.

Family factions in the face of Rome

Political splits, such as that between the two brothers of the Aeduans' ruling family, were by no means confined to Gallic political systems during the 1st centuries BC/AD. At least two British tribes are recorded by Roman authors as suffering similar divisions in broadly contemporary circumstances: the Iceni of East Anglia and the northern Brigantes. Both involved not siblings, but spouses. The more well documented of the two, recorded by Tacitus, occurred in the north, where queen Cartimandua was the reigning monarch. She was a Roman ally, a client-queen, while her husband and consort Venutius was fervently anti-Roman. History has frowned upon Cartimandua for her betrayal to Rome of the British freedom-fighter, Caratacus, after he had fled from his homeland in eastern England to her realm for refuge in AD 51.[38] As for Venutius, he had personal reasons to dislike his wife, beyond their political differences; he was understandably bitter as she had indulged in an adulterous liaison with his armour-bearer, Vellocatus,[39] thereby not only cuckolding him but dishonouring his family.

Although the documentary evidence concerning the Iceni is less clear, reading between the lines it is possible to infer that similar splits occurred along the marital fault-lines between the rulers Prasutagus and Boudica. Prasutagus was, like queen Cartimandua, a client-monarch and when he died he left his fortune and his lands jointly to his daughters and to the emperor Nero. One of the issues that incited his widow Boudica to lead the Britons into a calamitous rebellion against Rome was the brutal seizure of Prasutagus's assets by Decianus Catus, the Roman procurator (finance minister) assigned to Britain, which – according to Tacitus[40] –

included the raping of the Icenian princesses by Roman soldiers and the public flogging of Boudica herself. But why did Boudica's protest against Catus's action provoke such a ferocious response? It seems as if there must have been 'history' to Boudica's relationship with Rome and that, despite Prasutagus's pro-Roman ally status, she had a reputation for being a British agitator.

So how did these inter-family factions come about? This issue is a key factor in our understanding of British attitudes to the Roman presence. The answer, in part at least, lies in the relationship between Britain and Rome in the century prior to the Claudian invasion of AD 43. This was a time when the noble families, particularly in southeast England, were coming more and more into contact with the Roman world, particularly with respect to trade. But more significantly, certain British ruling families took the decision that *romanitas* was the future, so they sent their sons (and maybe daughters too) to Rome to be educated (see pp. 11–13). One of these, almost certainly, was the client-monarch Togidubnus, upon whom the Roman government bestowed large tracts of land in southeast England, in gratitude for his pro-Roman stance in the early years around the time of the Claudian invasion.[41]

When lordlings, such as Cartimandua and Togidubnus, returned to Britain after their sojourn in Rome, some of them might well have thrown their weight about, lording it over their fellows and scorning their parochial ways, breathing seditious allegiances to their foreign hosts and attempting to overthrow local traditions. No wonder, then, that factions thrived among these divided families. It is almost irresistible to make comparisons between this situation in ancient Britain, on the cusp of its engulfment into the huge maw of the Roman Empire, and the current divisions in Britain between the advocates of Brexit, fearful of the cosmopolitan influence of the European continent over 'traditional' British culture, and pro-European unionists following the historic national referendum that took Great Britain out of the European Union. In Britannia in the 1st centuries BC and AD, such schisms would have wrought profound changes to local attitudes towards politics, nationalism and, of course, religion.

CHAPTER ONE

Druids in the Roman Empire: disintegration or survival?

'There came a time when the emperor Aurelian, anxious to ascertain whether his lineage would continue to wear the purple after his death, sought to consult the female Druids residing in Gaul. They responded by saying that it would be Augustus's line, not Aurelian's that would be the most renowned in the Empire.' SCRIPTORES HISTORIAE AUGUSTAE[42]

Aurelian, commander of the elite Dacian cavalry, assumed the purple (that is, became emperor) in AD 270. He was a Dacian, from Transylvania, and he was put on the imperial throne by the army after the military deposition of his predecessor Gallienus. What are we to make of this writer's account of Druidic predictions of the new emperor's accession? The dubious nature of these late Roman texts, also known as the *Augustan Histories*, has long been appreciated by Classical scholars, one of whom scathingly referred to them as 'generally damned and generally used'.[43] Despite major problems and controversy surrounding their authorship, these documents cannot be completely discounted as literary evidence for the late Empire. A striking feature of the passage quoted here is that it is one of several prophecies within the *Histories* involving emperors-in-waiting and female Gallic Druids.[44] Behind the stories, we can glean that for each of these would-be-rulers the certainty of succession was bolstered by the prognostications of even the most obscure provincial religious leaders who upheld their Druidic traditions. If these tales tell us nothing more, at least they suggest that, far from being forgotten, the Druids remained within the Roman consciousness at the highest levels. The *Histories* are the only known ancient texts unequivocally to mention female Druids. The nearest equivalence comes from Tacitus two centuries earlier, in whose narrative of Paulinus's destruction of the Druidic stronghold on Anglesey mention is made of 'black-robed women with dishevelled hair like Furies, brandishing torches',[45] who stood alongside the Druids themselves on the shore to confront the Roman army.

The Chartres 'magician': shaman or charlatan?

The (albeit unreliable) testimony of the *Augustan Histories* challenges the claims of authors such as Pliny[46] and Suetonius, the gossipy biographer of 'the twelve Caesars', that the emperor Claudius wiped out the Druids completely.[47] But there is some eccentric and tenuous – but nonetheless plausible – archaeological evidence for Druidic survival (or even reinvention) in Roman Gaul, at Chartres, Roman Autricum, originally the capital of the Iron Age Carnutes tribe in northern France. On 20 July 2005, construction workers excavating the site for a car park in the centre of Chartres stumbled upon a small underground shrine beneath the burned-out ruins of a Roman house. The little sanctuary had been protected and preserved for two thousand years by the collapsed dwelling and, when the house was occupied, worshippers would have gained access to the basement-shrine by means of a wooden ladder, placed atop a short flight of stone steps. Safely concealed under the stairs was a cache of sacred material, including pottery vessels, oil-lamps and a broad-bladed knife, of the kind used in killing sacrificial animals.[48]

Why is the discovery of the Chartres shrine relevant to Druidic survival into Roman imperial times? The answer lies in the deposition there of at least three large inscribed pottery incense-burners (*thuribula*). Only one of the vessels survived intact but it was covered with four panels of cursive writing, scratched onto the outer surface of the censer with a pointed instrument, probably a *stylus*, when the clay was hard but before firing. Each block of script begins with the name of one of the cardinal points: *oriens* (East), *meridie* (South), *occidens* (West) and *septentrio* (North). Beneath each of these directional headings is a prayer to the 'all-powerful spirits', from one Caius Verius Sedatus, who states that he was their guardian, followed by a long list naming these spirits. It is these lists that point to a direct link between this shrine and the Druids, for one of the names appears to be 'Dru'. We should be cautious in assuming that this name explicitly designates a Druid, or even refers to Druidism at all, because 'dru' is a Gallic root-word meaning 'wise' and therefore with much broader potential applications; but these are the only surviving inscrip-

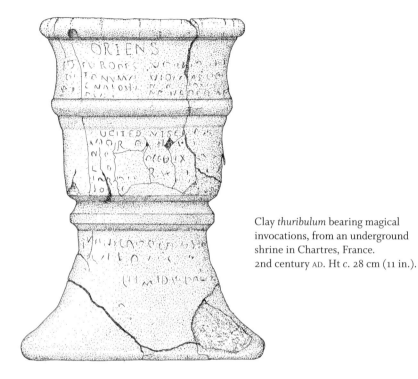

Clay *thuribulum* bearing magical invocations, from an underground shrine in Chartres, France. 2nd century AD. Ht *c.* 28 cm (11 in.).

tions that actually mention a word etymologically linked to the Druids. In support of a Druidic presence here in Roman Chartres, we should recall Julius Caesar's comment concerning an annual pan-Druidic assembly in a 'consecrated place' in the land of the Carnutes.[49]

Several issues arise from the messages on the Chartres incense-burners. Not least is the change of status for the Druids implied by the inscriptions, for here, the Druids are included as named spirits, while in the ancient literature they are unequivocally presented as religious leaders, not gods. Another challenge is to explain the calling up of Druidic spirits by a Gallo-Roman gentleman living in a Roman city in the 2nd century AD. Caius Verius Sedatus's three names (a *praenomen, nomen* and *cognomen* – together the *trianomina*) mark him out as a Roman citizen, so he may well have been a town councillor, eminently respectable and expected to toe the Roman party line rather than spend his time conjuring up obscure old Gallic deities. But herein may lie the secrecy, and fear of discovery, implied by the hidden sanctuary. Could it be that Sedatus (incidentally a name of Gallic origin) was a Roman official during the day but moonlighted in his leisure hours by donning the identity of a magician in his basement? If the word 'dru' in the inscriptions genuinely refers to Druids, Sedatus may not have been preserving an ancient tradition, but constructing it anew.

It is crucial to view the sacred inscriptions within both a micro and macro context. For the first, it is important to consider the *thuribula* not simply as vehicles to convey written messages to the gods but also as vessels for burning 'incense', whatever that comprised. Andrew Sherratt has made a convincing argument for 'narcotic archaeology', based on his observations of ceramic vessels probably made as 'aromatic burners' and of the presence of mind-bending substances such as *Cannabis sativa* and opium poppy seeds in prehistoric European contexts.[50] Cannabis was identified in the grave-goods accompanying the Hallstatt chieftain buried in his splendid, gold-rich tomb at Hochdorf in Germany in the late 6th century BC;[51] excavations at an early Romano-British site at Frensham in southeast England produced a series of deliberately deposited minia-ture votive pots, some containing cannabis residues;[52] and buried in the broadly coeval 'Doctor's Grave' at Stanway, Colchester (see pp. 119–23) was a copper-alloy vessel in whose spout remains of the hallucinogen *Artemisia* survived.[53] Mind-altering drugs were evidently far from unknown at the time that Sedatus was performing secret rituals in his dark cellar at Chartres. It is tempting to imagine the fragrant, psychotropic smoke emanating from the censers as thought by the celebrants here to represent the spirits arising in response to Sedatus's summons, particularly if they were high on the fumes. But what is more, some of the material in the cellar chimes with Greco-Egyptian cult ritual practices, including the use of cryptic magical spells, and, if that is correct, it may help to explain Sedatus's reference to 'Dru' as one of the *omnipotentia numina* rather than as earthly religious leaders. As a Roman citizen living in central Gaul in the 2nd century AD, two hundred years after the Caesarean conquest, he may well have been ignorant of the Druids' original role within Gallic society, and have cobbled together a mish-mash of esoteric-sounding rituals from different parts of the Empire in order to impress his followers, without much clue as to what he was doing. But why was Sedatus engaged in such clandestine religious activities? In presenting an alternative and arcane cosmology deep in the Roman city of Autricum, what was he trying to achieve? Was it simply a power trip or commercial venture, designed to impress gullible seekers after something spiritually new and engaging? Or was Sedatus a self-styled 'shaman', one of a number who, like 20th-century Russian and Siberian shamans living under Soviet rule, were potent foci of old traditions and religious freedom? Caius Verius Sedatus may have been a Roman citizen, but he was also a Gaul: so much is indicated by his Gallic *cognomen*.

The real significance of the Chartres inscriptions is the inclusion of the term 'dru' in the inscribed list of spirits' names on the three incense-burners in the basement sanctuary. If the term does refers to the Druids, their mention here indicates the retention of the 'idea' of this Gallo-British priestly class in the Gallo-Roman consciousness at least as late as the 2nd century AD. But the land of the Carnutes has produced yet more evidence for the survival of specifically native, non-Roman spiritual leaders and, what is more, this material has important links with the Chartres shrine. Book Eight of *de Bello Gallico* was written by Aulus Hirtius, an officer in Caesar's army and later governor of Transalpine Gaul, after Caesar's assassination in 44 BC. Describing the final episode in the conquest of Gaul by Caesar in 51 BC, when small, isolated pockets of resistance to Roman rule threatened the stability of the new province, Hirtius makes reference to a freedom-fighter called Gutuatrus.[54] The name means 'master of voice' or 'father of inspiration'; interesting epithets in themselves, but more significant is the archaeological evidence for Gallo-Roman inscriptions using *Gutuater* as a title, rather than a proper name. Might Hirtius have confused 'Gutuatrus' as a name with a descriptive or honorific title referring to the man's skill at oratory or divination? The link with Sedatus's shrine at Chartres is this: the list of obscure names, of which 'dru' is one, is full of 'plosive' sounds whose power would come from their being recited out loud, perhaps by a 'master of voice'. The association of *gutuatri* with religion is secured by two altars from Aeduan territory in Burgundy inscribed with the word *gutuater*. One from Mâcon is alas lost, but it recorded the presence of a *gutuater* of Mars and a priest of a native Gallic deity called Moltinus, putting this 'father of inspiration' clearly in a religious role. The other altar, from the Roman city of Autun (Augustodunum), dedicated to another local god, Anvallus, coupled with the Emperor, bears the word GVTVATE[R] on its base.[55] The territories of the Carnutes and the Aedui are relatively near one another geographically and, according to ancient literature, both have firm associations with the Druids: Caesar spoke of the annual Druidic assembly among the Carnutes, and, as we have seen, at least one Druid, Divitiacus, ruled over the Aedui (see pp. 23–24).

The testimony of Ausonius

The poet and rhetorician Ausonius was a Gaul, born at Bordeaux in Aquitaine early in the 4th century AD. He was of high rank within the western Roman Empire, being appointed by the emperor Valentinian I as tutor to his son Gratian. But Ausonius spent most of his working life in his native city. He is a person of interest here because of his authorship of a history of education called the *Commemoratio Professorum Burdigalensium* (*A Commemoration of Bordeaux University Teachers*), a work in which he makes specific mention of a Druidic family dynasty. One of these Druids was named Delphidius, a contemporary of Ausonius and a colleague at the University. He was the grandson of another Druid, Phoebicius, who Ausonius states was a priest at the shrine of the important Gallic deity Belenus, a god of light and healing equated with Apollo, who had similar roles in the Classical pantheon. Chadwick[56] connects the Greek names of these late Gallo-Roman Druids – both inextricably linked with Apollo – to Caesar's comment in the mid-1st century BC that these religious leaders used the Greek alphabet for 'public and private accounts'.[57] But what truth was there in this? Did Druids adopt Greek names, while upholding their old traditions and identities?

Caesar's commentary on the Gallic wars was designed to reach the ears of the Roman senate, and he may have mentioned the Druidic use of Greek characters only to enhance their status as an educated, 'civilized' group. After all, the Roman author's whole tone towards the Druids is generally respectful; he clearly admired them, and Divitiacus was his personal friend as well as his ally. Ausonius's emphasis on his dynastic Druids' Greek names appears to have a different purpose. We must remember that he was a poetic writer and rhetorician, who loved words for their own sake; he was not attempting to write objective history. The key lies in the association of these late Druids with the cult of Apollo, the Roman sun-god, and his holy of holies at Delphi, overlooking the Gulf of Corinth in southern Greece. The Delphic Oracle[58] was perhaps the most renowned prophet in the Classical world and, of course, one of the Druids' most important roles in the 1st century BC was as diviners of the future and the will of the spirits. So could it be that Ausonius's account of his 4th-century Gallic Druid family is largely fictitious, or at least heavily embroidered in order to enhance the romance and allure of his poem? In a sense, this does not matter too much for us, because whatever the truth (or otherwise) of the rhetorician's account, his testimony definitively shows that, even at this late period in the Roman Empire, the Druidic tradition maintained an active presence in the consciousness of Ausonius's contemporaries.

The degree to which the Druids maintained their authority in the Roman Empire after their last-ditch attempt to repel the invaders in AD 60, when they tried in vain to protect their sacred island of Anglesey from the Roman army, however, is open to debate. The evidence that some of the old ways survived – even human sacrifice[59] – and the multitude of British or Gallo-British divinities who strode through the centuries of Roman Britain alongside the new deities of the Empire would seem to suggest that they did. The long memories associated with sacred places argue strongly for the maintenance and fostering of ancient traditions.

We have only to look at sites like Fison Way, Thetford, in Norfolk, to acknowledge the importance of sacred memory. Here, around AD 60, the East Anglian tribe of the Iceni refurbished a massive timber assembly hall, a place to meet for political and ceremonial events. After Boudica's defeat, the Roman army carefully dismantled it, post by post, in order thoroughly to obliterate any trace of Icenian power and discourage the glorification of the site by any Britons still harbouring a rebellious spirit. But 300 years later, someone buried a votive deposit of precious jewelry and other treasures very close to the spot where the great wooden hall had been built. This hoard included more than thirty silver spoons, many inscribed with the names of local deities, some of them twinned with Faunus, an obscure Italian woodland god.[60]

Shifting sands: Druids and Christianity

'This is the penitence of a Druid or a cruel man vowed to evil, or a satirist or a cohabiter or a heretic or an adulterer, namely seven years on bread and water.'[61] AUTHOR UNKNOWN

After the fall of the Roman Empire, the Druidic 'signature' in mainland Europe dried up; the same is, to a high degree, true of Britannia, the exception being some passing allusions to Druids (*derwyddon*) in the medieval Welsh myths. They are mentioned in the 14th-century *Book of Taliesin*, a compilation of poetry that takes its name from the great Welsh poet and satirist of the 6th century AD, and in other 14th-century sources.[62] Indeed Taliesin, with his shamanic, shape-changing abilities, was very possibly a Druid himself.

By contrast, the Irish medieval mythic tradition is full of Druids. Medieval Irish prose literature relating to the Druids is sharply divided into pagan myth and overtly Christian texts. In the former, they remain heavily associated with prophecy and the ability to divine the will of the gods. The most notorious pagan Irish Druid was Cathbadh, one of the major players in one of the earliest texts, the *Táin Bó Cúailnge* (*The Cattle Raid of Cooley*). It was he who correctly predicted the short but glorious life of the Ulster hero Cú Chulainn.[63] The frequent references to Druids in the Irish medieval prose tradition pose the question of whether they were as prevalent and influential in Iron Age Ireland as in Gaul and Britain. Of course, we have no way of ascertaining their presence in Ireland at that earlier period because it never became part of the Roman Empire and Classical authors, for the most part, ignored it. The Irish Druids are a complex mystery to unravel, given that the individuals who wrote down the pagan myths were early medieval Christian monks in the monasteries that were the main foci of education in Ireland. These clerics were well versed in the Classical literary tradition, and so they may well have injected doses of Druidism into their stories, at least some of which were designed to ridicule and belittle paganism. So the presence of Druids in pre-Christian Ireland has to remain an unresolved enigma.

A unique phenomenon in the medieval Irish literary tradition is the connection between Christianity and the Druids. The *Lives* of two saints, Patrick and Brigit, date to the 7th century AD. The Druids play a prominent role in both, but for opposite reasons. The *Life* of St Patrick contains numerous references to the saint's battle with paganism, epitomized by his efforts to quash the Druids. The *Life* of St Brigit is quite different: her foster-father was a Druid, though he converted to Christianity when she was a child.[64] But of course Brigit herself was a transitional figure in Ireland; for pagans, she was a goddess of the dairy and of ale-brewing, and her festival was Imbolc, the beginning of spring and lambing. Even as a Christian saint, she retained many of her old divine responsibilities, particularly with respect to milk and ale.

But it is time to leave Iron Age traditions and their ancestral influence on and beyond the western fringes of the Roman Empire in Wales and Ireland, and turn attention to the seismic change brought about by the absorption of Britannia into the Roman world, with the dramatic effect its entry onto a global stage had on the religion and beliefs of this sacred island.

CHAPTER TWO

Foreign Conquest and Shifting Identities
New cults and old traditions

'I will buy with you, sell with you, talk with you,
walk with you, and so following, but I will not eat with you,
drink with you, or pray with you…'
WILLIAM SHAKESPEARE, *THE MERCHANT OF VENICE*[1]

Religion has so many, sometimes contrary, facets. It can be a powerful and positive agent for bonding people, but it can also be deeply divisive and disturbingly destructive. It can define who we are and who we are not. It can be used as a tool for 'othering' those who follow creeds and conventions different from what is considered 'standard' (whatever that may mean). In today's multicultural world, dress and hair codes, physical appearance, gender roles, food habits and ritual practices may all serve to mark religious affiliations, making adherents highly visible, sometimes seemingly intrusive and even aggressive to those outside their particular faiths. Shylock, Shakespeare's Venetian merchant, speaks simply and eloquently about what it meant to be a Jew in the early modern period. This seems a world away from Britain in the mid-1st century AD, when Rome sought to add the island to her Empire. Yet Shylock's words provide a timely reminder that religion is complex and that today's scholars need to scrutinize and interrogate the evidence from ancient literature, images and inscriptions carefully in order not to fall into the traps of over-simplification. Moreover, it is impossible to disentangle religion from 'secular' society. Even in the present Western world, where – in many places – formal religion is in decline, sacred architecture is everywhere: the spires of churches, mosques and temples punctuate city skylines, and a church or chapel sits at the core of nearly every British rural community.

Conquest and colonialism

'The Senate and Roman people [dedicated this arch] to Tiberius Claudius
Caesar Augustus Germanicus…because he received into surrender
eleven kings of the Britons conquered without loss and he first brought
the barbarian peoples across the Ocean under the authority of the
Roman people.' INSCRIPTION FROM THE ARCH OF CLAUDIUS, ROME[2]

The conquest of one people by another, more powerful one is never
bloodless or peaceful. By its very nature, conquest carries the inevitable
baggage of carnage, the appropriation of land and assets and the imposition of the 'superior' culture upon its subjects. In spring 2016 the author
travelled to Jamaica, in part to try to find out more about its original
Amerindian inhabitants, the Taíno (formerly known as the Arawak). When
Christopher Columbus arrived in 1494, the Taíno greeted him and his men
in friendship, but the Spaniards' greed for the gold they believed to be
there soon turned the encounter between the two worlds into a pitifully
asymmetrical conflict that caused the
virtual annihilation of the peaceful
Caribbean inhabitants of the island.
The Taíno possessed a rich spiritual
tradition, with a plethora of spirits
they called *zemís*, but in Columbus's
Christian colonization of Jamaica,
their religious beliefs, too, were all
but obliterated.[3]

The inscription on the Arch
of Claudius quoted above is full
of the brio, bravado and swagger

The inscription on the Arch of
Claudius in Rome, referring to the
emperor's conquest of Britannia.

of the *conquistador*. Claudius was flexing his muscles, asserting that – despite his physical infirmities (probably cerebral palsy) – he was a supreme ruler, capable of conquering not only the fabled island of Britannia but also Ocean itself, the boundary of the world. More evocative still (and much more disturbing) is the image of Claudius and the personified Britannia carved on a stone from the shrine to Aphrodite and the Julio-Claudian emperors at Aphrodisias in Turkey (see p. iv).[4] It depicts a brutal scene in which the emperor, naked but for a short cloak and helmet, kneels astride a bare-breasted woman, pinning her down in order to rape (even to sodomize) her. He is the all-powerful, muscular young hero (quite different from the middle-aged, physically impaired reality) in the ultimate act of subjugating the helpless female that is Britannia, in what Iain Ferris has aptly termed 'the pornography of conquest'.[5] The figure of Claudius is animated and full of vigour; his conquest, by contrast, is a disempowered female, her cowed demeanour vividly communicating her stress. This image and the inscription on the lost arch, together with Claudian triumphal victory coinage, leaves us in no doubt that the Claudian conquest of Britain was far from a bloodless fusion of different cultures.

Before Ground Zero

In order to understand the religious impact of the Roman conquest on Britain, it is necessary to take a backward glance at the Iron Age rituals already in place. Scholars struggle with Iron Age religions because – certainly compared with that of Rome – they appear muted, at least in terms of their archaeological voice. Of course, Classical literary sources are of limited use, containing little that is pertinent to Iron Age Britain, except for passing references to the Druids, and the pre-Roman Britons had no tradition of written chronicles. Chapter 1 dealt with the Druids, arguably the overarching authorities on later Iron Age cult practices. But what of local cults, those followed in the numerous settlements and farmsteads scattered about Britannia? Archaeology has detected no more than a handful of firmly recognizable shrines, the best example being the circular sanctuary at Hayling Island, Hampshire.[6] Its form echoes the typical Iron Age roundhouse, and it is significant that many rituals actually did take place in domestic contexts. A good example of this is the Iron Age roundhouse at Thornwell Farm near Chepstow, where the inhabitants appear to have placed special deposits of pottery and animal body parts around the southeast-facing entrance,[7] as if to mark its symbolic significance (perhaps because it represented the most vulnerable part of the house).

More widespread was the practice of so-called 'structured deposition', where assemblages of objects were deliberately buried in pits and ditches or put into aquatic places, as if to placate the underworld or water spirits. Llyn Cerrig Bach (pp. 19–21) is a prime instance of the latter.[8] Iron Age objects whose primary use was undeniably sacred are rare, though the newly discovered bronze figurine from Culver Hole Cave on Gower (see p. ix) and some wooden images, notably the early Iron Age group from the Humber Estuary at Roos Carr,[9] buck the trend of iconographic silence. Set against this tradition of sporadic, non-formalized and largely personal expressions of worship, the religious changes in Britannia following the Roman conquest, epitomized by the triumphal trumpet-blast that was the new temple to Claudius at Colchester, represented an upheaval of truly epic proportions.

Gods for all seasons

'Each god used to dine at home; there was not such a mongrel galaxy of the divine powers as we have today. The stars were content with a few divinities; thus with a lighter burden they didn't overdo the load on poor Atlas.' JUVENAL, *SATIRES*[10]

The Roman annexation of new provinces was far from simple, in both cultural and religious terms. It is necessary to appreciate that, by the mid-1st century AD, the Roman army consisted not only of Romans from Rome or even Italy, but contained recruits from many previously subjugated peoples, including Gauls whose culture and belief systems were quite closely connected to those of Britannia. Accompanying the warrior elite, the legions, were large auxiliary forces, non-citizen military units recruited wholesale from different parts of the Empire for their particular fighting expertise, for example as archers or cavalry. The funerary inscriptions on early Roman military tombstones from Corinium (Roman Cirencester) clearly display this diversity; among those commemorated were one Dannicus, a Raurican who enlisted in the Rhenish *Ala Indiana*, a cavalry regiment raised by a Treveran from the Moselle Valley; and one Julius Indus Genialis, a Frisian from the Netherlands, who belonged to a mounted unit raised in Thrace.[11] Both men died in about AD 60. The cultural mix in the invading force was reinforced by groups of merchants, speculators and entrepreneurs, all hoping to milk the fledgling province of its resources and take advantage of new trading opportunities, as well as to make money by providing the army with food, wine, clothes and equipment. These diverse troops brought with them their own gods and goddesses, whom they worshipped alongside the State gods of Rome.

Tombstones of Genialis (above, ht 210 cm/ 82½ in.) and Dannicus (right, ht 108 cm/ 42½ in.) from Corinium. Genialis wears a Roman army helmet, in contrast to bareheaded Dannicus, who has long curly hair.

The Romans' attitude to religion was complex. At its heart was polytheism, the acknowledgment and veneration of a plethora of deities. Some were 'high' gods, divinities of the State, worshipped throughout the Empire. At the opposite end of the scale were the local spirits of groves and springs, and the *augenblickgötter* (literally, 'gods who supervise the blinking of the eye'), who watched over all human activity. It was this multiplicity of gods and godlings that was being mocked by the Roman satirist Juvenal, writing in the earlier 2nd century AD.

At the apex of the hierarchical pyramid of the Roman pantheon was the Capitoline Triad: Jupiter, king of the gods, his consort Juno and their daughter Minerva. Like most of the Roman 'high' gods, these three were the direct counterparts of Greek deities, in this case the ruling trio Zeus, Hera and Athene. Worship – particularly of Jupiter – was to a degree more about pledges of loyalty to the emperor and the Empire than religious devotion. This was especially pertinent to the Roman army: military units erected new altars to 'Iuppiter Optimus Maximus' (Jupiter Best and Greatest) every year on the god's official birthday, early in January.[12] When a new shrine was set up, the previous year's dedication was ceremoniously buried. Excavations of auxiliary forts on Hadrian's Wall, such as at Castlesteads, Birdoswald and Maryport, have revealed several such altars. Intriguingly, some of these characteristically Roman altars betray more local concerns than statements of loyalty to the emperor and the motherland: small, unobtrusive symbols of a solar wheel, the emblem of the Gallo-British equivalent to the Roman sky-god, often feature in the archaeological assemblage. We will explore such issues of cultural fusion in Chapter 3.

Worshipping the emperor

For the newly acquired Roman province of Britannia, perhaps the most crucial part of the State Religion was the Imperial Cult: the divine sanction of Roman authority. This was a strange phenomenon that took different forms depending upon where in the Empire its worship took place. According to a long-standing Roman tradition in which both kings and the deification of living people were anathema to government and people alike, reigning emperors could not be gods, but were elevated to divine status only after their deaths. But the Imperial Cult within the eastern Empire was readily absorbed into a tradition wherein living potentates, such as the Egyptian pharaohs, were already accepted as divine, and here there was no stumbling-block to the veneration of a living emperor-god. In the west, the cult of the emperor was more subtle: during an emperor's lifetime, the cult consisted of the worship of the 'spirit' of empire, represented by the current ruler, and of Rome. Like the veneration of Jupiter in the provinces, the Imperial Cult was actually more a recognition of fealty to the sovereign power of Rome than a function of deep religious conviction. (Indeed, when Christianity first came to the attention of the Roman government as a significant new religious movement, the monotheistic denial of the emperor as a god was the chief source of friction and persecution, largely because Christians' refusal to worship the emperor was perceived as sedition.)

Despite the Roman central government's rule that living emperors could not be gods, in the provinces, the subtle distinction between a dead emperor-god and a living one was probably often missed.[13] This became especially apparent – and problematic – in early Roman Britain in the furore caused by the insensitive (to say the least) erection of a large stone temple to the Imperial Cult at Roman Camulodunum (Colchester) in AD 49. Camulodunum had been the tribal capital of the Trinovantes, whose heartland was Essex; the town's name itself is telling, for it enshrines the veneration of the tribal god Camulos, an image of whom might have survived. For an immediately pre-conquest potsherd from Kelvedon, Essex, not far from Colchester, depicts a bearded Trinovantian horseman, with stiff, lime-washed hair.[14] In his left hand he carries a trapezoidal shield and in his right is a curious crook-headed staff, perhaps a ceremonial sceptre but just possibly a *lituus*, an object used in Roman divination rituals, but familiar to southern British tribal leaders.[15] Whether the Kelvedon image represents a god or a warrior, it serves to make visible the indigenous Trinovantian presence; and if it is an image of Camulos, it is an indicator of the tension between local religious tradition and the brash new cult of the Roman emperor. For just a few years after the Claudian invasion, Camulodunum, with its modest wooden shops and houses, was transformed both by the construction of a huge Classical temple of gleaming white stone – set high on a podium, a triumphant trumpet-blast of foreign victory – and by the settling of veteran Roman legionaries there in what became the model Roman town of Colchester, a *colonia*, built not simply to house ex-soldiers but as a statement to the Britons of Classical civilized living. And the twist of the knife was that the locals, particularly the Roman-appointed Trinovantian priests (called *severi Augustales*) had to foot the bill, both for the erection of the sanctuary itself and for its maintenance. This burden was in addition to other crippling taxes levied on the population, and the confiscation of parcels of land as allotments for the retired soldiers. It was little wonder that when the Iceni rose up in rebellion in AD 60, led by Boudica, the Trinovantes gladly joined forces with their northern neighbour to throw off the Roman yoke.

Just outside the temple-steps there stood a life-sized bronze equestrian statue of the emperor Claudius, just to remind the locals whose temple it was. In his *Annals*, Tacitus describes the construction of the temple as 'erected to the divine Claudius…during his lifetime', and the author goes on to comment, with penetrating insight, that the building was 'a blatant stronghold of alien rule, and its observances were a pretext to make the natives appointed as its priests drain the whole country dry'.[16] Very little trace of the image survives but his head, brutally hacked off the body in antiquity, was found nearby, tossed into the river Alde in Suffolk; and some enraged British warrior struck off a hoof from Claudius's bronze mount and carried it all the way from Colchester to Ashill in Norfolk, where it was deliberately deposited as a votive act, perhaps in thanks to the British gods who gave strength to the freedom-fighters. But was something else going on here? Is it possible that the treatment of Claudius's bronze head was not simply a matter of contemptuous discard? For the Britons (and the Gauls), the human head was deemed especially iconic, the power-source of the body. Enemies were beheaded and their heads collected for display in shrines or on gate-posts of important buildings. Stone images of the severed heads of gods or humans with overlarge heads indicate the significance and reverence accorded this motif.[17] In Iron Age religious traditions, both within Britain and elsewhere in western Europe, the human head was treated as an object of veneration,[18] and the skulls of the dead were sometimes ritually deposited in watery places. Perhaps, in a deliberately ironic twist, the head from the hated image of imperialist domination was not thrown away, but subverted to become an icon of nationalist religious fervour.

Religion and rebellion

'The gods gave the Romans advance warning of the disaster: during the night a clamour of foreign voices mingled with laughter had been heard in the council chamber, and in the theatre uproar and lamentation, but it was no mortal who uttered those words and groans; houses were seen underwater in the river Thames, and the Ocean between the island of Britain and Gaul on one occasion turned blood-red at high tide.'[19]

So wrote Dio Cassius of the sinister omens surrounding the Boudican army's sack of Londinium, a Roman port and entrepôt whose location on the great tidal river Thames caused its early florescence during the period of conquest and beyond.[20] The Romans were extremely superstitious. Their world view admitted that the gods constantly intervened to control humans and bend them to the divine will through the medium of portents. The more significant the subject of the omens, the more extraordinary the spirit-manifestation might be. The incomprehensible and sinister mutterings heard in the Roman basilica (city hall) and the moaning and groaning issuing from the theatre fanned the flames of dread in a colonial community already on high alert in the face of the imminent danger from the savagery of the rebel forces bearing down upon their city, which had no walls and was virtually devoid of defence.

Similar doom-laden stories circulated around the Britons' attack on Colchester. Tacitus goes into graphic detail about the strange prophetic happenings there, most disturbing of which was the collapse of a huge statue of the Roman goddess of Victory, which fell down 'with its back turned as though it were fleeing the enemy'.[21] Not only that, but the Roman author describes how Maenad-like women (Maenads were the frenzied followers of the Greco-Roman god Dionysus/Bacchus), in trance-state, howled gibberish in the local Roman senate-house, and tells of the phantom appearance of London in ruins. Tacitus's account tallies in many respects with that of the later writer Dio, and it may be that the latter used Tacitus's testimony and embroidered it. In both accounts, we may be seeing hindsight in action, but it is clear that the Roman settlers in the new province were seriously spooked – and rightly so – by prophecies of disaster (quite possibly initiated by the Druids).

Britannia erupts

One well-known Roman exploiter of Britain in the early post-conquest days was the unscrupulous Stoic philosopher Lucius Annaeus Seneca, born in Cordoba in southern Spain in about 4 BC, who became chief advisor to the emperor Nero. He was a master of the double-standard: Stoicism involved personal integrity and austerity, yet Seneca was an immensely wealthy imperial official, who perceived that rich pickings were to be had from the new province.[22] He lent tribal leaders in southeast Britain vast amounts of money, in the expectation of gaining lucrative returns on the loans. When the Boudican rebellion erupted, however, Seneca realized that his investments could be at risk, so he immediately foreclosed on the deals and called in the loans for repayment. Seneca was probably only one of many foreign speculators and usurers who sought to suck the life-blood from the new province by ruthless exploitation and the promise of 'cheap' loans to help fund the building of new roads and public buildings (like the temple of Claudius) and the extraction of new Roman taxes.[23]

So in the early post-conquest years, the Trinovantes were simmering, full of smouldering resentment for the Romans, and especially because of the seizure of lands that had belonged to them and their ancestors (including their god Camulos) since time immemorial. Enter Boudica, the catalyst for full-blown revolt. Her tribe, the Iceni, who shared a border with the Trinovantes, were nursing their own grievances. Prasutagus, their king, had been a client-ruler, a Roman ally who, in exchange for his loyalty to the emperor and his promise to keep the peace in his realm, had received assurances that he would keep his kingdom and be protected against hostile neighbours. But in AD 60, Prasutagus died while the Roman governor Suetonius Paulinus was far away with much of his army, smashing the Druidic stronghold on Anglesey, at the opposite end of the country. Tacitus takes up the story:

> 'While Suetonius was thus occupied, he learnt of a sudden rebellion in the province. Prasutagus, king of the Iceni, after a life of long and renowned prosperity, had made the emperor co-heir with his own two daughters. Prasutagus hoped by this submissiveness to preserve his kingdom and household from attack. But it turned out otherwise. Kingdom and household alike were plundered like prizes of war, the one by Roman officers, the other by Roman slaves. As a beginning, his widow Boudica was flogged and their daughters raped. The Icenian chiefs were deprived of their hereditary estates as if the Romans had been given the whole country. The king's own relatives were treated like slaves.'[24]

This episode has been touched upon in Chapter 1, in the context of native British pro- and anti-Roman factions just before and during the conquest-period of the mid-1st century AD. The client-king Prasutagus seems to have disinherited his wife in favour of his daughters as well as the emperor Nero, and it is possibly because Boudica was as anti-Roman as her husband was friendly to the new regime. This split between the Icenian king and his consort might also explain Boudica's savage and – given her probable status as a Roman citizen – likely illegal punishment for resisting the rapacious demands of the finance minister, the procurator Decianus Catus.[25]

Just as Roman religion – in the shape of the intrusive Imperial Cult – played a crucial role in the British rebellion of AD 60, so too did British divine matters. We saw in Chapter 1 that the Druids represented a very real threat to Roman domination and that their resistant influence had to be erased. Dio Cassius's account of the Boudican revolt[26] reveals that Boudica herself exercised divinatory powers; he describes her use of a hare, released from her tunic to see which way it ran, in order to predict victory for the Britons before the final pitched battle with Paulinus's forces. This ritual act took place in a sacred grove presided over by Andraste, a British goddess of victory; the wider ceremonies included well-born Roman women being impaled on sharpened stakes, and their breasts being cut off and sewn into their mouths so that it looked as though they were devouring them. Boudica's status as a religious as well as political leader may even mean that she herself was a Druid, though there is no documentary evidence for British Druidesses, and the literary references to Gaulish female Druids all date much later than Boudica.[27]

Beyond Boudica: reconciliation and rebuilding

'Still, the savage British tribesmen were disinclined for peace, especially as the newly arrived imperial agent Gaius Julius Alpinus Classicianus was on bad terms with Suetonius, and allowed his personal animosities to damage the national interests. For he passed round advice to wait for a new governor who would be kind to those who surrendered, without an enemy's bitterness or a conqueror's arrogance.'[28]

So, what was going on in the aftermath of the Boudican revolt? The rebellion itself shook the Roman Empire to its foundations, and the fledgling province of Britannia was almost lost. Under the leadership of one woman, Boudica, three major Roman towns – Colchester, London and Verulamium – had been sacked, and the 9th Legion savaged. In the wake of the final pitched battle between Paulinus and Boudica, when the British forces were defeated, the Roman governor appears to have behaved with excessive brutality towards the survivors, so the province was in meltdown. Nero made the only possible decision if Britannia was not to be lost: to replace his senior ministers in the region. The emperor's first act was to embark on a major cabinet reshuffle in Britain, and to sack Decianus Catus, whose disastrous appointment as chief finance officer had lit the flames of rebellion. We don't know much about Decianus Catus's background, but he was already hated because of the high taxes he was levying on the Britons, and may also have had a hand in the dispossession of the Trinovantes from their lands to make way for the settlement of retired Roman legionary veterans. It was his high-handed behaviour in seizing Icenian assets and brutalizing its royal family after the death of king Prasutagus that had sparked the terrible events that followed, and it was clearly felt that he had to go immediately, and that the restoration of financial security in Britannia was even more crucial than Suetonius's removal. Significantly, his replacement as procurator, Classicianus, was not a Roman but a provincial from northeastern Gaul. Appointing him to Britain was a shrewd move on Nero's part, for although technically subordinate to the provincial governor, *procuratores augusti* were independent of his authority and reported directly to the emperor. As a Gaul, Classicianus was likely to have empathy (if not sympathy) for the Britons, and he was clearly effective, for he warned Nero of Suetonius's excesses and ensured that the next governor, Turpilianus, was not a career soldier like his predecessors but a man skilled in administration and arbitration, who would consolidate the parts of Britain already annexed rather than attempt to beat the fringes of the province into submission.

If Classicianus was a key player in the future of Britannia as a Roman province, his death also provides significant information concerning religious ritual. His Gallic origins were no bar to his achievement of high office in Roman provincial administration. Despite his conciliatory attitude to the Britons, he was, by allegiance, a Roman first and foremost, and his status is reflected in the rites surrounding his death and burial. In 1852, a fragmentary inscription was found on a stone reused in the Roman wall that was raised to defend Londinium after the rebellion.[29] It was part of an elaborate Cotswold limestone tombstone, with an ornamental 'bolster' design on the top that was erected over the procurator's cremated remains in about AD 65. His tombstone is a very direct statement of *romanitas*, being utterly Roman in every way, not least in its adherence to the Roman custom of committing the dead man's soul to the Roman spirits of the Otherworld. The inscription tells us a great deal about this man, including that he died when still in office and that his widow, Julia Indiana Pacata, daughter of Indus, had the gravestone built in his

The tombstone of Gaius
Julius Alpinus Classicianus,
found in London.
162.5 × 155 cm (64 × 61 in.).

memory. Classicianus's names indicate both that he came from northern
Gaul and that he was a Roman citizen (at this period, only this chosen
few possessed three names). His widow's father, Indus, belonged to the
tribe of the Treveri, in the Moselle Valley, though Tacitus comments that
Julius Indus had been a Roman collaborator during the great rebellion of
the Rhenish tribes led by Florus and Sacrovir in AD 21.[30] So Classicianus
came from a northeastern Gaulish family who had prospered by becom-
ing Roman, but who were particularly useful to Rome because of their
provincial origins.

Bodicacia's tomb

There is no direct archaeological evidence for Boudica's existence. It is
even possible that she was entirely a figment of the Roman imagination,
a trope of barbarism, with her long red hair, masculine appearance and
harsh voice – even her name straightforwardly means 'victory'. However,

in February 2015, excavations on the Bridges Garage site outside the Roman west gate of Corinium (Cirencester) yielded a startling find: an early 2nd-century AD Roman tombstone set up in memory of a twenty-seven-year-old British woman called Bodicacia, a name closely connected etymologically to Boudica (see p. vii). Could it be that Bodicacia was a relative of Boudica, or simply that she, too, bore a name meaning 'victory'? The gravestone was not found *in situ* but had been moved from its original position and placed face-down on a much later Roman inhumation grave.[31] The significance of the Bodicacia tombstone does not end with the inscription itself; its form, its iconography and its later reuse also reveal early Romano-British religious beliefs and practice.

Bodicacia's tombstone came from a cemetery used throughout the Roman period, whose early phase saw the construction of a square stone edifice, possibly a mausoleum. The tombstone itself is topped with a decorative triangular pediment, as if to mimic a Roman temple. Within the triangle was carved the face of Oceanus, the sea-god who, according to Classical tradition, was thought to gird the known world, with the wild land of Britannia lying beyond its boundaries. The depiction of Oceanus on a tombstone is extremely rare, but other, similar imagery from a stone sculpture[32] and a mosaic[33] from Corinium suggests that he, or a local river-deity, may have been accorded special significance here. On Bodicacia's tombstone, Oceanus's long, flowing hair and beard and his crown of crabs' claws survive, but sometime in antiquity his image was literally defaced, the facial features deliberately obliterated. While the other Corinium sculpture is worn and battered, there is no firm evidence that it was similarly defaced. Was somebody trying to erase it because of a change in ideology or religious thinking later in the stone's history, perhaps when it was reused as a grave-cover? There is another dimension to the Oceanus head. Although the protruberances sprouting from his hair are undoubtedly the claws of a crustacean, as befits a sea-deity, they look remarkably like the antlers surmounting the head of another stone image from Cirencester showing a seated male figure clasping a pair of ram-horned serpents, often interpreted as the Gaulish stag-god Cernunnos, whose worship is known elsewhere in Britain (see pp. 142–43).[34]

Bodicacia's tombstone is otherwise in near-perfect condition, its surface unweathered, the inscription as sharp as the day the *scriptor* cut it. This is because more than a century after it was raised in the young woman's memory, the stone was removed from her grave and repositioned, face-down, to form the lid of a later inhumation burial. Why was the stone inverted? Was it to appease the spirit of its original owner or, more likely – in my opinion at least – a deliberate act of engagement between past and present souls? By placing the inscription facing down into the new grave, perhaps the newly and older dead were able to communicate, and the ancestor able to provide comfort for the fresh corpse.

The turbulence of the eastern tribes, which culminated in the cataclysmic Boudican rebellion, should not lead us to imagine that the whole of southern England was in turmoil in the years after the Claudian invasion. The very Roman tombstone commemorating a woman with the very British name of Bodicacia reminds us that early Roman Britain was complicated. The Corinian woman was a member of the Dobunnic tribe, whose incorporation into the Roman province is mentioned only briefly by ancient commentators. Dio Cassius remarked that the first governor, Aulus Plautius, 'secured the surrender on terms of part of the Bodunni [Dobunni] tribe who were subject to the Catuvellauni', and left a garrison there.[35] This laconic statement by a late Greco-Roman historian contains the important point that at least part of the Dobunnic people and their territory had been in vassalage to its more powerful eastern neighbour. So it may well be that the intervention of Plautius was welcomed by the Dobunni as being more palatable than their previous domination by the Catuvellauni. We know from coins that a local Dobunnic king, Bodvoc, ruled the tribe in the earlier 1st century AD.[36] It is possible that he, or a successor, became a client-king of Rome, like Togidubnus in West Sussex (see pp. 12–13) and Prasutagus. The discovery of Bodicacia's tombstone may be taken as an example of early interconnectivity between Britons and Romans in the first days of the province, as exhibited in the mixture of funerary and religious symbolism and in the adoption by British mourners of Roman ways of remembering their dead.

New gods and old beliefs

'Though he slays, in Numa's fashion,
lambs and russet steers,
He swears before Jove's high altar
By none but his revered
Goddess of horses, and images daubed
On the stinking stalls…'

JUVENAL, *SATIRES*[37]

In this early 2nd-century AD poem, Juvenal jeers at a Consul called Lateranus, who was probably of Gaulish origin. The reference to the 'goddess of horses' is to the Gallic horse-deity Epona. Juvenal does not approve, sneering at Lateranus for paying lip-service to the Roman State gods, Numa and Jove, aping the most respected of the early Roman kings, while implicitly venerating his favourite local animal-divinity. Juvenal disapproved of a lot in Roman society; he did not like foreigners and he particularly objected to those jumped-up provincials who assumed high office and threw their weight about while pretending to possess a Roman pedigree. I am sure that Juvenal was far from being alone in his 'us' and 'them' attitude to people and cults he considered strange, vulgar and inherently un-Roman.

On 25 May 2016, *The Times* published an article by Alice Thomson about the rise in the number of faith schools in Britain, and the increase of religious prejudice in some of them, thereby exposing students to a culture of intolerance and perhaps even extremism.[38] This piece prompted a riposte in a letter from the Rev. Nigel Genders the following day: 'But for children, learning about faith is about discovering themselves, their identity and how they relate to their friends.'[39] These two notions of faith-teaching encapsulate just how emotive issues of belief and religion can be. The underlying message of Thomson's original article can be perceived as one of imbalance between two ideologies, where one displays far more zealousness in its presentation than the other; in Genders' response, the emphasis is on the fundamental importance of religious faith, not just for its own sake but also as a platform for informed and curious enquiry about differing secular views of the world. Divergent though they seem, both viewpoints can contribute to the question of religious interaction between Roman incomers and the indigenous British population during the years immediately following the establishment of Britannia as Rome's newest imperial acquisition.

In trying to understand religious beliefs and rituals in early Roman Britain, a different kind of asymmetry from that examined in Thomson's article is manifest. Roman religious systems appear to have had far more formalized structures than those of native Britons and, just as importantly, the physical expression of such systems was much more tangible and visible than was the case for local British cults (at least in the archaeological record). Two traditions were vital for the intense physicality of Roman religious expression: the epigraphic habit and the iconographic habit, added to which was the choice of permanent material – stone or metal – for building temples and making divine images. For pre-Roman Iron Age Britain, as for its Gallic neighbour, religion was a more 'silent' affair, with virtually no inscriptions, few formally structured sanctuaries – certainly nothing comparable to the architectural templates adhered to by the Romans – and scarce images, most of which were probably made of wood and thus perishable.

There is little literary or archaeological evidence for religious persecution in Britain during or after the conquest, the exception – of course – being the attempted annihilation of the Druids, though this was largely motivated by the recognition that they were powerful political agents for resistance and rebellion. Indeed, the Romans have a reputation for being 'tolerant' towards the cult-systems of their provinces and for being receptive to the adoption and absorption of foreign deities into their own pantheon. This is at least partly due to the multi-god cosmologies that existed in much of the ancient world; tension did, of course, arise when Roman polytheism clashed head-on with monotheistic Judaism and then with Christianity. However, while monotheism was not present in early Roman Britain, it would be rash to assume a complete absence of religious tension following annexation. Juvenal's attitude makes Roman prejudice seem very real, even if he was only speaking for one who lived in the city of Rome itself. So the study of religious epigraphy and imagery in Roman Britain can be meaningful only if approached not through a lens of neutral ideology or benign syncretism, but against a model of competitive power-hierarchies.[40] The interaction between official Roman religion and the belief systems of the peoples colonized under imperial expansion was by no means an anodyne 'marriage'. Feelings of colonial superiority, tensions and subversions must have marched alongside the religious connections between Rome and Britain. The hated temple to Claudius, brashly erected at Colchester only a few short years after the invasion of AD 43, would not have been easily forgotten or forgiven by those who had to see it daily where their old shrine had stood, and not least to pay for it. Yet at about the same time as this temple was built and destroyed, another was constructed at Chichester by a British king, Togidubnus, who adopted the name of his emperor, Tiberius Claudius, and who dedicated his sanctuary to 'Neptune and Minerva, for the welfare of the Divine House [of the emperor]...'.[41] But even Togidubnus, Rome's friend, ally and client-king, stressed in his temple dedication that he was a great *British* king. Early tensions within the new province are exemplified by Suetonius Paulinus's destruction of the Druids' holy of holies on Anglesey. British subversion to Rome and a counter-religious movement *may* be expressed by the human sacrifice of Lindow Man (see p. 17), if he was ritually murdered as part of a last-ditch attempt to avert the Roman army's push towards the island.[42]

As we explore the cults that proliferated in Britannia in the post-conquest period, it will become increasingly clear that post-colonial perspectives on Romano-British religion can only take us so far. Yes, the introduction of Roman methods of cult-expression, like epigraphy and image-making, appears to skew the balance between Roman and native, so that *romanitas* is the more visible. But cultural interaction, even in a colonial situation, was a two-way street (a principle explored in Chapter 11). Given that there was undoubtedly a degree of coercion and 'conqueror-muscle' in the early days, religion in Britain became more Romano-British than either Roman or native. But the persistence not only of local beliefs but also of the long-standing spiritual ties with neighbouring Gaul is abundantly expressed in the developing arenas of epigraphic and iconographic cult-expression. These multi-cultural religious issues are explored in the pages that follow.

Marching as to War
Religion and the Roman army

'For the welfare of our lords, the most invincible emperors,
to the Spirit of the Place Flavius Longus, military tribune
of the Twentieth Legion Valeria Victrix, and Longinus,
his son, from Samosata, fulfilled their vow'[1]

This dedication was inscribed on the front of a large stone altar found in the Roman legionary fortress at Chester in 1693. Inscriptions like these, from military installations across Britannia provide a mass of information not just about religion but also about the soldiers enlisted into the Roman army and sent to the distant provinces to keep the *pax romana* (peace across the Empire). We cannot be sure precisely when this altar was erected, but the mention of two emperors narrows the field to the end of the early 3rd century AD at the earliest.[2] The altar was dedicated to the *Genius loci*, the 'Spirit of the Place' (presumably Chester), and reflects a common habit among army personnel: when soldiers were first drafted to a particular provincial location, they made it their business to ascertain who the local gods were and to worship them alongside their own deities. So this *Genius loci* might have been an indigenous

Altar to the *Genius loci* ('GENIO LOCI'), dedicated by a legionary officer from Samosata, found at Chester. Ht c. 81 cm (32 in.).

British divinity or the spirit of the Roman fortress, or both. But Longinus certainly came from a very distant place: Samosata was a town on the Upper Euphrates in Mesopotamia.

The wording on the altar erected by Longus and Longinus ends with V S, (v)otum (s)oluerunt, a common formula explaining that father and son were making a votive offering together. The Romans had a somewhat curious attitude to the gods (to a modern, Western viewpoint at least), believing that they were engaged in a kind of contractual relationship whereby if a person asked for a divine favour and it was granted, it must be 'paid for' by a votive gift. So prayers had two distinct parts: the first, called the nuncupatio, or 'asking-ritual', included both the request and the vow of a particular present to the spirit if the prayer was answered; the second, the solutio, was the tangible gift itself, in this case the stone altar, the fulfilment of the original vow. We cannot know what Longus and his son asked of the gods, but the inclusion of his son's name in the dedication was perhaps because the boy had been ill. After all, the tribune was a serving officer and may well have been the father of a young child or, perhaps, of a young man about to enter military service himself, with all the risks that entailed. This altar from Chester is one of numerous examples of epigraphic communication with the gods by soldiers from all over the Empire. Perhaps for those stationed a world away from home, such vows had – and have – particular poignancy.

Ridley Scott's iconic film *Gladiator* (2000) portrayed Roman soldiers' attitudes to the gods remarkably accurately. Central to the beleaguered and betrayed Roman general Maximus's character was his veneration of his personal household gods. Everywhere he travelled he carried with him three small figurines, the *Lares et Penates*, his personal spirits who watched over him and kept him grounded in his Spanish farm and homeland. Each day, he would unwrap the sacred images from the cloth in which he concealed them, recite prayers to them and pour them a small libation (gift) of wine or oil; then he would bury them for safe-keeping until the following day. In a sense, the fictitious Maximus was engaging in a private ceremony essentially analogous to the public displays of devotion demonstrated by Longus and Longinus at Chester. All places, whether military fortresses or

Relief-carving of the
Genii cucullati from
the fort of Housesteads
on Hadrian's Wall.
Ht 41.5 cm (16¼ in.).

private dwellings, possessed their own spirits, who had to be propitiated
so that they would continue to look after those who lived and worked
there. One possible manifestation of the *Genius loci* worshipped both by
the army and by the civilian population comprised images of a triad of
distinctive little godlets, known as *Genii cucullati*, 'hooded spirits', because
they are shrouded in the peculiarly Gallo-British hooded cloak called
variously a *sagum* or a *birrus britannicus*. One image from Housesteads,
Northumbria, shows three ostensibly gender-neutral figures, swathed in
heavy woollen hooded capes, staring out at their worshippers.[3] If these
figures did represent the spirit of the place, then they are a powerful
reflection of synthesis between Roman and native religious tradition: a
combination of the Roman *Genius loci* and the British reverence for the
sacred number three (see Chapter 7).[4]

The impact of the army on religion and its expression

The Roman army in Britain was a highly significant force in matters over
and above the strictly martial sphere. It is striking that those regions in
which we observe a strong and enduring military presence are also those
in which religion left its heaviest footprint. Guy de la Bédoyère[5] comments
quite rightly that the distribution of surviving cult-material, particularly
of inscriptions, correlates closely with the regions where the army was at

its strongest. Conversely he cites the South West Peninsula, land of the tribe of the Dumnonii, where the military appears to have been virtually absent west of Exeter and where there is thus an almost complete absence of Roman culture, whether religious or secular.[6] It is clear from the pattern of finds that the army played a crucial role in the spread of the 'Roman brand' (*romanitas*). So we might be forgiven for assuming that cultural and religious interaction was largely a one-way street, and that the adoption of Roman religious ideas and beliefs was a unilinear affair in which natives in colonized areas were afforded little choice in the matter and did not make an impact upon their invaders' culture. But this was demonstrably not the case, for the epigraphy and iconography in militarized areas indicate a strong presence of British religion, albeit presented in a Roman manner. And, of course, into this mix was added the polyglot nature of the Roman army, which brought with it a kaleidoscope of cults and rituals from all over the Empire.

John Creighton's *Britannia: The Creation of a Roman Province* draws attention to 'the creation of the familiar':[7] the manner in which Roman colonists, whether military or civilian, sought to construct environments, both physical and emotional, in which they felt at home. An obvious example of this is the recurrent formula of building – forts, temples and houses erected according to uniform architectural plans – imposed upon annexed regions. In terms of the spiritual, one method of bringing the familiar to religion was to discern which deities belonging to conquered territories best fitted with Roman perceptions of their own pantheon, and to 'join up' certain Roman and native deities. Such an exercise may be termed conflation, fusion, equation or synthesis, but the result is consistently expressed epigraphically by linking two names – one Roman, one indigenous – or by merging elements of the imagery associated with each original god. So while much of the evidence for religion in Roman Britain may represent ethnic singularity (whether that be Classical, Oriental or Gallo-British), there is a significant amount of evidence for the construction of strong connections between gods of widely divergent origins. This concept of bridging religious divides, often termed syncretism by anthropologists,[8] is addressed in detail in Chapter 11.

The other way in which the army 'created the familiar' was by the constant repledging of fealty to the spirit(s) of Empire/the emperor(s) and to the head of the Roman pantheon, Jupiter [Iuppiter] Optimus Maximus (I.O.M) through observance of the Imperial Cult (see pp. 42–43). The excavation of multiple altars to Jupiter found at such northern forts as Maryport, Birdoswald and Castlesteads is indicative of an annual military ritual in which, every 3 January (Jupiter's birthday), a new altar to this most powerful of gods was dedicated and erected and the previous year's commemoration ceremonially buried. In a sense, this practice was much more about reaffirmation of connection to the motherland of Rome than about spiritual belief but, nonetheless, Jupiter was a multi-functional god; not just lord of all gods, ruler of the skies and bringer of thunder, but also a solar rider and a fighter against evil (see Chapter 5), and it behoved an army far from home to pay him homage.

Being a soldier: cults of war, triumph and fate

Hosts of Mars

'To the god Mars and the Spirits of the Emperors the Colasuni [brothers], Bruccius and Caratius, presented this [figurine] at their own expense at a cost of 100 *sesterces*; Celatus the bronzesmith fashioned it and gave a pound of bronze made at the cost of 3 *denarii*'[9]

This inscription is cut into the base-plinth of a bronze image of Mars, naked but for a flamboyantly crested helmet; his hands once held weapons, perhaps a spear and a shield. The statuette was found in 1774 on the course of the Foss Dyke canal in Lincolnshire. It is interesting to attempt a rough calculation to find out the kind of outlay involved for the Colasuni brothers (it is not an easy sum to do, because the value of different coin denominations fluctuated significantly depending, as in all monetary systems, upon changes in the economic situation). The annual pay for a Roman legionary (the elite of the army) at the time of the Claudian conquest was *c.* 225 silver *denarii*, so a citizen soldier's weekly pay-packet was roughly 4.5 *denarii*. A *denarius* was worth between 4 and 6 *sesterces*. The brothers therefore may have paid 28 *denarii* for the statuette, the equivalent of seven weeks' wages for a regular Roman soldier.[10] We do not know the occupations of Bruccius and Caratius, but their names are British, and by the mid-2nd century AD, when the figurine was probably commissioned, monetary values were probably quite different from Claudian times, but at least we can say with confidence that the brothers contributed a substantial portion of their income in this dedication. Although the dedication on the Foss Dyke Mars makes no mention of their status as soldiers, for these British brothers the Roman war-god was worthy of veneration. However, as we shall see, funny things could happen to the worship of Mars in the hands of British (and Gallic) devotees, including a radical change to his perception as a bloody god of the battlefield.

The figurine of Mars from Foss Dyke appears to conform to the Classical idea of a god of war (except, perhaps, for his nakedness). But at Maryport, a Roman fort on the Cumbrian coast south of the western edge of Hadrian's Wall, soldiers worshipped a war-god whose image could not provide a greater contrast to the Lincolnshire Mars. This little figure, roughly carved on a piece of sandstone, depicts a warrior-god, also with a spear and shield, but it is aggressively British in its style, with a huge head surmounted by bulbous horns. It, too, is naked, but is additionally ithyphallic, and the point of its clumsy-looking spear also resembles an erect

Inscribed bronze figurine of Mars, from Foss Dyke, Lincolnshire. Ht c. 27 cm (10½ in.).

Relief-carving of a
horned warrior-god
from the Roman fort
of Maryport, Cumbria.
Ht 34 cm (13½ in.).

phallus.[11] So what does the Maryport image represent? Is it meant to be
Mars or is it, instead, a kind of subversion of the Roman war-god, a British
'counter-Mars'? The influence of indigenous tradition is very marked,
particularly in the giant head and the horns, both entirely foreign to the
iconography of the Roman Mars. Who commissioned this image: a soldier,
of British or Gallic origin, or a local civilian? Roman soldiers stationed
at Maryport set up a number of altars specifically dedicated to 'Military
Mars',[12] stressing their veneration of him as a warrior-deity. The inscriptions on these stones proudly state that the members of this army-unit,
the 1st Cohort of Baetasians, were Roman citizens, a comparatively rare
status for auxiliary troops on active service. Baetasians were a German
tribe whose homeland was in the Roman province of Lower Germany,[13]
near the mouth of the Rhine. The cohort was raised there in the mid to
late 1st century AD,[14] but the altars to Mars probably date to the later 2nd
century. I would be wary of assuming that these soldiers were responsible for the somewhat risqué image of the horned god found at the fort.
Another inscription from Maryport might provide the solution: an *optio*
(a deputy centurion)[15] called Julius Civilis commissioned the erection
of an altar dedicated to Belatucadrus, 'the Fair Killer', a local northern
British war-god worshipped widely in the region of Hadrian's Wall and

sometimes given the forename Mars.[16] Could the little naked, horned image from the same fort have been he?

Belatucadrus is one of many northern British war-gods with local names whom native worshippers linked with the Roman war-god. A fellow indigenous warrior-deity was Cocidius, his name translated by Anne Ross as the 'red god', perhaps a reference to blood-letting in battle. While the great majority of inscriptions from the region of Hadrian's Wall were carved on stone, the headquarters building in the fort of Bewcastle, Cumbria, produced a rare find of two small silver plaques, both inscribed 'to the god Cocidius' and each bearing an image of an armed man (see p. 219).[17] The warrior on the smaller plaque has a spear and shield and appears to be wearing a rudimentary mail-coat; on the larger one, Cocidius only has a spear, but the fuller inscription provides information that the dedicant was a military tribune with the splendid name Aurunceius Felicessimus. The silversmith who made these plaques stamped through the imagery from the back; the figures are simply and schematically rendered, as are many Romano-British stone images, but all the essentials for the presentation of the god have been observed: he is fully armed and named.[18] Cocidius was a popular deity in the military north: in the western region of Hadrian's Wall he was very much a warrior-lord, but to the east he was linked with the Roman god Silvanus, perhaps in the latter's capacity as a hunter (another blood sport!). The Bewcastle finds suggest the presence of a shrine here or nearby, for decorated plaques like these are usually designed to be displayed on the walls of religious buildings in order to show the devotion of the dedicant to the god and to display the fulfilment of his or her vow. There is some corroborative evidence for a *fanum* (small shrine) to Cocidius in the region of Bewcastle, for a *fanum Cocidii* is mentioned in a strange document known as the *Ravenna Cosmography*, compiled by an anonymous cleric in Ravenna, Italy, in about AD 700. Although according to David Mattingly 'the *Cosmography* is an error-strewn and disorganized listing of place-names from all over the empire',[19] and so we might dismiss the location of the Italian monk's *fanum Cocidii* as at best vague and at worst virtually random, the silver plaques from Bewcastle mean he might just have been right.

Roman soldiers worshipped a plethora of Mars or Mars-related gods in Britannia. Belatucadrus and Cocidius may have been well established in northern Britain before the army arrived, and the connection with the Roman war-god made by Roman military men who perceived equations or at least similarities between their own Mars and the British warrior-deities. Sometimes, army-recruits brought their own local gods to Britain with them, already linked up with Mars. One such was Mars Thincsus, worshipped by a German military unit at the wall-fort of Housesteads in Northumbria. Thincsus was a Germanic deity who migrated to Britain with the German cohort where he was coupled with the Roman god of war (as happened with the British spirits Belatucadrus, Cocidius and their brothers). His devotees set up a sanctuary to him here; of a once imposing temple-building, an inscribed altar and an associated fragmentary carved stone arch from a gateway survive.[20] The inscription reads: 'To the god Mars Thincsus and the two Alaisiagae, Beda and Fimmilena, and to the Deity of the Emperor, the Germans, being tribesmen of Twenthe, willingly and deservedly fulfilled their vow'. Twenthe is in what is now the Netherlands. Another altar from Housesteads gives further information: it is dedicated to Mars and the Two Alaisiagae, also by people from Twenthe, who identify themselves as 'of the formation of Frisians of Vercovicium [Housesteads]...styled Severus Alexander's'.[21] This probably refers to the existence of a personal imperial military unit raised around the mouth of the Rhine in the early 3rd century AD, when Severus actively campaigned against the powerful German tribe of the Alemanni.[22] Eric Birley has suggested that the term 'Alaisiagae' might mean 'all-honoured ones'. Beda and Fimmilena may be titles respectively meaning 'prayerful one' and 'skilful one'.[23] All their names are female, and they were probably helpers to Mars Thincsus: the arch depicts the war-god holding his sword, shield and spear, and accompanied by a goose, a symbol of alertness and aggression; he is flanked by two naked goddesses, members of the Alaisiagae, each bearing a sword and a victory-wreath. While Thincsus was assimilated with Mars, the Alaisiagae remained determinedly foreign, German goddesses who escaped overt linkage with *romanitas*.

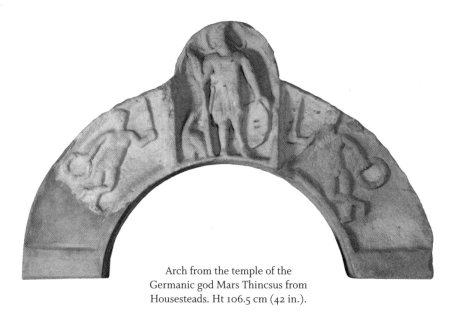

Arch from the temple of the
Germanic god Mars Thincsus from
Housesteads. Ht 106.5 cm (42 in.).

Geese seem to have been popular birds with Romano-Germanic gods of war: far away in Caerwent, South Wales, the Silures worshipped a Treveran god named 'Mars Lenus or Ocelus Vellaunus'. This god's name was inscribed on the base of a statue that has virtually disappeared, except for a pair of human feet standing next to those of a goose.[24] A second altar from Caerwent was dedicated to the same god, though simply called 'Mars Ocelus'.[25] The association of Mars with these Gallo-British deities raises questions concerning the wholly military nature of their responsibilities. Lenus Mars presided over a great healing sanctuary at Trier (Augusta Treverorum) in the Moselle Valley, where his Treveran name always comes first on inscriptions, indicating that the local god was pre-eminent in the partnership.[26] The peaceful function of Lenus is endorsed by an inscription on a small altar from the great Roman villa at Chedworth, in rural Gloucestershire, where the god's name was scratched on a stone beneath a roughly incised human figure holding a spear and an axe that seem to have represented protection against disease.[27] The role of 'Mars' as a healer seems rather odd, but it is widely accepted, at least among French and German scholars, that one quirk of Gallo-British religious manipulation of the Roman pantheon is reflected in the reinterpretation of Mars's warlike qualities as a force for protection against disease. We will return to this subject in Chapter 6.

Regiments of divine military women

'To the goddess Fortuna, Julius Bassus, camp-prefect, set this up.'[28]

'Lady Nemesis, I give thee a cloak and a pair of boots; let him who wore them not redeem them except with the life of his Blood-red charger.'[29]

Roman soldiers worshipped a plethora of goddesses, each of whom appears to have tapped into a military need. The Roman goddesses Fortuna and Nemesis were deities of Chance and Fate: important to keep them in one's corner when facing the enemy! Victory needs no explanation; as a matter of course, soldiers would pray to her before battle. Unlike this trio, the mother-goddesses, themselves often presented in groups of three, were born and bred in Gaul and the Rhineland, but they were eagerly adopted by the Roman military because they represented succour, protection and sustenance on the battlefield. Divine personifications of abstract concepts were often perceived as female. The dedication to Fortuna by Julius Bassus was found on the site of the great baths at the legionary fortress of Caerleon in South Wales. Bassus held the post of *praefectus castrorum*, which meant that he was third-in-command of Legio II Augusta. Fortuna (Chance) was not a military goddess *per se*, but Roman soldiers were careful to propitiate her so that she would protect them on the battlefield. Fortuna is often found in military bathhouses, because the bathers believed they were at particular risk from evil forces when stripped naked. Several gemstones, once mounted in rings and lost when the steam from the baths loosened the glue holding them in place, bear the image of Fortuna, for a soldier's personal protection. At the northwestern legionary fortress at Chester, the goddess was invoked, rather wistfully, as 'Fortuna Redux' – Fortuna the Home-bringer – and the altar was also dedicated to the healing-deities Aesculapius and Salus ('Health') by the freedmen and slaves in the household of a senior army officer.[30]

The personification of Victory was another important military cult strongly tied up with fealty to the emperor and winning wars for the expansion and consolidation of imperial provinces. So it is no surprise that the apparently spontaneous collapse of the great statue of the goddess Victoria at Camulodunum (Colchester), its back turned as though running away from danger, just before Boudica's army attacked it was seen as an evil portent of terror to come.[31] Both legionaries and auxiliary soldiers frequently dedicated altars to Victory. A rarer find is a beautifully evocative little bronze plaque from Caerleon that depicts winged Victoria bearing a trophy of war: a breastplate and helmet flanked by two shields, which she brandishes in triumph on a long stave (see p. viii). The plaque is thought to have come from a piece of parade armour,[32] proudly worn by an army officer on ceremonial occasions.

A close relative of Fortuna was Nemesis, or Fate. She was invoked on a lead *defixio*, or curse tablet, placed in the amphitheatre at the fortress in Caerleon by someone with a personal grievance who wanted revenge. The writing on the curse tablet does not tell us what the unknown recipient of the spell had done to invoke such invective. He was probably a fellow

Lead curse tablet invoking Nemesis from the amphitheatre of the fortress at Caerleon. Ht *c.* 7.5 cm (3 in.).

gladiator who had brought his cloak and boots into the cloakroom of the amphitheatre. Maybe he played dirty in the arena, and his injured opponent called upon Nemesis for justice. Far away at Chester, another legionary soldier set up an altar to Nemesis, once again in the amphitheatre.[33] Why was Fate invoked at these places? Military amphitheatres were mainly used for parades, ceremonies and military drilling, but they also sometimes hosted games, including gladiatorial combat. Was Nemesis called upon to give favours in betting, or was she propitiated for a more sinister purpose, to bring curses down upon individuals at these dangerous events? The *defixio* from Caerleon specifically calls for the slaughter of a war-horse.

The cult of the mother-goddesses was not of Roman origin, seeming rather to have had its origins in Gaul, but its outward manifestations only occur as a result of the epigraphic and iconographic habits introduced by the Roman army and administration.[34] The *Matres* (called *Matronae* in the Rhineland) were very frequently perceived in triplicate, whether as three distinct entities or as three aspects of the same goddess. These triple goddesses are explored in more detail in Chapter 7, but it is important to mention them here because, despite their overt symbolism of fecun-

Three mother-goddesses from Cramond on the Antonine Wall, Scotland.

dity and motherhood, these divinities enjoyed considerable popularity among the Roman military in the frontier regions of both Britain and the Rhineland. A cohort raised among the Tungrians of Belgium, stationed at Housesteads, venerated the Mothers,[35] as did troops also raised in Gaul based at Vindolanda, Chesterholm, just south of the Wall.[36] It is very likely that these units imported the mother-goddess cult from Gaul to Hadrian's Wall. It is perhaps significant that the worship of the *Matres* in military Britain was expressed mainly in epigraphic dedications, with the notable exception of multiple images from Housesteads, where there must have been a major sanctuary for them,[37] while the other main cluster of devotees in the Cotswolds (see Chapter 5) displayed their veneration for these goddesses almost solely through iconography. By contrast, the cult of the *Matronae* followed by army officers on and around the Rhine frontier was expressed in monumental stone altars that combined a unique form of imagery with well-cut and detailed inscriptions, often indicative of the senior rank of the dedicants.[38] Whatever the precise role the mother-goddess cult played in military Britain, it is likely that these triple goddesses were worshipped as protectors and nourishers of soldiers' lives and welfare.

Riding into battle

I am no rider. Until a few days before writing this section, the only encounters I had enjoyed with horses comprised slow, sedate ambles on the little white horses of Provence through the rice-fields of the Camargue. So it was not until I met Jazek, a Polish-Arab horse, that I realized what a strong bond there is between riders and their animals. Jazek is twenty-two years old and suffers from arthritis, so he can no longer be ridden for more than short canters. His owner, a former research student of mine, stables him a few miles from where she lives and visits him at least twice a day. When I was taken to meet Jazek, I was amazed at his greeting of her: nudging her shoulder with his head in a long, loving massage. We took him for a walk through the woods near Newport in South Wales and, by the end of the hour, I was treated to the same gesture of affection, and felt oddly at one with this powerful but gentle creature. His owner explained that when she rides Jazek, there is a real sense that he is careful to protect and look after her, instinctively seeking to avoid tricky situations, such as low boughs or treacherous ground. All the sentimentality expressed here does have a purpose: to emphasize how close the bond must have been between cavalrymen and their war-horses in the Roman army. Little surprise, then, that deities associated with horsemanship were popular with mounted soldiers. After all, riders and their horses were dependent upon each other for their survival, and mutual empathy was crucial to their successful partnership.

Epona, goddess of cavalrymen

'To the spirits of the departed (and) to Aventinus, *curator* of the Second Cavalry Regiment of Asturians, of 15 years service; his heir Aelius Gemellus, *decurion*, set this up.'[39]

The tombstone bearing this inscription comes from the fort of Chesters on Hadrian's Wall. Military *curatores* and *decuriones* were army men with administrative roles within their units. Another tombstone from Chesters has a barely legible inscription, but above it is the image of a horseman brandishing a sword,[40] and it is possible that a similar image once adorned Aventinus's memorial tablet too. We met two early cavalrymen – Dannicus and Genialis from Cirencester – in Chapter 2, both of whom are depicted on their tombstones trampling prostrate enemy Britons.

Roman cavalry were specialized auxiliary troops from areas within the Empire with strong riding traditions; Aventinus's regiment was raised in Asturia, northern Spain. Cavalry units were crack fighting corps, their speed and manoeuvrability vital in outflanking enemy armies in pitched battle. Unsurprisingly, many of these horsemen worshipped deities associated with horses.[41] The Cumbrian coastal fort of Maryport was home to several cavalry units over time; one was the 1st Cohort of Spaniards, a part-mounted regiment.[42] Two carved stones at this site may be connected: one is a tombstone depicting a cavalry-officer; the other

Carvings of the Gallic horse-goddess
Epona (above, ht 65 cm/25½ in.)
and on a tombstone of a cavalryman
(right, ht 134 cm 53 in.) from
Maryport, Cumbria.

is an image of the Gallic horse-goddess Epona,[43] a rare depiction within
Britain. These two carvings, both on red sandstone slabs, are very similar
to one another: indeed it is tempting to see the same sculptural hand
at work. But unlike the cavalryman, who sits astride his mount, Epona
adopts her typical side-saddle position.[44] Another dedication to Epona
was written on an altar set up in the 2nd century AD at Auchendavy on
the Antonine Wall in Scotland by a legionary centurion called Cocceius.
The Auchendavy altar comes from the outer northern limits of Empire
and its dedication is telling for it places a Gallic goddess alongside high-
ranking Roman martial deities.[45]

From her distribution in her Gallic homeland, Epona seems to have
appealed to Roman soldiers and Gallo-Roman civilians alike. She was
extremely popular on the Rhine frontier, with a particular concentration of dedications from legionary fortresses east of the Rhine and in the
Danube Valley.[46] Her symbolism suggests that she was associated primarily
with fertility. Epona is often depicted with a suckling foal, particularly in
Burgundy, and corn-sheaves adorn a little bronze image of the goddess

with two ponies from southern England.[47] The common imagery of the goddess bearing a key also suggests her role both as guardian of stables and – more significantly – of the gateway to the afterlife. So why was such a 'homespun' deity as Epona worshipped by army officers? She never appears as an overtly military figure, unlike Victory. But her role as a horse-guardian (maybe even as a horse-whisperer) probably appealed to her military devotees, particularly cavalrymen, because they saw her as a protector of their mounts, and by extension themselves. And it is easy to see why people engaged in the risky business of fighting called upon a deity who could lead them safely to the Otherworld should they die in battle.

Divine horsemen

Sometime in the Roman period, a dead man was buried in a grave with an exquisite little bronze figurine of a mounted warrior at Westwood Bridge, Peterborough.[48] He wears a flamboyantly crested helmet, a cuirass and a cloak; in his left hand he carries a diamond-shaped shield, and in his right he once held a spear. He sits astride a chunkily built pony with a stylized mane and tail. He looks like a Roman cavalryman, but the rider and his mount betray local craftsmanship: the man's head is too big for his body, his shield too small to be functional, and the horse's incised eyes and mane suggest indigenous schematic tradition.[49]

Bronze figurine of an armed cavalryman, found at Westwood Bridge, Peterborough. Ht 9 cm (3½ in.).

The same is true for a small stone carving of a mounted warrior from the Roman town of Margidunum in Nottinghamshire, depicted in an even simpler fashion. The horseman's head is just a sphere above a rectangular slab of torso and diminutive legs, an immense spear in his hand, riding a horse smaller than a Shetland pony. The artist's intention was clearly not to reflect realism but to present the essentials: armed warriors on horseback.[50] But who were these deities? Despite the apparent *romanitas* of the Westwood Bridge figurine, I suspect that both these images depict local (though to us) nameless warrior-gods. Perhaps, like Epona, they represented the crucial role played by Roman cavalry on the battlefield; they may have been perceived as local deities, but were accorded the physical form of a Roman mounted soldier. But at Margidunum, at least, the craftsperson who fashioned the image played only lip-service to Classical iconographic traditions (see also Chapter 7).

Antenociticus: a British deity on Hadrian's Wall

'Two vast and trunkless legs of stone stand in the desert…Near them, on the sand,
Half sunk a shattered visage lies…'[51]
PERCY BYSSHE SHELLEY, *OZYMANDIAS*

Were it not for the accompanying inscriptions from his shrine, the fractured remains of the god in a fort at Benwell would be just as enigmatic as Ozymandias's shattered statue in the Egyptian desert. Once a life-size statue, only the head and a few fragments of Antenociticus's image survive. Both images are full of pathos, ruined but retaining hints of former splendour. Just outside the fort, towards the eastern end of Hadrian's Wall, the soldiers stationed here built a rectangular stone sanctuary to a local British god called Antenociticus.[52] It is a happy, though fairly unusual, happenstance that the site yielded epigraphic and iconographic evidence for his worship as well as for the building in which he was venerated. Three inscriptions tell us his name, which was entirely British, with no Roman name added, but the status of the dedicants indicates that his was a

Stone head of the British god Antenociticus, part of his cult-statue from his temple at Benwell on Hadrian's Wall. The curly horns in his hair are clearly demarcated. Ht of head *c*. 30 cm (1 ft).

'high-end' cult whose devotees included a legionary centurion and a prefect of cavalry. The name Antenociticus itself provides no key to the god's identity but the fragmentary statue, including the head, depicts him as a youthful deity. His face was carved in the British tradition, with lentoid eyes, a wedge-shaped nose and thick, coarse hair, and he gazes serenely out over his sanctuary and those gathered to do him homage. One feature of the carved head has caused controversy: two locks of hair fan out from the middle of his head to just above each eye. Although dismissed by one scholar as a simple vagary of the hairstyle,[53] others are of the view that these strands represent not hair but a pair of horns.[54] The latter reading is supported by the remains of a torc (a Gallo-British necklet) on Antenociticus's neck, broken from the body. These torcs were not only symbolic of high status but were also frequently associated with horned deities, such as Cernunnos (see Chapter 7).

So what was Antenociticus doing at Benwell? Was he brought to Britain by soldiers from elsewhere in the Empire? One of the altars dedicated to him was set up by a cohort originally recruited among the Vangiones, a tribe whose lands lay in northeast Gaul near the west bank of the Rhine. Was he an entirely British god, known only in this one remote spot and, perhaps, silently existing before the army arrived? Or was he, as Jane Webster has suggested for a number of the British-named deities that sprang up all over Hadrian's Wall, an 'invention of a god at need'?[55] I suspect that, in any case, the adoption of Antenociticus's cult by the army at Benwell was relatively short-lived, at its peak in the mid-2nd century AD, when all the surviving altars were erected, but perhaps not lasting long beyond that time. The altars were deliberately buried – significantly – face-down in a corner of the shrine, and the statue broken up: only the head was preserved: was that because it was felt to be too impious an act to smash it, when the human head was such an important cult-signature in Roman Britain?

Rule Brigantia

'Sacred to Brigantia; Amandus the engineer,
  by command fulfilled the order.'[56]

Antenociticus is just one example of an apparently British deity worshipped by Roman soldiers in the frontier zone of the province. While he appears to have been confined to Benwell, the goddess Brigantia had devotees in several places in the territory of the eponymous northern tribal hegemony of the Brigantes, a huge region stretching from Yorkshire to Dumfries and Galloway. Brigantia was the personification of the tribe and she was perceived as an armed woman, not unlike Britannia, with her shield and trident, as represented on pre-decimal British coins and other imagery. Several altars to Brigantia record her worship, by people of Gallic or British origin and by senior Roman military personnel alike.

By far the most interesting dedication to Brigantia is from the Roman

Monumental relief-carving of Brigantia from the Roman fort at Birrens, Scotland. Ht 93 cm (37 in.).

fort at Birrens in southwest Scotland, where a relief-carving of the goddess is accompanied by the inscription quoted above.[57] She stands more than 45 cm (18 in.) high, facing the spectator, wearing an elaborate helmet surrounded by a crown representing a turreted wall, holding a spear and a globe, with a shield resting on the ground beside her. The head of Medusa is carved between her breasts and she is winged. So, in iconographic terms, she resembles a blend of the Roman goddesses Minerva and Victory: her imagery could not be more Roman, yet her crown and her name proclaim her as a guardian-spirit of British Brigantian territory. A rather eclectic dedication to Brigantia comes from Corbridge,[58] an army depot just south of Hadrian's Wall. Here a Roman centurion of the 6th Legion called Gaius Julius Apolinaris commissioned the erection of an altar to a range of gods including Jupiter Dolichenus and Caelestis Brigantia. Dolichenus and Caelestis were Syrian divinities (see Chapter 8), and it is likely that Apolinaris himself came from the east, bringing his gods with him and relating them to both the Roman and British panthea.[59]

The army and its gods

This chapter has had the space only to focus on a handful of the more prominent cults practised by the army in its forts and fortresses. As might be expected, the bulk of appeals to the gods made by soldiers were dedications to those appropriate to the welfare of fighting men: Mars, Victory and Fortuna. Other prominent deities of Roman origin popular with army personnel have not yet been discussed because their cults belong principally to later chapters; this is especially true of Jupiter Optimus Maximus, the focus of the Imperial Cult, Mithras, a god of Persian origin (to whom we shall return in Chapter 8), Mercury and Minerva. But it is striking how many Gallic and British divinities were worshipped by soldiers: Epona, for instance, and, curiously, the mother-goddesses. But it is time to leave the army and military cults for the present and to explore, in the next chapter, the shrines and temples built in the towns and the countryside of Roman Britain.

CHAPTER FOUR

Town and Country
Urban devotions and rural rituals

'I am told by the *haruspices* that I must rebuild the temple of Ceres which
stands on my property; it needs enlarging and improving, for it is certainly
very old and too small considering how crowded it is on its special anniversary,
when great crowds gather there from the whole district on 13 September and
many ceremonies are performed and vows made and discharged. But there is
no shelter nearby from rain or sun, so I think it will be an act of generosity and
piety alike to build as fine a temple as I can and add porticoes – the temple
for the goddess and the porticoes for the public.' PLINY[1]

This is an extract from a letter written by Pliny the Younger to his architect
Mustius. Pliny was an inveterate writer of letters, many of which were
directed to the emperor Trajan when the author held the appointment
of imperial special advisor in Bithynia (Asia Minor). Pliny was born in
the early AD 60s at Comum (Como) in northern Italy. On the death of his
uncle, he inherited his estate in the same region. The letter to Mustius
about Ceres' dilapidated shrine on Pliny's land reveals fascinating details
concerning temple ownership and its attendant responsibilities, as well
as pilgrimage and ritual in the Italian countryside. Equally interesting is
Pliny's stated reason for renovating the shrine on his estate: a command
from *haruspices*, professional seers who acted as intermediaries between
the spirit and human worlds. The letter goes on to discuss the refurbishment of the temple, proposing the use of marble and other expensive
materials, and the replacement of a wooden image of Ceres, so old that
it was falling to pieces, with a more permanent statue of stone.

Urban centres and sylvan spaces

> 'No one shall have gods to himself, either new gods or alien gods, unless
> recognized by the State. Privately they shall worship those gods whose
> worship they have duly received from their ancestors. In cities they
> shall have shrines; they shall have groves in the country and homes
> for the *Lares*.' CICERO[2]

The high-flying writer, rhetorician and politician Marcus Tullius Cicero
set out his opinions on how religion should work in his ideal state, within
an Italian context, in his law manual, the *De Legibus*. Without going into
the minutiae of what exactly Cicero meant by 'shrines' or 'homes' for the
Lares (the household spirits), the interest of this piece lies in the distinc-
tions he makes between holy spaces in towns and in the countryside. At
first glance, it appears that he advocated built sanctuaries only for urban
environments, and believed that rural worship should take place in natural
locations. Cicero wrote *De Legibus* in the mid-1st century BC, while Pliny's
description of his rural shrine to Ceres dates to more than a hundred years
later. The sanctuary that Pliny planned to restore on his country estate was
definitely a temple-building, so it hardly conforms to Cicero's guidelines
on country worship. It is telling, too, that such authors as Lucan,[3] Tacitus,[4]
Dio Cassius[5] and the Elder Pliny[6] talked about sacred groves as barbarous
places in Gaul and Britain, where Druids lurked and dark sacrifices were
carried out. So Cicero's view was markedly divergent from those of this
group of later authors. The latter were likely simply using the theme of
Druidic groves as ammunition in their emphasis on barbarity, making a
false distinction between the 'order' of civic worship and the 'wildness'
of the foreigners on the western edge of the Roman Empire.

The Greeks and Romans perceived a firm distinction between cities and
the countryside, the latter often viewed as wild and chaotic, in contrast to
the settled order of urban spaces. In his disturbing and contrapuntal play
The Bacchae, the Greek tragedian Euripides uses the tensions between
nomos (order) and *physis* (disorder) to explore attitudes associated with
both gender and species. To *nomos* belonged cities, civilization and men;

physis was the realm of chaos, women and beasts. This kind of thinking likely affected the reportage of 'barbarian' ritual practices of Gaul and Britain in Classical literature, as taking place in sinister secret woodland places where dark, chaotic things lurked and the trees dripped with the blood of human sacrificial victims, all seemingly anathema to the urbane, educated and ordered Roman mind. But for Pliny the Younger at least, the rural position of a sanctuary was no bar to its possession of a formally built structure, adorned with costly marble and stone statuary.

In Roman Britain, too, both urban and countryside shrines conformed to similar architectural formulae. In some instances, it is possible to identify pre-existing Iron Age sanctuaries, sometimes nebulous in form and often discerned not by the presence of a structure but only by the remains of ritual activity beneath or alongside Roman sacred buildings. A perception common to both urban and rural sanctuaries was that building structures on holy ground represented an 'invasion' of spiritual space, and it may well be that foundation-rituals played a major role in the establishment and consecration of religious buildings. But one feature that is likely to have distinguished certain country shrines from city temples is that of pilgrimage. The location of certain rural sanctuaries in Gaul and Britain, at about a day's walk apart, and sometimes visible from each other, suggests that the sacred journey was an important way of congregating to worship deities in non-urban areas.[7] Of course, some city temples, too, attracted their pilgrim-devotees. The great temple to Sulis Minerva at Bath (see Chapters 5 and 6) is a good example of a Romano-British town-shrine that drew supplicants from Gaul and beyond as well as from elsewhere in the province of Britannia.

The Romans built imposing, Classically styled temples in both cities and the countryside in Britain. These were large rectangular structures built on platforms (*podia*), reached by steps leading to pedimented entrances supported on columns.[8] A popular architectural form for temples in Roman Britain and Gaul – but solely confined to these provinces – was the type today known as 'Romano-Celtic', simply by dint of its distribution. These shrines could be circular, polygonal, rectangular or square, but all shared the common feature of concentricity. They varied considerably in size but

The foundations of a late Romano-Celtic temple at Caerwent, South Wales.

were generally small compared to temples of the Classical type. They had an inner *cella*, the holy of holies, that only the priest could enter, typically surrounded by a public roofed portico with open walls for the display of votive objects by dedicants. Archaeologically, this structural footprint can be identified by the more solid inner wall-foundations, built to support the two-storeyed *cella* that stood inside the less robust walls of the gallery or portico.[9] Romano-Celtic temples were used as centres for worship and ritual all over Britannia, whether in major cities, like Caerwent, tribal capital of the Silures in South Wales, or remote rural areas, such as Woodeaton, Oxfordshire, a shrine deliberately positioned between the two powerful tribes of the Catuvellauni and the Dobunni.

Urban hymns

John Creighton[10] draws attention to the formulaic layout of Roman towns, in which public buildings, including temples, were positioned so as to enable prominent citizens to perambulate between the forum and basilica, the public baths, the library and the favoured place of worship, with just the right amount of distance between them to enable the patron, followed by his *clientes*, to show himself off to the populace. So the location of temples in major cities was not always dictated according to strictly spiritual criteria.

Verulamium

During the later Iron Age, what was later to become the Roman town of Verulamium was called Verlamion.[11] It was a major centre of the great Catuvellaunian tribe, that same tribe whose king, Cassivellaunus, had confronted Caesar's invading army with a huge phalanx of war-chariots in the mid-1st century BC. A hundred years later, in about AD 55, a man of the highest status, probably the tribe's chief or king, died and his funeral was conducted at Folly Lane, Verlamion, with great solemnity and ceremony. We do not know his name, but his body lay in state for some time, surrounded by elaborate grave-furniture, and then he was burnt on a huge pyre, along with large numbers of artefacts, including pottery vessels and metal goods. An enclosure was built around his cremated remains and, flanking its entrance, the bodies of three women were interred, possibly after being sacrificed to honour the dead man's spirit and accompany him into the afterlife.[12]

When the new Roman town grew up and its public buildings – including several temples – were constructed, its orientation was clearly focused on that earlier burial-site, as if it retained a powerful significance even in the new order of *romanitas*. What is more, in the 2nd or 3rd century AD, a large sanctuary was built at Folly Lane, perhaps on the site of a cenotaph to that long-dead chieftain. A grisly feature of this Roman shrine was a deep shaft, one of several, dug in front of the temple-building, in which the deliberately defleshed skull of an adolescent boy was interred, upright, with a puppy and a whetstone (see pp. 17–18). The gruesome, bloodstained head was then displayed for a time outside the temple before being interred in the shaft nearby.[13] The proximity of this deposition to an important sanctuary and the singular treatment of the skull make it difficult to argue that this was anything other than ritual activity involving human sacrifice. So it looks as though such barbaric (to the Romans) rites were still taking place well into the Roman period, even in one of the principal towns of Roman Britain, a *municipium*, which gave the people of Verulamium so-called Latin Rights – not quite as prestigious as the full Roman citizenship accorded the *coloniae* (towns built for veterans of the Roman army), but still 'a little piece of Rome, far far away'.[14]

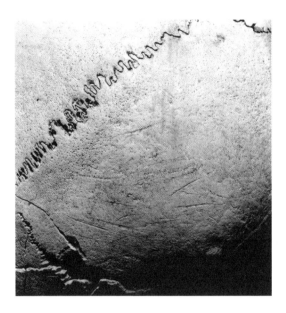

Detail of the boy's skull
found at Folly Lane,
Verulamium, showing
the marks of the
defleshing knife.

Cirencester (Corinium)

Unlike Verulamium in southeast England, the tribal capital of the Dobunni
at Corinium (Cirencester) in the Cotswolds has revealed no unequivocal
architectural evidence for temples. There were formal ritual structures:
the tombstone of Bodicacia (see Chapter 2) was found in close proximity
to a square, walled cemetery, perhaps a mausoleum, built in the late 1st
or early 2nd century AD, but no shrines *per se* have been discovered in
Corinium. However, there is abundant iconographical evidence in the
form of a rich group of stone images that must once have adorned sanctuaries. The 1972 excavations at Price's Row in Watermoor Road revealed
the presence of 4th-century Roman shops built in a line. Outside one of
these was a row of sculptures, including depictions of a mother-goddess
or *Mater* accompanied by three *Genii cucullati* (hooded deities), an altar
dedicated to Mercury and the *Matres* and the carving of an eagle along
with a column-base.[15] Significantly, nearly all these stones had been broken
in antiquity: the eagle's head had been taken off, and the column-base
had been deliberately halved.[16] Is it possible that these sculptures came

from a lost – or destroyed – temple and that their fragmentation and redisposal were associated with religious tensions, intolerance and the reappropriation of old, curated images?

Even more evocative of a city shrine here is a group of stone carvings from the Ashcroft area of the Roman city, found in 1899. Nearly all these sculptures were dedicated to the Gallo-British cult of the Three Mothers, who are depicted with babies, small children or the fruits of the earth. An inscribed altar dedicated to the 'Suleviae' also comes from the site; these were versions of the mother-goddess worshipped also at Bath, their name perhaps deriving from that city's principal deity, Sulis. The *cucullati* are represented here too, as are other deities, including a hunter-god.[17] Neil Holbrook has suggested that this group of sculptures may, like the stones from Price's Row, have been originally located at a temple-site elsewhere, and redeposited as a cache after the shrine was either sacked or fell out of use.[18] Both the *Matres* and the *cucullati* were venerated among the rural Dobunnic population as well as in the tribal capital. These deities were overtly associated with fecundity and prosperity: their portrayal with small children and fruit or bread represents a relationship with their worshippers that included requests or thanksgiving for good harvests and the gift of healthy offspring.

Cirencester was a vividly religious Romano-British town. Its inhabitants worshipped divinities that ranged from the decidedly Gallo-British antlered god Cernunnos (whose cult is explored in Chapter 7) to the Roman State gods that included Jupiter, Mercury, Minerva and Diana. But even Roman gods had their 'Celtic' side. In Gaul and Britain, Mercury acquired an indigenous consort, Rosmerta, and she is represented with him in the town,[19] alongside other, more conventional depictions of the god.[20] Mercury's popularity here may be explained by the fact that in Britain and the Gallic provinces his principal function was as a god of commercial transactions, so people running urban businesses would naturally have been attracted to his cult. Rosmerta's name is Gallic and means 'goddess of prosperity', and so she complemented the concerns of her divine partner.

Jupiter, lord of the Roman gods, wielder of thunder and ruler of the sky (see Chapter 5), was also worshipped in Cirencester, but his cult,

Two views of Bacchic figures carved on the
capital of a Jupiter-column from Corinium. On the left
is a Maenad grasping a *tympanum* (drum); on the
right is Silenus holding a *rhyton* (drinking horn).
Ht *c.* 106 cm (42 in.).

too, was touched by traits whose origins lay in Gaul. Fragments of a
'Jupiter-Giant' column reveal Jupiter's veneration as a sky-horseman at
Cirencester. These monuments were especially popular in eastern Gaul
and in the Rhineland, where they were frequently set up by soldiers on
the *limes* (the military frontier zone that formed the imperial boundary in
Germania). Jupiter-Giant columns present a wonderful blend of Roman
and non-Roman iconography and religious thinking. They consist of a
rectangular or polygonal base stone, decorated with (usually) Classically
inspired divine images and a dedicatory inscription to Jupiter. Above this
a tall pillar, topped by a Corinthian capital, soars towards the sky, and on
its summit is a sculptured group, and this is where the mixture of Gallic
and Roman culture shows itself. The carved group represents a primeval
battle between good and evil, light and dark, sky and underworld: typically,
Jupiter is depicted as a horseman, the front hooves of his mount trampling
a prone 'giant', a sub-humanoid figure with a large head and its lower
limbs replaced by snakes.[21] The sky-rider wields Jupiter's thunderbolt and
his shield wards off the giant's evil gaze. But the Roman Jupiter is never
mounted, and this Gallic version sometimes bears a solar wheel instead

of a shield (see Chapter 5). Cirencester is rare in its evidence for one of these monuments in Britain. The surviving stones include an elaborate Corinthian capital upon which Classical gods, such as Bacchus, disport themselves among the acanthus leaves, and a rectangular base bearing a dedicatory inscription that reads:

> 'To Jupiter Best and Greatest, His Perfection Lucius Septimius…
> governor of Britannia Prima, restored [this monument], being a
> citizen of Rheims.'

And on another face:

> 'This statue and column erected under the ancient religion Septimius
> restores, ruler of Britannia Prima.'[22]

This inscription packs a lot of information into a few words. It tells us that the monument, including a column and the statue of Jupiter, was dedicated by a *very* high-status person from Rheims, a Roman city in northeastern Gaul, who must have commissioned its construction after AD 296 when the emperor Diocletian split Britain into four provinces.[23] Septimius was making a conscious decision to resurrect an obsolete cult that had been at its most popular in the Rhineland from the mid-2nd to 3rd centuries. It is clear from this inscription, and from other evidence such as the tombstones of the Roman cavalrymen Genialis and Dannicus, who hailed from these regions,[24] that Cirencester enjoyed a close association with Rhenish communities. It is likely that the antlered god Cernunnos was also imported by individuals from eastern Gaul, where his cult was especially popular.

Great Chesterford

Very different from the official Roman *municipium* at Verulamium and the *civitas* (tribal) capital at Cirencester was the small walled town of Great Chesterford in Essex. A high-status burial and a rectangular timber shrine, predating a Roman temple, at the site provide evidence of late Iron Age religious activity. Soon after the Claudian conquest a Roman fort was built here, either before or because of the Boudican revolt, strategically located at the junction between two powerful tribes – the Catuvellauni and the Trinovantes,[25] both of whom were heavily involved in the Boudican rebellion. But the military site was dismantled less than two decades after its construction, as the threat of revolution had subsided, and in its place a town grew up, with public buildings, houses and, towards the end of its life, a town wall, erected in the 4th century, presumably in response to a real or perceived threat.[26] A mile to the east of the town a religious precinct was established, its focus a Romano-Celtic temple built on the site of the Iron Age sanctuary, thus making a deliberate statement of engagement with its Iron Age past. The siting of the original shrine may have been chosen because of its proximity to a stream, and there are hints that a sacred tree or grove stood nearby, the latter possibly an artificial structure with trees or tree-trunks planted close together to replicate a natural grove. Close to the Iron Age sanctuary and to its north was a pit containing two complete ceramic vessels buried in about AD 60–70.[27] The shrine's position on this inter-tribal boundary may also have been deliberate, occupying a neutral territory where ceremonial assemblies and tricky negotiations, perhaps conducted by priests – even Druids – may have taken place. After all, Caesar draws attention to the role of the Gallic Druids as arbitrators in disputes.[28]

The Roman temple that succeeded the Iron Age shrine was built directly on top of it in the late 1st or early 2nd century AD, shortly after the Roman town was established. It was a substantial structure of traditional Romano-Celtic rectangular form, with an outer portico ambulatory and a taller *cella* inside, the sanctuary-building surrounded by a *temenos*, or external sacred precinct, bounded by a stone wall. The *cella* and the outer ambulatory were both decorated with mosaic floors. The archaeological evidence for ritual activity here chimes with the pattern of use discerned in other Romano-British and Gallo-Roman temples in so far as the active area seems to have been the *temenos* rather than the innermost shrine itself. Its interest lies in its evidence for highly organized and repetitive acts of worship that must have been controlled or overseen by a (probably resident) professional clergy.

Central to the ritual activity here was the deliberate deposition of special objects – particularly ironwork – and the whole or partial bodies of animals, mostly newborn chicks and the right sides of lambs in pits. The remains of sheep-pens in the precinct indicate a concern for convenience: apparently pilgrims could come to the sanctuary empty-handed and select and purchase an animal for slaughter, rather than bringing their sacrificial lamb with them from home. Analysis of the bones revealed signs of butchery, leading to the conclusion that the animals were killed and partially consumed in acts of commensality (ritual feasting), wherein the cooked sacrificial meat was shared with the gods. Clearly the people involved in these ritual practices considered the right side of the animal the more valuable and efficacious part of the body; it was therefore given to the gods while the less favoured left side was eaten by the worshippers. Cattle were also used in the ceremonies, but in a different way from the lambs: the skulls of five cows and a horse, all with their lower jaws missing, were carefully placed upside-down in a hole outside the precinct.

There is other evidence for how visitors used the shrine, for little gold and silver plaques in the form of feathers or leaves were left by pilgrims as offerings. This type of object was a comparatively common gift found on many Romano-British temple-sites, and again it seems likely that these could be bought in a special shrine-shop near the temple.[29] This sanctuary fell into decline in the 3rd and 4th centuries AD, and while attempts were made to refurbish it late in its life, their success was limited and the building gradually fell into disuse during the early 4th century.[30]

Not all the religious activity at Great Chesterford took place in this one temple. There were other sanctuaries in and around the town, and the habit of depositing offerings in pits was repeated in many parts of the built-up area and its environs. Some of these offerings – including pottery, money, animals, human foetuses and personal objects such as cosmetic sets – may well have been foundation deposits, made to bless new shops or dwellings. But one religious item stands out as a public monument rare in Roman Britain: the remnants of a Jupiter-column, part of an octagonal base saved from its use as a cooling-trough in a smithy in 1803 by a local antiquarian named Foote Gower. (Half a dozen fragmentary Jupiter-columns are known in Britain, compared to over two hundred in eastern Gaul and the Rhineland.) Four carved heads depicting Classical deities can be seen, each set within an arched niche: their identities are uncertain, for the stone is very worn, but at least one may represent Jupiter and others may be the faces of Mars or Mercury and Venus or Luna. Its original provenance is unknown, but when complete it would have towered over the town, at a height of some 15 m (46 ft),[31] just as its fellow did at Corinium, dominating the landscape for miles around. If the pits and shafts that were dug throughout the town seem to reflect a preoccupation with underworld spirits, the Jupiter-column represents an ebullient hymn to the lords of the sky. There are many other signs of the ritual activity that took place at Great Chesterford, including a whole range of deposits in ritual shafts, but one object is worthy of special mention: the ceramic *thuribulum* (incense-burner) found in the mid-19th century,[32] not unlike the ones from the 'Druidic' shrine in Chartres (see pp. 29–32). This vessel provides a chink in the door to imagining the experience of worshipping in the town, for its use involved the burning of aromatic and quite possibly mind-altering substances that could lull devotees into a trance-state in which they received visions of the spirit world.

Rural worship

In July 2016 I went with my small *a cappella* choir to sing Choral Evensong at the tiny 12th-century church of Llanfrynach near Cowbridge in the Vale of Glamorgan, South Wales, an annual summer event. The church stands in the middle of a field, its medieval village deserted after the ravages of the Plague, and it has no electricity supply, so we sang by the dimming light of the windows and by candlelight. It occurred to me as I crossed the field, with its tall nettles and long damp grass, that Romano-British pilgrims approaching rural temples would have experienced something very similar. The countryside was a hive of religious activity in Roman Britain. Sanctuaries ranged from isolated wayside shrines to monumental temples that enjoyed a wide-ranging reputation and to which pilgrims flocked from far and wide. The rural sanctuaries considered here provide a curious contrast to the urban temples of Verulamium and Great Chesterford, where it is unclear to which deities they were dedicated. The shrines at Nettleton Shrub, Wanborough and Lydney were all built for the worship of specific divinities: Apollo Cunomaglus at Nettleton, a sun-god, perhaps Jupiter-Taranis at Wanborough and Nodens at Lydney.

Nettleton Shrub

'Life is a series of adoptions'[33]

It is by no means always possible to tell which god or gods were venerated at temples in Roman Britain, particularly in the absence of epigraphic dedications or iconographic representations. Fortunately, both survive at the temple at Nettleton Shrub in Wiltshire,[34] and so we know that the principal deity worshipped here was Apollo Cunomaglus, his composite Roman and native British name a proclamation of his cross-cultural identity. 'Cunomaglus' means 'Hound-Lord', so the cult at Nettleton was tapping into Apollo's function as a hunter. The temple was built deep in beautiful countryside but was situated on a Roman arterial road, the Fosse Way, and so would have attracted travellers making the journey between the two important towns of Cirencester and Bath, the former being the tribal

Reproduction of an inscribed bronze plaque depicting the young sun-god Apollo from the temple of Apollo Cunomaglus at Nettleton Shrub, Wiltshire. Ht 11 cm (4¼ in.).

capital of the Dobunni, and the latter a major religious settlement as important, in its way, as Canterbury Cathedral or Westminster Abbey are today.

The dedication of the temple to a god with a native name strongly suggests that local people were worshipping him prior to the Roman conquest.[35] Before the temple itself was built at Nettleton, a military base was established in the AD 40s. But a few decades afterwards, a round stone shrine was constructed on the site of a spring, and there is evidence of ancillary buildings in its environs, including a strong-room, a meeting-hall, what may have been a resident priest's house and a hostel where weary pilgrims who had travelled from afar could stay overnight in the hope of receiving dream visions from the gods, as at the shrine at Lydney. This sanctuary went through several phases of minor alteration and refurbishment, and major new construction work took place in the mid-3rd century, when an octagonal *podium* was built surrounding the original circular temple. But soon after the construction of this platform, fire destroyed the sanctuary, and it was replaced by a bigger, more solid and elaborate octagonal temple-building, its arcades and painted wall-plaster displaying the increased popularity and prosperity of the cult-centre. Other buildings adorned Apollo's sacred space here, including a second temple of rectangular design. After the sacred precinct fell into disuse in the early 4th century, attempts were made to restore the cult as part of the mid-4th century pagan revival seen elsewhere in the southwest of the province, probably triggered by the apostate emperor Julian, who made a short-lived attempt to veer away from the Christianity adopted and disseminated by Constantine earlier that century (see Chapter 9).

Of the many votive finds from the main temple, the most revealing is an inscribed altar that reads 'Deo Apollini Cunomaglo Corotica Iuti Filia VSLM' ('to the god Apollo Cunomaglos Corotica, daughter of Iutus, willingly and deservedly fulfilled her vow').[36] Another dedication took the form of a small bronze pedimented plaque depicting the head of a young god with an inscription from a suppliant called Decimius to the god Apollo.[37] Many pilgrims left their mark at Nettleton. Two other rural divinities associated with hunting – the Roman Silvanus and Diana – were worshipped here, along with Mercury and his Gallo-British consort Rosmerta, showing that shrines like this need not be the exclusive domain of a single deity. Visitors to the sanctuary offered coins, jewelry and other personal items to the presiding god or one of his divine companions, including human and animal figurines, together with pottery and glass vessels. Signs of heavy wear in the entrance are testament to the shrine's popularity over centuries and sponsorship by people with money to spend on elaborate stone architecture and painted walls at a wayside shrine.

Why was Apollo Cunomaglus's sanctuary such a popular focus of pilgrimage and worship? The hound-motif suggests hunting, and that would be fitting for a rural shrine. But what of Apollo himself, and was there a deeper symbolism associated with dogs? In order to resolve these issues, Nettleton's physical proximity to the thermal-spring sanctuary at Bath, sacred to Sulis Minerva, is relevant in more than one respect. Not more than a day's walk from each other, the cults of both Apollo and Sulis were associated with light, heat and spring-water, and each may have been on recognized and regular pilgrim-routes. The Classical Apollo was, first and foremost, a sun-god, and Sulis's name suggests that she, too, was a solar deity (see Chapters 5 and 6). Sulis was principally concerned with healing, the hot springs a magnet for sick pilgrims. But Apollo, too, was concerned with health for, according to Classical mythic tradition, he was a wielder of plague, so he may have been propitiated in aversion ceremonies by suppliants anxious to avoid disease. Dogs were also connected with healing cults in the ancient world. The great medicinal sanctuary and theatre dedicated to Asklepios at Epidaurus in the Peloponnese[38] was dedicated to healing (ear complaints in particular, perhaps because of the astounding acoustics of the temple-theatre), and its priests kept live dogs because of the legendary therapeutic properties of their saliva. So, against this cultural backdrop, it is valid to theorize that Nettleton had a role as a sacred place of healing. The personal items the pilgrims left here included things they wore, such as brooches, bracelets and pins (for clothing or hair), these last being votive objects perhaps – because of their phallic shape – associated with the desire for pregnancy.[39]

Wanborough

The discovery of the temple-site at Wanborough, Surrey, is noteworthy for both positive and negative reasons. While the excavation of the shrine produced a wealth of evidence for the activities of both worshippers and – importantly – clergy, the systematic and greedy looting of the site, particularly of its huge assemblage of coins, by metal-detectorists robbed the temple of some of its most significant finds. This is not an out-and-out criticism of metal-detector users. Indeed, the introduction of the Portable Antiquities Scheme in the late 1990s has encouraged increasing and fruitful cordiality between museums and other heritage bodies and metal-detectorists in Britain. Most of the latter are responsible individuals interested in the past for its own sake. Unfortunately, Wanborough was the victim of a less worthy minority who sold what they found for monetary gain,[40] so a great deal of information about this rich site has been lost.

The Wanborough temple-complex has several idiosyncracies, not least of which is the huge number of Iron Age and Roman coins deposited as offerings. But the really important material comprises the highly revealing group

One of the bronze chain-and-wheel headdresses from the temple at Wanborough, Surrey.

of liturgical regalia, including sceptres and headdresses, testament to a thriving clerical presence at the shrine. The headdresses are particularly fascinating because in the absence of inscriptions at the site, they provide clues as to the nature of the presiding deity; the wheel-symbols forming the apex of the ritual headgear are associated elsewhere with the Romano-Celtic sky-god Jupiter-Taranis.[41] These 'crowns' consist of fine bronze chains supporting the wheel-models, presumably mounted on caps made of leather or textile.

There was probably a shrine at Wanborough in the late Iron Age, though no trace of this early building has survived, and the first *locus sanctus* may have been ephemeral, perhaps focused on a sacred grove or tree. Very soon after the Roman conquest a large coin-hoard was buried here, comprising a mixture of Iron Age and Roman issues. Then, in the mid-2nd century AD, a number of large dedication-deposits were made in advance of the construction of the temple itself. The most prominent features of these foundation offerings were redeposited Iron Age coins (perhaps as a way of expressing the shrine's rootedness in the ancestral past) and the liturgical regalia. Soon afterwards the temple of typical Romano-Celtic form was built, with a square inner *cella* surrounded by an ambulatory. Two hundred years later the temple was deliberately demolished.

The presence of sceptres and unusual headdresses at Wanborough invites further consideration, for it is rare for such a concentration of priestly regalia to be found at a Romano-British temple-site. It is possible only to guess at what kind of ceremonies and festivals were celebrated here, but the number of pieces suggests that they included processions in which several clergy took part, each resplendent in their wheel-surmounted headdress. When new, the chains and wheels would have glinted like gold in the sunlight, fitting tributes to a god who, though linked to the Roman Jupiter, had his ancestry in the Gallo-British cult of the sun.[42] The temple at Wanborough had a relatively short life but a rich one, full of pageantry and benefiting from wealthy pilgrims who left pots of food and liquor as well as personal items and, of course, money. So many coins were found here that the temple may, like many Classical sanctuaries, have acted as a community treasury.[43]

Lydney

> 'To the god Nodens: Silvianus has lost his ring and given half its value
> to Nodens. Among those who are called Senicianus do not allow health
> until he brings it to the temple of Nodens'[44]

The lead plaque upon which this inscription was written was found at the imposing stone temple at Lydney Park, Gloucestershire, built high above the river Severn in the late 3rd or early 4th century AD. The sanctuary was dedicated to the British god Nodens, whose name is philologically connected to an Irish god-king, Nuadu, who is chronicled in the early Irish myths.[45] The plaque belongs to a group of objects known as *defixiones*, or curse tablets. These vengeful messages were used by aggrieved parties to implore or demand divine punishment – frequently in the form of ill-health – from the gods for personal crimes such as theft.[46] The Lydney curse is especially interesting, for someone called Senicianus lost a gold ring inscribed with his name far away at Silchester in Hampshire, where it was found early last century. Was this the malefactor who stole a fellow pilgrim's ring on Nodens' holy ground? It would be nice to think so, and to speculate whether the god's hand stretched out far enough to punish him.

The temple at Lydney was built late in the Roman period but, like other shrines in southern England,[47] it was deliberately sited inside a defunct Iron Age hillfort. Iron mining took place here too, and two votive objects associated with the mine consisted of miniature miner's picks, each made of iron,[48] though most model implements made for religious offerings were of bronze.[49] Of the other numerous votive objects, including personal possessions, such as pins, rings and brooches, among the most revealing were two more inscribed dedications to Nodens, both on sheet-bronze plates,[50] and no fewer than nine small votive images of dogs, including a beautiful figurine of a recumbent deerhound.[51] The last-mentioned group suggests that, like Apollo Cunomaglus at Nettleton, Nodens was a hound-lord, perhaps associated with hunting. But the presence of votive dog-figurines may have other meanings. The link between these animals and healing has already been considered, and at least two other gifts brought by pilgrims

suggest a therapeutic aspect to Nodens' responsibilities: a figurine of a
pregnant woman clutching her abdomen, and a model arm, its fingers
displaying a malformation due to iron deficiency, a problem that might
well have been alleviated by drinking or bathing in the red, iron-rich water
of the stream flowing through the site. An oculist was present at Lydney,
leaving behind him a stamp from a pot of eye ointment, enhancing the
notion that Nodens was a divine healer. There is also evidence at Lydney
for an *abaton* or dormitory, where a sick pilgrim might stay overnight in
the hope of a healing vision from the god.

The finds from Lydney demonstrate the presence of professional clergy
here. They wore chain headdresses, similar to those from Wanborough,
and the regalia of one consisted of a splendid bronze diadem depicting
one of the sun-gods, Apollo or Sol, standing in a *quadriga* (a four-horse
chariot) and armed with a flail.[52] We are fortunate in being able to put
names to individual religious officials who presided over the rites at Lydney,
for the *cella* of the sanctuary was adorned with a beautiful mosaic pavement depicting the Severn Bore (the great tidal wave that sweeps down
the river at particular times),[53] together with dolphins and other water
creatures. It bears a highly informative inscription telling visitors to the
temple that one Titus Flavius Senilis dedicated the mosaic to Nodens'
holy place. Senilis calls himself a 'superintendent of religious rites'. The
man who supervised the laying of the mosaic was Victorinus, but he was
not simply a craftsman, for the inscription mentions that he was an *inter-
pres*;[54] it is highly likely that this means he was an expert in reading and
interpreting the dreams and visions of pilgrim-visitors and of decoding
the obscure messages that came from professional oracles who had the
ear of the god (see Chapter 6).

So what sort of god was Nodens? Was he primarily a healer-deity, or
a hunter (as implied by the deerhound figurine)? Could he have been
involved with both? Was he also a god of water, the sun and iron-produc-
tion, as some of the deposits from the site suggest? The cult of Nodens
seems to have been complex and multifaceted. The temple was situated
in an area that, even today, is rural and remote. Yet it was a sophisticated, Classically styled building, with resident clergy and a rich variety

Reproduction of a bronze figurine of a dog with a human face, from the temple of Nodens at Lydney, Gloucestershire. Ht c. 6.5 cm (2½ in.).

of sacred objects. The apparent ambiguity of Nodens may be explained partly by a small figurine that seems to be highly significant, depicting a dog with a human face.[55] Shape-shifting was a common phenomenon in Gallo-Roman and Romano-British cult imagery, and this statuette may well represent the involvement of shamans in ritual activities. Shamans traditionally act as conduits between the material and spirit worlds, and they often have animal-helpers who facilitate such transitions. Shamans are frequently associated with healing because in antiquity (as in some traditional societies today) disease was commonly thought to have been caused by the intervention of maleficent spirits, whom the shaman sought to control.[56] It may be that the idea of transformation is key to understanding the complexities of Nodens' cult at Lydney. In hunting, life and death are exchanged, and in many traditional hunting communities, venery is hedged with ritual and taboo to ensure that the killed animal's spirit is appeased and that the herd of deer, or the slain hare, would return to the earthly world reborn. Ideas of transition between states may also explain the two votive inscriptions at Lydney to Mars Nodens.[57] Chapter 6 explores the manner in which the traditional role of Mars as a warrior-god, patron of soldiers, was reinterpreted in Britain and Gaul as that of a fighter against illness. Such perceptions were underpinned by ideas of changed states: from life to death in hunting and war to transformation from sickness to health.

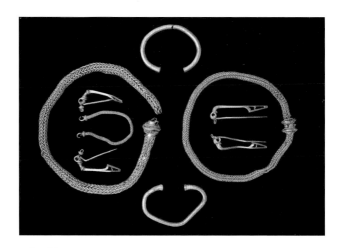

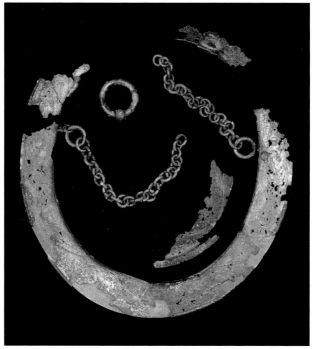

PREVIOUS PAGE Silver dish from Mildenhall, Suffolk, its central roundel depicting Oceanus, the great river believed by the Romans to encircle the world. (diam. of dish 61 cm/2 ft). The dish comes from a cache of silver treasure deliberately buried in the 4th century AD (see p. 6).

TOP Late Iron Age hoard of Greek-made gold jewelry found near Winchester, Hampshire (see p. 11).

ABOVE The Iron Age headdress as discovered at Cerrig-y-Drudion, North Wales (see p. 22).

OPPOSITE Modern reconstruction of the Cerrig-y-Drudion headdress.

ABOVE Sculpture showing
the violation of Britannia
by the emperor Claudius,
from Aphrodisias,
Turkey (see p. 39).

OPPOSITE Life-sized decapitated head
from an equestrian statue of the emperor
Claudius that once stood outside the great
temple at Colchester, found in the river
Alde, Suffolk (see p. 44).

BOADICEA

OPPOSITE Edwardian stained-
glass window depicting
'Boadicea' (Boudica) from
the 'Queens' Window' in
the Moot Hall at Colchester
Town Hall (see p. 47).

ABOVE The tombstone of an early 2nd-century AD
British woman called Bodicacia, found in 2015
in a Roman cemetery at Corinium. In the apex
of the monument the deliberately defaced head
of Oceanus, with crab-claws in his hair, is
clearly visible (see p. 51). Ht 134 cm (53 in.).

Bronze plaque depicting Victory,
from the legionary fortress of
Caerleon, South Wales (see p. 67).
Ht 26.2 cm (10½ in.).

CHAPTER FIVE

Cosmology in Roman Britain
Sky, earth and water

'When mistletoe is discovered it is gathered with great ceremony, and particularly on the sixth day of the moon, because it is then rising in strength and not one half of its full size. Hailing the moon in a native word that means "healing all things" the Druids prepare a ritual sacrifice and feast beneath a tree and bring up two white bulls. A priest wearing a white robe climbs the tree and with a golden sickle cuts down the mistletoe, which is caught in a white cloak...'PLINY[1]

This famous passage by Pliny the Elder hints at the part played by observation of the natural world in Gallo-British belief-systems. Although Pliny was making specific reference to Gallic Druids, both he and Caesar mention their influence in Britannia. What is so telling about Pliny's comments is the emphasis on the moon's physical properties: its changefulness and its gleaming whiteness. The moon's brightness is acknowledged in the white robes of the priests, the choice of white bulls for sacrifice and the attraction to the pale luminescence of the mistletoe berries.[2] The 'golden' sickle was almost certainly gilded bronze, but its pale, shining surface and the curved shape of its blade would seem, once more, to reflect the character of the rising moon.

Antiquarian picture of Pliny's Druids cutting the mistletoe from the sacred oak on the sixth day of the moon.

Songs to the moon

The river Witham in Lincolnshire has long been recognized as a place where Iron Age Britons came to offer precious gifts, including decorated military equipment, to the gods.[3] But archaeologists became particularly interested in the region when, in 1981, a metal-detectorist found part of a sword inlaid with red coral. This led to the mounting of an excavation on the north bank of the river at Fiskerton that revealed something very odd indeed: rows of wooden posts that formed a timber trackway over the low-lying boggy ground. It was possible to date the trackway very accurately by means of dendrochronology (tree-ring dating), which determined the very year that the trees used were felled. The result was quite startling, for a pattern of continuous construction was revealed. Over a period of one hundred and fifty years beginning in 457 BC the posts were removed and replaced every twenty years or so, during ten episodes of activity, and although not every timber post used in the causeway fits the pattern precisely, it has been possible to identify a rhythm of renewal that would appear to have broadly coincided with lunar eclipse events[4] and continued until the 4th century BC.

The focus on Fiskerton as a sacred site was not confined to the wooden causeway. In the later Iron Age and Roman periods, people were making offerings here in the form of martial equipment, ornaments, two log-boats and part of another whose form suggests a Roman date.[5] A more sinister find, made during the excavations in 1981, was part of a human skull whose owner received a deadly head-wound from a sword.[6] While it is impossible to be certain, it is entirely feasible that the despatch of this individual – probably a young man – was an act of human sacrifice, and that the body was cast off the causeway into the water, maybe during the Roman period, in the same fashion as other votive offerings. It would be rash to make a firm assertion that all this ritual activity was associated with the moon, but sacred memory can be long, and if the renewal of the trackway was a ritual connected with lunar eclipses, it may be that the continued sanctity of the site also had links with the moon. Archaeological evidence from the European continent may corroborate such a theory. Certain Iron Age

Iron Age silver coin from Drayton,
Hampshire, depicting a horse beneath
a crescent, or partially eclipsed, moon.
Diam. *c.* 2 cm (¾ in.).

iron swords or daggers from central Europe are ornamented with gold inlaid symbols representing full and crescent moons.[7] An Iron Age silver coin from Drayton, Hampshire, depicts a galloping horse, above which is a motif that seems to depict either a crescent moon or a moon in the process of eclipse.[8] Finally, Caesar's observation that Gallic people counted time by night rather than by day supports the theory that night possessed a particular significance, at least in Gaul (see Chapter 10).[9]

In the summer of 2016, a cave explorer in the Gower Peninsula in southwest Wales found human bones trapped beneath a roof-fall, along with a small copper-alloy statuette (see p. ix). The figure stands some 10 cm (4 in.) high; its gender is uncertain, but probably female, to judge by the absence of obvious male genitalia. Its head is overly large and its physiognomy, with its lentoid eyes, wedge-shaped nose and the slit of a mouth, betrays its local, perhaps Iron Age, manufacture. But most striking is the huge crescent headdress it wears, and it is tempting to interpret the image as that of a moon-deity. Between its feet is a small hole, probably for the insertion of a staff, suggesting that the figurine was carried in ceremonial processions or other ritual activities, perhaps taking place in the torch-lit darkness of the cave.[10]

The Romans introduced the moon-goddess Luna to Britain. A vivid relief-carving from the thermal-spring sanctuary of Sulis Minerva at Bath shows Luna in front of a lunar crescent, a riding whip in her hand. The stone formed part of a temple-pediment and would have been visible to anyone visiting the shrine.[11] One of the votive finds from the reservoir of the main hot spring was a silver moon-pendant,[12] probably once attached to a sceptre carried by a religious official in processions or other religious duties. There is little evidence that Luna was a popular goddess in Roman Britain, but in the temple to Sulis at Bath at least, with its emphasis on heat and the sun, Luna played a prominent role, demonstrating that worshippers recognized the importance of acknowledging the moon as ruler of the night skies.

Gods of the heavens

'Those who propitiate with horrid victims ruthless Teutates, and Esus whose savage shrine makes men shudder, and Taranis, whose altar is no more benign than that of Scythian Diana...' LUCAN[13]

'Teutates who inspires terror with sacrificial blood, and whose altar bristles with weapons, is called Mercurius Teutates in the language of the Gauls. He was venerated with human blood. Esus Mars is appeased thus: a man is suspended in a tree until his limbs fall apart in a bloody sacrifice. They propitiate Taranis Dis Pater by cremating several men in a wooden trough'. BERN SCHOLIAST ON LUCAN[14]

In AD 60, the Roman poet Lucan published the first three books of his epic poem the *Pharsalia*, commemorating the last great battle for leadership of Rome, between Julius Caesar and Pompey in 48 BC at Pharsalus in Thessaly. In the first passage quoted here, he describes three Gallic gods encountered by Caesar's army near Massilia (Marseille): Teutates, Esus and Taranis. The second, more detailed account is by a medieval Swiss author from Bern, writing his commentary on the *Pharsalia* in the 9th century AD. The latter presumably drew on ancient texts that are now lost. All three fearsome deities feature – albeit rarely – in the epigraphic record of Britain and Gaul.[15]

Lucan's first two deities bear Gallo-British names that reflect their status: 'Teutates' means 'tribe', the name being cognate with the Irish *tuath*, and 'Esus' means 'lord'. Both are thus associated with titles of rank, rather than particular abilities or affinities. Taranis is different, for his name is functional: it means 'Thunderer', from the Celtic word for thunder (surviving in the Welsh *taran*). While the medieval Bernese 'scholiast' conflates Taranis with the Roman Dis Pater, god of night and darkness, the few surviving inscribed dedications refer to him either alone or coupled with Jupiter. Of these, the sole British example is a sandstone altar with a now virtually illegible inscription from the legionary fortress at Chester.[16] It was found in the mid-17th century while a cellar was being excavated for a householder named Richard Tyrer, and it is probably because he kept it in his garden for over twenty years that the inscribed surface is so worn. The dedication was made to: 'Jupiter Best and Greatest Tanarus, Lucius Bruttius Praesens, of the Galerian voting tribe, from Clunia, *princeps* of Legion XX Valeria Victrix, willingly and deservedly fulfilled his vow, in the consulships of Commodus and Lateranus'. The inscription, fortunately transcribed before being worn away, is full of information: the dedicant was a centurion who hailed from Spain.[17] The slight variation in the deity's Gallo-British name is probably due to a mistake made by the *scriptor* (the text drafter) or the *ordinator* (the stone-cutter), either (or both) of whom may never have seen the god's name in writing, being quite possibly illiterate and reliant on dictation from a third party.[18]

The altar to Taranis/Tanarus from Chester is indicative of how far interconnections between Roman and provincial religion could develop. Here was a high-ranking citizen soldier, a leader of men in the Roman army, yet he openly proclaimed his allegiance to a foreign Gallic sky-deity whose cult he clearly perceived as being suitably coupled with the highest of the Roman State gods. As was considered in Chapters 2 and 3, the veneration of Jupiter by the military blended religion with politics, the latter being closely associated with repeated declarations of loyalty to the emperor and the spirit of Rome by army personnel, however far they were from the imperial centre.

Altar dedicated to Jupiter Optimus Maximus set up by soldiers at Maryport, Cumbria, with detail of the Gallo-British solar wheel. Ht 79 cm (31 in.).

And was it this same hybrid sky-lord, Jupiter Taranis, whose wheel-symbol was surreptitiously carved on the sides or the backs of altars overtly dedicated to Jupiter Best and Greatest at forts on Hadrian's Wall, such as Castlesteads, Maryport and Birdoswald? And what did this wheel represent? Did it belong to Jupiter's chariot, rolling thunder across the heavens? Or was it the motif of the Gallo-British sun-god, whose flaming wheel depicted solar force?[19] The wheel as a sacred symbol was deeply entrenched in Gallo-Roman religious thinking, and it was present in Roman Britain, too, albeit less commonly. In the 3rd century AD, an individual deposited a hoard of religious bronzes in a pot at Felmingham Hall, Norfolk. The vessel contained a range of priestly regalia and figurines, including ravens, a model wheel and a human head apparently radiating light and surmounted by a crescent moon,[20] this last lending credence to the interpretation of the wheel as a celestial symbol. In Gaul and the Rhineland, the horseman depicted on the summit of Jupiter-columns sometimes carries a sun-wheel in place of the more usual shield (see Chapter 4).[21] The sky-god used the solar disc as a means of combating the 'dark side' represented by the human-snake monster.

The complex symbolism demonstrated in the representation of the sky-father clearly reflects its one-time background in ancient mythology. Two striking objects from Roman Britain perhaps allow a glimpse into the story behind the celestial cult of Britain and Gaul. Each is part of a ceremonial sceptre. One comes from a temple at Farley Heath, Surrey: a sheet-bronze strip originally wound around a wooden stave, it depicts a range of images including wild and domestic animals, a 'smith-god' carrying a long-shafted hammer and a pair of tongs, and a human head associated with a sun-wheel and a thunderbolt.[22] The other sceptre-piece comes from a sacred hoard at Willingham Fen in Cambridgeshire. This sceptre-head was cast in bronze and contains what must relate to a hidden story of light and darkness told in images: a god with a solar wheel, accompanied by

Bronze sceptre-terminal depicting the solar wheel-god with his eagle, a triple-horned bull's head and underworld creature trampled beneath the god's foot, from Willingham Fen, Cambridgeshire. Ht 12 cm (4¾ in.).

an eagle and the head of a bull with three horns (see Chapter 7), grinds an underworld monster into the ground underfoot.[23]

Earth matters

Sun- and sky-cults were necessarily closely associated with the land: put at its simplest, the sun, rain, storms, drought, heat and cold have direct consequences for the fertility and well-being of livestock and crops, and thus for the communities that rely upon them. It is no surprise, then, that Romano-Britons acknowledged these connections in religious representations. A stone carving from the Cotswolds near Cirencester depicts three mother-goddesses seated in a niche in whose gable is a solar wheel.[24]

Stone carving depicting a *Genius* whose usual *patera* (offering-plate) is replaced by a solar wheel, from Netherby, Cumbria. Ht c. 43.5 cm (17 in.).

The female images on this stone are simple or stylized in form and their 'Britishness' is emphasized by their over-large heads.[25] Each woman holds a product of the harvest – probably bread or fruit – in her lap. At the other end of Roman Britain, at Netherby near Carlisle in Cumbria, the stone figure of a *Genius loci* (a spirit of place) carries a solar wheel in place of the *patera* or offering-plate usually held by such figures.[26] Both carvings appear to reflect the need to propitiate the spirits controlling the sun, and the earth's consonant fertility.

The sacred marriage

A prominent theme in early Irish mythology is the notion of sacral kingship, wherein the divine female personification of the land wed the mortal king in order to secure and enhance the land's prosperity. This holy union was symbolized by the goddess's act of passing a wine-cup to her mortal spouse. But the goddess was fickle and, if her royal husband was not up to the mark, she abandoned him for a more likely partner, thus ensuring that the land continued to flourish. For under a miserly and ineffective king, Ireland's fertility was doomed to fail.[27] Although the Irish myths were assembled in written form during the medieval period (between about AD 800 and 1200),[28] it is likely that they contain grains of material from earlier, pre-Christian times. It is certainly true that both sculptures and epigraphy in Roman Britain (and Gaul) reflect divine partnership. In certain Gallic sculptures depicting such couples, the male deity actually holds a cup of wine, as if to indicate his legitimation as king by his consort.[29] What is particularly interesting is that, where the names are recorded, the goddess frequently bears a local Gallo-British name, while that of her consort is more often of Roman derivation, or he might have a Roman and a local name (see Chapter 11). Perhaps the female partner represented the spirit of the land, joined in marriage to an intrusive, foreign (Roman) partner. Rosmerta and Mercury (see pp. 228–29) are a good example of this pattern of representation. On one image of the couple from Gloucester, the god is portrayed in fully Roman form, with his signature emblems of *caduceus* (herald's staff), purse and cockerel, while his consort's imagery owes much less to Classical tradition and is far more inventive. And, in the context of the 'sacred marriage', her symbolism is telling, for she holds a small skillet poised over a casket of ale, perhaps ready to hand to her partner, chiming with the Irish mythic union between goddess and king.[30]

A pilgrim called Peregrinus from Trier in the Moselle Valley set up an inscribed dedication to his local gods, Loucetius Mars and Nemetona, while visiting the thermal-spring sanctuary at Bath.[31] The name 'Loucetius' comes from a Gallic god of light, often twinned with Mars, perhaps because of his common function in the western provinces as a healer and protector.[32] Nemetona's name reveals her identity as a goddess of the land, and specifically of the sacred grove or *nemeton*. Several Gallo-British place-names have this word as their root, including Vernemeton ('the most sacred of groves') in Nottinghamshire.[33] The pairing of a god of light with a goddess of the land chimes with the connection between the solar wheel and the mother-goddesses or *Genius loci* mentioned earlier; perhaps the appearance of the sun-symbol with these earth-spirits is a way of expressing the partnership depicted more overtly with Loucetius and Nemetona.

Earth mothers

The most prominent evidence for deities connected with the fertility of livestock, crops and humans is provided by the popular cult of the *Matres* or mother-goddesses, so often depicted in triplicate. We have touched upon their cult in Chapters 3 and 4, and the habit of multiplying gods by three is considered further in Chapter 7. But the mother-goddess cult, as presented especially in southwest England, repays investigation here in terms of the way the goddesses were depicted. Divergences of style in the iconography of Cirencester and Bath betray the mind-set of the sculptor or the patron who commissioned it (or both). The little schist plaque from Bath[34] depicts three female figures standing side by side (and looking irresistibly like the 'three little maids from school' in Gilbert and Sullivan's *Mikado*). They have disproportionately large heads, large bulging eyes, bare torsos from the waist up and long pleated skirts. They are not identical: the position of their hands and arms is different, and they are of slightly different sizes, the largest occupying the central position. Their underdeveloped breasts and youthful physique suggest they are young girls, possibly adolescents. A close look at their prominent eyes reveals the possibility that they are either blind or suffering from goitre[35] – in which case, they might represent not goddesses but supplicant-pilgrims visiting Sulis's thermal spring to be healed.

The mother-goddess figurines from Cirencester provide a sharp contrast to the little figures on the plaque from Bath, for they are much more naturalistically portrayed, but again where they occur in triplicate each female has her own persona, and is not just a clone of her colleagues. Three relief-carvings from the town that depict the three mothers are treated very differently one from the other. Two come from what must have been a shrine in the Ashcroft area of the town, and accompanying

Schist plaque depicting triple goddesses, from the sanctuary of Sulis Minerva at Bath. Ht 24 cm (9½ in.).

them was an inscription (one of two from Cirencester)[36] to the 'Suleviae', clearly a local name for the goddesses. The mothers were also known by this name at Bath,[37] so it is likely that this little plaque shows the same goddesses. The link between the two Roman towns is Sulinus, a sculptor who dedicated altars to the *Matres Suleviae* in both. The connection between his name and that of his chosen goddesses is interesting. Maybe he selected them for their names, or did he, perhaps, name himself after them, as a sign of special devotion and as a way of giving himself to the divinities?

Two of the Corinium mother-goddess carvings show the women seated stiffly in a row, staring out at their spectators.[38] On each of the two stones, the women are given separate identities, with unique quirks in hairstyles and clothing. On one, the three hold trays of produce on their laps; two of them wear pleated robes but the one on the right (facing the viewer) wears a cloak pinned at the breast, more appropriate to a male deity, and close inspection even reveals possible traces of a beard. So the sculptor may have been 'playing with' or subverting gender, as if to shock, to jolt supplicants into challenging assumptions concerning the categorization of divinities as exclusively male or female. The second stone shows a different set of mother-goddesses, with long hair and robes to the feet; the two outer figures each have dishes of food on their knees, while the central woman holds a tightly swaddled baby. The final carving is very different: it displays three women looking relaxed, as if gossiping together in a playgroup, their toddlers frolicking around them with a small dog.[39]

Stone statue-base dedicated to the Suleviae by a stonemason called Sulinus, from Bath. Ht 58.5 cm (23 in.).

There is one very simple, 'matchstick' carving from the Cotswold Roman villa-site of Chedworth[40] that seems to resonate with several features of the earth-goddesses from the region already considered here. It depicts a robed figure with spiky hair, standing in a niche, its right hand poised over a cylindrical bucket, like Rosmerta's. But in its left hand it holds a spear. The image itself appears 'gender-neutral', but a very faint inscription scratched on the base reads 'Dea Riigina', 'the goddess queen'. It is always possible that the name could have been added to the stone some time after the figure was carved but, if not, the title is suggestive of the 'sacred marriage' alluded to in the context of divine partners. And the presence of the spear is interesting, too, because it is unusual to find a weapon in a woman's hand and the image itself bears no resemblance to the Roman armed goddess Minerva. The spear's position in the *left* hand may also be revealing,[41] since then, as now, only a small proportion of the population was left-handed – so the spear may have been consciously placed in that hand to convey a non-aggressive attitude more appropriate of a guardian, communicating latent, but reserved, power. But, as perhaps with one of the Cirencester *Matres* carvings, was gender, again, perceived as a contested, questioned and perhaps fluid issue?

Stone relief-carving of a goddess with a spear; on the base is a scratched dedication to 'Dea Riigina' (the goddess queen). Found near Chedworth, Gloucestershire, and almost certainly from the precincts of the Roman villa. Ht 26 cm (10¼ in.).

The water-spirits

'And the lakes in particular provided inviolability for their treasures, into which they let down heavy masses of silver and gold. The Romans indeed, when they conquered the area, sold the lakes by public auction, and many of the purchasers found there hammered mill-stones of silver. In Toulouse, moreover, the temple was a revered one, greatly esteemed by the local inhabitants and for this reason the treasure there was unusually large since many made dedications and none would dare to profane them.' STRABO[42]

The Greek geographer Strabo lived from c. 63 BC to AD 21. His *Geography* draws heavily upon the lost works of the earlier author Posidonius, who travelled in Gaul in the early 1st century BC. Here, Strabo was describing the rituals of the Tectosages, a tribe who lived in southwest Gaul, their capital being Toulouse. The passage is important for its emphasis on the sanctity accorded the deposition of precious objects in watery places, a practice we have already encountered. Strabo was writing about a specific region in southern France but Iron Age sites such as Fiskerton, Llyn Cerrig Bach (see pp. 19–21) and rivers, such as the Thames and Witham, indicate the importance of aquatic sanctuaries in Britain. Given this background, it is entirely understandable that water-cults played a prominent role in Romano-British religion.

The sacred river

According to early Irish mythology, the most sacred river was the Boyne, which winds through the present-day counties Meath, Kildare and Louth. One medieval mythic document, the *History of Places*, describes the way in which the goddess Boann was transformed into the great river as a punishment. She was married to a water-god named Nechtan, but when she disobeyed his command never to visit his holy well, he cast a spell so that the spring-water boiled over the well-head and surrounded her, sweeping her up in its torrent and turning her into a water-spirit.[43] Many Irish legends focus on the magical properties of Boann's great river, most famously in

Stone image of a river-god, from the Walbrook Valley,
London (very possibly from the Mithraeum).
Ht 34 cm (13 in.).

the story of the young hero Finn and Finnegas the Bard.[44] When he was still just a child, Finn came upon Finnegas, near his house on the banks of the Boyne, where he was fishing for the legendary Salmon of Wisdom, which dwelt in a river pool. Just as Finn approached, the bard caught the fish and instructed Finn to cook it. As the boy did so, he inadvertently touched the scorching flesh with his thumb and instinctively sucked the sore place. And so it was that, by accident, the salmon's vast knowledge was passed to Finn and he became a fount of all wisdom. The river Boyne was clearly a 'thin' place, a portal to the Otherworld, whence the spirits strayed into the domain of people and changed their lives forever.

But what of rivers in Roman Britain? Were they, too, invested with sacred power? Some of the divine personifications, like the bearded reclining river-gods from the Walbrook Valley in London[45] and at Cirencester,[46] were depicted in the manner of the Roman water-god Neptune. But the names of several indicate that they were perceived as female: Verbeia was the goddess of the river Wharfe in Ilkley,[47] and Sabrina was the personified spirit of the Severn.[48] But it is, perhaps, Tamesa, the goddess of the Thames,[49] for whom there is the most evidence for persistent veneration. It was into this great river that Iron Age communities living in the vicinity of what would become the bustling Roman port city of Londinium cast exquisitely decorated metalwork, particularly military parade-gear, such as the Battersea Shield and the Waterloo Helmet,[50] presumably as offerings to the spirit of the tidal waters. What is more, a series of disembodied human skulls have been found in both the Thames and its tributary the Walbrook: they belonged to young men and some have been dated to the early Roman period.[51] Were these also offerings to the river-gods, perhaps made at a time of deep crisis in the province? Could it be that these young adults were sacrificed at the time that Boudica's army was marching on Roman London, and buried within the waters? Or perhaps the heads were deliberately removed from corpses and deposited in a sacred river as some act of reverence to the spirit within. Might they, like the objects from the Thames, have been offerings to the river-goddess Tamesa?

Fire, sun and steaming water: the healing sanctuary to Sulis at Bath

'In Britain there are hot springs furnished luxuriously for human use. Over these springs Minerva presides and in her temple the perpetual fire never whitens to ash, but as the flame fades, turns into rocky lumps.' SOLINUS[52]

In the early 3rd century AD, Solinus wrote thus of the hot and sacred springs at Bath, part of a series of strange phenomena from all over the Roman Empire that he gathered from other people's anecdotes. Ancient chroniclers[53] called Bath *Aquae Calidae* ('hot waters'), but the town is better known as Aquae Sulis, after the local name of the presiding goddess. The thermal springs here gush out of the ground beside the river Avon at a rate of over a million litres (a quarter of a million gallons) a day at a temperature of 46° C (114.8° F).

Solinus's comment about fire has gone generally unnoticed, but it is potentially important, for the worship of the goddess Sulis (whose name is related to the Celtic 'Sul' meaning 'sun') was all about heat. The first image seen by pilgrims visiting the town's sanctuary would have been the intimidating, moustachioed head of the 'male Medusa' that glared out at the world from the temple-pediment (see p. x, top).[54] The eels and serpents in his hair suggest that gorgon-, solar- and water-symbolism all influenced the sculptor's representation. But it is tempting to see the swirling tendrils surrounding this head as flames.[55]

The Romans made much of the hot springs at Bath. Indeed, the highly visible and odour-laden billows of steam emanating from the hot water would have struck any visitor with wonder. Only a few decades after the Claudian invasion, engineers (probably from the military) were deployed to build a great stone temple and precinct around the bubbling waters, and not only were the military involved in building the sanctuary to Sulis; the sacred complex may have been originally established by and for Roman soldiers. There is paltry evidence for exploitation of the site in the Iron Age[56] and, if the springs held significant pre-Roman sanctity, any ritual activity during this period has left virtually no footprint. But the sacred springs of Aquae Sulis were a magnet for Romans and Roman Britons. During a massive and integrated construction programme, the reservoir containing the principal spring, the temple and the bathing complex were built in homage to the goddess and to accommodate large numbers of pilgrims.

The local spring-deity was Sulis and her responsibilities were clearly perceived as akin to those of the Roman State soldier-goddess Minerva, perhaps in her role as guardian, a protector against disease and misfortune. Were only the imagery of Sulis Minerva to have survived, she would be interpreted as a wholly imported Classical divinity, for the life-sized gilded bronze head, severed from the body in antiquity and originally bearing a helmet, appears to depict the young Minerva in typically Roman style (see p. xi.[57] But the epigraphic evidence tells us her true identity: the

Stone relief of Minerva, from the sanctuary of
Sulis Minerva at Bath. Ht 69 cm (27 in.).

dedications made to the goddess address her as Sulis Minerva, or simply as
Sulis.[58] A lead *defixio*, or curse tablet, from the spring-reservoir mentions
Fons Sulis (the Spring of Sulis), clearly in reference to the divine personification of the miraculous steaming waters constantly bubbling up from
underground.[59] And close scrutiny of some of the iconography appears
to acknowledge local traditions alongside those of Rome. One image of
Minerva,[60] standing in a gabled niche, depicts a rather ungainly woman
with a heavy woollen robe (suitable for Britannia's fickle climate) and
with the typical Minervan *gorgoneion*[61] (head of Medusa) on her breast but
otherwise distinctly British in style, with flame-like hair and a very Celtic
face that has a marked resemblance to the head on the temple-pediment.
It is true that Sulis's sanctuary attracted many cults besides her own, so

we should make only a tentative interpretation of this triple-image as Sulis rather than any other local female divinities, but it is nevertheless possible that the charming trio of schematized 'mother-goddesses' on the little schist plaque from the town (see p. 106)[62] represented Sulis in local triplistic tradition.[63]

The hot water of the springs (though foul to taste and at times toxic to drink) was recognized by Romans and Britons to possess curative properties, particularly for inflammatory disorders such as gout and rheumatism. Pilgrims travelled here from far-flung places in the western Roman Empire: Peregrinus from Trier was just one of many who undertook a gruelling journey to a sanctuary whose presiding spirit clearly had a profound and widespread reputation beyond Britannia. Sulis's popularity came from her thermal springs. Bath was one of a host of healing sanctuaries in Britain and the western provinces that grew up around springs and sacred pools. In Gaul, these curative shrines are characterized by the presence of model body-parts presented by sick pilgrims in the hope that the healer-deity would accept these offerings in exchange for healthy organs.[64]

British pilgrims left fewer of these anatomical votive gifts at the curative shrines they visited but, as noted at Lydney (see pp. 94–96), they are occasionally found here. Two offerings in the form of miniature pairs of breasts are recorded from the main spring at Bath; perhaps the women who left them for Sulis did so in hope of, or gratitude for, successful lactation.[65] Female pilgrims cast other personal possessions into the sacred spring, intimate items worn on the body, as if to establish direct connection between supplicant and goddess. As was so often the case in antiquity, spiritual healing went hand in hand with empirical medicine. An eye-doctor called Janianus perhaps held a regular surgery here, leaving stamps for eye-ointment inscribed with his name at Sulis's sanctuary.[66] Ironically, the spring-water in the baths at Bath may itself have been a source of eye infections, providing eye-physicians like Janianus with an ever-burgeoning and lucrative trade.

Whatever the nature of ritual that went on at this great spring-shrine, the principal focus was the enclosed reservoir that Roman engineers built to control and enclose the sacred spring and its magical hot waters.

Countless objects were deliberately cast into the pool: from pewter vessels, used to douse pilgrims or for drinking-cups, to a washer from a catapult, an offering from a soldier.[67] But the most striking group of objects cast into the reservoir is the *defixiones*, the curse tablets, with vengeful inscriptions scratched onto the soft lead or pewter, demanding justice and retribution for wrongs done to pilgrims, usually involving theft. We will return to these fascinating objects in the next chapter.

What exactly was the status of Aquae Sulis? Was it a Roman town that happened to have a spa and temple, or was it principally a sanctuary to a powerful goddess, with thriving pilgrim visitor numbers, around which the settlement grew and from which it drew its economic prosperity, rather like Lourdes? And what of the relationship between Bath and other Roman sites in the region? We know of connections between the temple-spa and Corinium, where the same sculptor, Sulinus, plied his trade. And some deities, like the Suleviae, were also shared by Bath and Corinium. Bath also possessed links with the temple of Mercury at Uley, Gloucestershire, where the same scribes were employed at both sites to write out curse tablets on lead or pewter sheets (see p. 192). So several sites in the vicinity of Bath and the Cotswolds appear to have enjoyed close-knit connections with each other.

In the archaeologist Barry Cunliffe's words, 'Bath is a peculiar settlement, in size much smaller than typical Roman market towns, in elaboration much greater'.[68] It is impossible to resolve Bath's role, if any, in the politics of the province, whether it 'served as a centre for regional government'[69] or not. Bath was perhaps essentially a cathedral city, like Salisbury or Wells: small but rich and powerful beyond its size, and a centre for cult and pilgrimage. We may imagine regular pilgrimages that could take in a number of the neighbouring holy places during spiritual journeys. However, during the 4th century AD, rising sea levels affected the water-table and the baths suffered disastrous flooding. They eventually closed, and the demise of the spa and temple's prosperity marched alongside the end of *romanitas* experienced by Britain as a whole, exacerbated by tensions within the religious community, as we shall see in Chapter 11.

Coventina's Well: a 'northern power-house'

'To the goddess Coventina for the First Cohort of Cubernians Aurelius
Campester joyously set up his votive offering.'

'To the goddess-nymph Coventina Maduhus, a German, set this up for
himself and his family, willingly and deservedly fulfilling his vow.'[70]

If Sulis's sanctuary is the most significant reflection of sacred water-power
in southwest Britain, Coventina perhaps fulfilled a similar role in the
north. When the Roman army settled at Carrawburgh, a fort on Hadrian's
Wall, they built a sanctuary in the nearby valley, which contained several
streams forming a marshy area with a number of springs at the bottom.
The water was famous in the 19th century for its purity, and it was this
freshness that attracted the attention of the military units stationed at the
fort, causing them to build a shrine to Coventina, the deity of the springs.[71]

The square structure was built of local stone and left open to the air, so
it was not a true temple, but consisted of a concentric square building, the
inner square enclosing the spring-well and the outer forming the boundary
of the *temenos* (the sacred area surrounding the shrine). The spring-fed
well was personified as a goddess, Coventina. Epigraphy shows that many
of her devotees came from the Rhineland, including the 'Cubernians'.
She was not twinned with a Roman goddess and probably belonged to
this single location. Many individuals or units set up altars thanking the
goddess for her help, and the presence of incense-burners (not dissimilar
to the 'Druidic' ones from Chartres), one of them inscribed,[72] indicates
that religious ceremonies took place here. The inscribed altar stones were
placed in groups around the well, and some were ritually buried so that
they could never be desecrated or reused. Central to the devotional acts
by supplicants here was the casting of personal possessions and money
into the holy water. They included bronze figurines of human faces and
animals, jewelry, leather shoes and glass and pottery vessels.

It is likely that, like Sulis at Bath, Coventina's popularity lay in her
perceived ability to heal. But in addition to a wealth of inscriptions

Stone relief-carving of triple Coventina (ht 52.2 cm/20½ in.) from Coventina's Well at Carrawburgh (bottom right).

providing her name, stone relief-carvings reveal her physical form too. Two sculptures depict Coventina as a water-spirit: one, inscribed with a dedication to her, shows the goddess lounging at ease on a waterlily-leaf, holding a frond languidly aloft; the other represents a triple goddess (or three separate deities) each reclining, as if on a bed, and holding a beaker of spring-water in one hand while pouring it out from a pitcher with the other. The 'Celtic' style in which their faces are treated betray her origins – or those of her sculptor.[73]

Coventina's cult resonates with all those discussed in this chapter. The gods of the cosmos – of sky, earth and water – all demonstrate in their different ways how communities and individuals perceived the spirits to whom they prayed and offered gifts. Whether a soldier stationed in the cold north on Hadrian's Wall or a wealthy pilgrim bringing riches to the steaming atmosphere of Aquae Sulis, worshippers accepted *romanitas* but constantly sought to adapt as well as adopt, and to use the new ways of expressing their devotion to make visible their own local deities whose pre-Roman form had previously been hidden.

CHAPTER SIX

Gut-Gazers and God-Users
Divination, curing and cursing

'Now he was teaching in one of the synagogues on the Sabbath.
And just then there appeared a woman with a spirit that had
crippled her for eighteen years. She was bent over and was
quite unable to stand up straight.' LUKE[1]

The perception that illness – whether of mind or body – was caused by the
invasion of evil spirits lurked at the heart of many societies in antiquity
(and still lingers in certain traditional communities to this day). Luke,
Christ's chronicler, describes just such a diagnosis for the unfortunate
woman in the passage quoted. The connection between disease and the
spirit world was, and is, one of the fundamental tenets of shamanic belief-
systems, and a principal role of the shaman is to take 'soul-flight' between
the material and spirit worlds in order to vanquish the maleficent ghosts
and accomplish feats of healing by their banishment from the afflicted.[2]
In traditional medicine, whether in Classical antiquity, medieval Britain
and Europe or in modern-day non-Western communities, the work of
empirical physicians marches alongside that of the spiritual healer: indeed,
the two professions are frequently combined in one person. The fictional
Brother Cadfael, a medieval monk of Shrewsbury Abbey in Ellis Peters's
crime novels and the consonant television series, is a physician whose
skill lies both in his knowledge of herbal remedies and his faith in God.[3]
The combined practice of fact-based medicine and spirit-healing may
have been true of a Briton who died at Camulodunum and was given a
ceremonial burial during the earliest years after the Claudian invasion,
for his tomb produced grave-goods that indicated his professional status
in both realms of the curative art.

The shaman-doctor of Camulodunum

According to Roman law, the dead could not be buried within the precincts of towns because of the fear of pollution that might infect the
living (see Chapter 10). In about AD 50, a Briton of high rank died and
his cremated remains were interred in a richly furnished tomb that has
been called 'The Doctor's Grave'. His was one of several wealthy tombs
within enclosures located at Stanway, just outside the Roman city of
Colchester (formerly the Trinovantian tribal capital of Camulodunum),
dating to the post-conquest period. These interments were discovered
in the late 1980s and mid-1990s as the result of rescue excavations
undertaken by the Colchester Archaeological Trust in advance of quar-
rying activities that threatened to encroach upon and destroy evidence
for late Iron Age and Roman occupation here.[4] The Doctor's Grave is
particularly special because of its singular grave-goods. The most striking of these consist of a gaming board, its glass counters positioned as if
in mid-game between two players; a spouted bronze vessel; a set of iron
and copper-alloy rods; and a surgeon's tool-kit,[5] hence the grave's name.
The medical equipment (including a surgical saw, scalpels, forceps, a
retractor, needles and scoops)[6] betrays a mixture of Roman and Gallo-
British traditions, appropriate to the date of the grave, only a few years
after the Roman invasion of AD 43. While twenty-five comparable medical
implements were recorded as having been found in Cirencester in the 19th

The board-game, rods,
spouted vessel and medical
tool-kit found in the
Stanway Doctor's Grave.

and 20th centuries, none has a precise provenance and there is no reason to assume they were originally a group, as those in the Doctor's Grave evidently are. But the Cirencester finds also include oculists' stamps, one of which, sadly lost, was apparently adorned with the Christian chi-rho monogram (see Chapter 9).[7]

Alone, each object placed in the Doctor's Grave is highly significant: combined, they allow glimpses into the complex persona of the dead person. A physician's medical kit was an intensely valuable and personal possession. Certain pieces among this set demonstrate their probable local manufacture, and it is almost certain that some were individually made to the doctor's specifications. The saw was designed for bone surgery, while the retractor, forceps, hooks and needles would have been essential tools for probing, internal investigations and suturing wounds.

The bronze strainer bowl and the sets of metallic rods from the tomb may be considered together, for both suggest a sacred and arcane dimension to the physician's craft. What makes the vessel so special is the presence of an organic deposit lodged in the spout: a plug of various plant-materials, with a high concentration of *artemisia vulgaris* (mugwort) and *artemisia absinthium* (wormwood).[8] Both forms of this herb have proven therapeutic powers, employed by early doctors and by practitioners of herbal medicine even today to treat internal complaints such as worm-infestations and other gut disorders.[9] Taken as an ingested infusion, it would have been extremely bitter to taste, but the presence of pollen in the vessel's spout suggests that honey might have been mixed with the drink to make it palatable. But it is also possible that the herbal brew in the Stanway vessel was inhaled rather than drunk and that it was used as a narcotic in spiritual healing. Studies of psychoactive substances used for current transcendent rituals in Africa and the New World consider a whole range of alkaloid hallucinogens, presenting evidence for the use of *artemisia* as a 'marijuana substitute' in Central American spiritual ceremonies.[10] So could it be that the physician who died at Camulodunum was combining empirical and sacred crafts in order to heal the bodies and minds of his patients? The strainer bowl from his grave might have acted in much the same way as the incense-burners found in the secret underground 'Druidic' shrine at Chartres (see pp. 29–32). Ceramic *thuribula* were also present at Romano-British shrines such as Coventina's Well at Carrawburgh (see pp. 116–17), which contained two clay incense-burners, of which one bears an inscribed dedication to Coventina Augusta.[11] As we saw earlier, archaeological evidence that psychotropic substances were ingested as part of ritual experience is not uncommon in prehistoric Europe, from the later Neolithic to the Iron Age and beyond.[12]

By itself, the evidence from the strainer bowl might not be sufficiently convincing to interpret the Stanway 'doctor' as having dabbled in ritual behaviour. However, the set of iron and bronze rods, together with the board-game, may add colour to the picture of someone who attempted to cure ailing minds and bodies, using a variety of empirical and spiritual means by which to do so. The eight rods break down into four groups, consisting of four longer ones, two of bronze and two of iron, and four shorter ones, again comprising two of each metal. Seven of the rods were clustered in a heap near the gaming board, rather as in the pointed sticks used in the game of spillikins (pick-up sticks),[13] but a single iron rod lay diagonally across the board, between the opposing rows of counters.[14] What was the purpose of these rods? Their form resembles that of Roman pens (*styli*), with one flattened end used to erase words written in wax and the other with a blunt rounded terminal that (if these rods were pens) would originally have been fitted with a sharp point.[15] But the number and varying sizes and metals of the Stanway rods suggests a different function from writing implements.

What if the Stanway rods were used for a ritual, even shamanic purpose? More than one ancient writer recorded the use of wooden rods for casting of lots, a practice employed in divination. Describing the Germanic tribes in the late 1st century AD, Tacitus reported that in consulting the gods these northern communities cut wood from fruit trees and whittled it into thin rods.[16] Then runes were written on each rod and a bundle of them was cast onto a white cloth, to be 'read' by the priest who interpreted the will of the gods according to the positions in which the sticks had fallen and by the message inscribed on three rods he chose to examine. There are certain similarities between Tacitus's testimony and the rods from the Doctor's

Reconstruction drawing of ritual lot-casting among ancient Germanic tribes, as described by Tacitus.

Grave at Stanway although – alas – no runes appear to have been engraved on these. But Tacitus's comment that wood from specific trees had to be selected puts in mind the special choice of different metals (and sizes) for the Stanway rods. There is one other possibly significant factor for the bundle of rods, for if they were thrown onto the gaming board from any height, they would clang together as they landed, adding an auditory dimension to the ritual experienced by the mourners at the grave.

The board-game, too, hints at ritual connections within this burial. What part did it play in the funerary activities at Stanway? Its centrality to the event is suggested by the way the medical kit, the rods and the straining-bowl lay on top of it or close beside it.[17] The gaming board is not unique to the Doctor's Grave; another has been found in a nearby grave thought to accommodate a soldier, so, by itself, it does not necessarily point to ritual behaviour. But the soldier's counters were placed in a neat pile beside the board, as if awaiting play,[18] while in the doctor's tomb the twenty-six glass counters, half blue, half white, were positioned as though a game between two people had begun, and one blue counter was inverted, probably deliberately. What is more, as well as the metal objects – the rods and the spouted bowl – placed on the board, a small heap of cremated human bone had been tipped out onto its surface.[19] There is some evidence to suggest that gaming boards in antiquity were not only valued personal possessions but in some contexts, such as medieval Wales, also played a role in the ceremonies surrounding the installation of prominent people in public office.[20] For instance, the game *gwyddbwyll* (Welsh for 'wood-sense') is recorded as being played by high-ranking individuals in medieval Welsh mythic literature, such as Arthur in the tale *Peredur son of Efrog*.[21]

To judge by the grave-goods that his community felt appropriate to inter with him, the Stanway doctor appears to have been a complex individual whose skills and responsibilities included surgery and religious duties including divination and the manipulation of minds by the use of psychotropic substances. If so, it is tempting to think of him as a kind of shaman, a 'two-spirit' person who was able, through drug-induced trance, to move between the worlds of people and the gods and to fight disease by combating evil spirits and predicting the divine will, as well as healing through conventional medicine. His double persona (as doctor and shaman) may even have been displayed by the two players represented on the gaming board.

A gut-gazer from Bath

'To the goddess Sulis, Lucius Marcius Memor, *Haruspex*, gave this gift'[22]

The priests who maintained the great healing shrine at Bath, presided over its rituals and attended to the spiritual needs of its supplicants have left their archaeological mark. They are represented by their ceremonial regalia, such as headdresses and a sinister-looking tin mask, used in processions and concealing the face of the wearer. These objects are anonymous, but inscriptions provide the names of two of the clergy. One, we can discern, was a seventy-five-year-old priest of Sulis called Gaius Calpurnius Receptus[23] (see also Chapter 10). About the other we can glean considerably more. His name, Lucius Marcius Memor, proclaims his Roman citizenship, and his presence at Bath is recorded on a statue-base, presumably once bearing an image of Sulis. He held the very Roman title of *Haruspex*

Life-sized tin mask from the sanctuary of Sulis Minerva at Bath.

Dedication to Sulis ('SVLI') by the *haruspex* Lucius Marcius Memor, Bath.

('gut-gazer'), signifying a specialist in reading portents from the entrails of sacrificed animals, but since the inscription that mentions him clearly shows that the statue (and its base) was a gift to the goddess, it appears that this man's business at Bath was as a pilgrim-supplicant rather than as a religious practitioner. His name is significant, for his *cognomen*, Memor, perhaps referred to his expertise as a curator of sacred memory and oral tradition, and we know from Julius Caesar's observations that the Druids were keepers of memory and holders of their communities' past. Of course, Memor might have been both pilgrim and official gut-gazer at the site. Perhaps, because of his specialist skills, local priests had called upon him to help in their shamanic task of divining the future and Sulis's will by reading the signs in the bloody innards of sacrificial victims.

The Lydney 'dream doctor'

The *cella* mosaic at the rural temple of Lydney incorporates an inscription mentioning an important man called Victorinus, an 'interpreter of dreams'. It is likely that this individual was a professional religious practitioner, perhaps resident at Lydney, for dreams were an important part of the complex relationship between people and the gods. In the Roman world, the dreams of supplicants in sacred places were perceived as one of the pathways of spiritual communication; but to the recipient of a god-given dream, its meaning was opaque and required someone skilled in 'translating' its message, to make it accessible and to interpret the meaning behind it.[24] Dreams were deemed so important in healing sanctuaries

The inscribed *cella* mosaic at the temple of Nodens, Lydney,
Gloucestershire, mentioning Victorinus, the 'interpreter of dreams'
('Victorino Interp...').

in the Classical world that many curative shrines had a special *abaton* (a
dormitory) to house sick pilgrims, who hoped that they would receive a
divine visitation while they slept on holy ground. It is tempting to think
that when pilgrims awoke after their stay in the *abaton* or large guest-house
at Lydney, they told their dreams to Victorinus, and he would act as the
mouthpiece of the spirits, instructing supplicants what they should do for
the gods in order to be healed. A suite of bath-buildings here demonstrate
that – as at Bath – washing was a central part of the healing process.[25]

Music: the 'perfume breath of God'

'There are also lyric poets whom they call Bards. They sing to the
accompaniment of instruments resembling lyres...' DIODORUS SICULUS[26]

In the summer of 2016, sixteen years after his release from his four-year
incarceration as a hostage in Beirut, Brian Keenan broadcast a talk about
his psychological experiences of being shut up on his own in a dark cell
so small that he could touch all its walls without moving.[27] He explained
that one of the imaginary people who inhabited his suffering mind during

that time was a 17th-century blind Irish harpist called Turlough Carolan, who used his music and his poetry to heal. After Keenan's release, he was invited to speak about his experience of captivity at the University of Fairbanks in Alaska. He told of an email he received from an Inuit woman after his talk. She explained to him that Carolan was a 'dream-walker' who, after his death, became a wandering spirit-healer, or shaman, who came to the aid of damaged minds. The woman told Keenan that dream-walkers worked on the principle that those whom they helped to heal were obliged to pass on the curative gift to others. Keenan's address in Alaska – and other talks – served to fulfil that obligation.

How does Brian Keenan's story of Turlough Carolan inform healing-cults in Roman Britain? To my mind the connection is music; the use of harmonious sound to access the spiritual dimension. There is compelling evidence for the playing of musical instruments in ancient religious contexts. In the later Iron Age, ceremonial trumpets were ritually deposited in watery places, such as the little pool at Loughnashade in County Armagh, Ireland,[28] and at Llyn Cerrig Bach on Anglesey.[29] And in a sacred deposit of material deep underground by a subterranean stream at High Pasture Cave on the Isle of Skye,[30] someone deliberately interred part of a lyre, as if to reflect the musical contribution to ritual and its resonant sound in that enclosed dark space. Like Keenan's blind harpist, the musician here very likely accompanied his playing by song or sacred verse. The quote from Diodorus Siculus that opens this section describes this practice in ancient Gaul.

Part of a ceremonial trumpet from the late Iron Age ritual deposit in a pool at Llyn Cerrig Bach, Anglesey (above), and part of an antler bridge from a lyre, deposited in about 180 BC at High Pasture Cave, Skye (left).

There is plenty of iconographic evidence for music in the Gallo-Roman provinces.[31] In Britain, the record is more mute, but the little bronze figurine of a girl flautist from Silchester may well have come from a sanctuary; likewise the stone image of a 'mother-goddess' from Cirencester who holds what looks like a drum on her lap.[32] In traditional societies, shamans use drums to communicate with the spirits, and among the Sámi communities of northern Europe and Siberia these instruments act as 'cognitive maps' that help the shaman to navigate, and gain insights into, the spirit world[33] – the drums are covered with images and symbols that represent the triple-layered cosmos at the heart of Sámi shamanism, and these markings are read and interpreted by the shaman according to the seasons or other time-centred events.[34] While it may be a leap to

Drawing of the bronze figurine of a flute-girl from Silchester, Hampshire.

imagine that the Cirencester carving represents a shaman, her 'drum' may indicate that percussive sounds were employed by priests in order to attain altered states and, like shamans, to enter the spiritual realm and thus to combat the evil spirits that caused harm.[35]

Healing and harming on holy ground

'to the goddess Sulis…whether slave or free, whoever he shall be, you are not to permit him eyes or health unless blindness and childlessness [...] so long as he shall live, unless he returns these to the temple.'[36]

The curious thing about certain healing sanctuaries in Roman Britain is their presentation of a dichotomous association between help and harm. The lead curse tablet on which the above message was written comes from the thermal shrine to Sulis Minerva at Bath. It was one of a host of small lead plaques which, once inscribed with the wished-for act of vengeance, were tightly rolled for secrecy and thrown into the sacred spring-reservoir. This short but venomous letter to the goddess expresses much, not least about the relationship between the person doing the cursing and the deity to whom the request was addressed. The tone is far from that of a humble suppliant; it is a curt and urgent demand that the goddess grant revenge. The fragmentary inscription does not tell us what the cursed miscreant had done, this section sadly being lost, but, on analogy of numerous others from the site, it almost certainly involved theft: of clothing, jewelry or money. As in many *defixiones*, the retribution sought for the misdemeanour seems excessively harsh. But this may be to do with the fact that the crime took place on sacred ground, the supplicant apparently requesting that the items be returned to the place from which they went missing – the temple. It is telling, too, that the penalties demanded of the healer-goddess Sulis were the blight of ill-health and the terrible afflictions of blindness and infertility.

Eyes, light and water

Sulis at Bath and Nodens at Lydney both appear to have been associated with an ability to cure eye afflictions. That eye-doctors practised at these shrines is confirmed by the medicine-stamps on sticks of eye ointment that have been discovered at them.[37] Tiberius Janianus lost his stamp at Bath, and Iulius Iucundus mislaid his in the Lydney temple.[38] Excavations of the rich deposits from the healing sanctuary at *Fontes Sequanae* near Dijon, France, have revealed a great deal of evidence for eye-disease and the rituals used to combat it.[39] Pilgrims journeyed to this remote spot to implore the presiding goddess for eye-cures, and left votive offerings in the form of images of themselves in wood and stone, their eyes deliberately emphasized to hammer home their message. Small bronze plaques simply depicting pairs of eyes were a similarly popular gift.

Water played a key role in the sanctuaries of both Sulis and Sequana. Like Sulis, Sequana was a water-goddess, and it seems as though pilgrims suffering a variety of ailments were drawn to watery shrines in the belief that the healing touch of the deity was transmitted through sacred water.

Fontes Sequanae was built where the infant river Seine bubbles out of the ground in a series of springs and pools, its water pure and fresh but with no particular curative properties. Sulis's springs, conversely, contain many minerals, including sulphur, and the stream running through Lydney is rich in iron. Some of the 'selfies' from Sequana's shrine display tell-tale lumps in the neck that suggest some pilgrims suffered from goitre, a condition caused by iodine deficiency that can result in not only thyroid-swelling but also exophthalmic (prominent) eyes.

In addition to its real or imagined healing properties, water is associated with light, with its reflection and translucency endowed by light on clear springs and pools. Even the cloudy, spring-turbulent bath-waters of Aquae Sulis shine with a lambent green glow, as though lit from beneath. There is an obvious connection between eyes and light. Sulis was a goddess of both light and water, and it is surely no accident that the fierce bearded face that greeted pilgrims at the entrance to her temple was carved with piercing eyes that seem to look right through to the soul. One inscribed dedication from Bath, on a stone broken off a building block, is particularly striking in this context: '...son of Novantius, set this up for himself and his family as the result of a vision'.[40] So the inward eye, too, is represented at Bath. The dedication brings to mind Victorinus, the 'interpreter of dreams' whose name and profession was written in tesserae on the mosaic floor within the inner sanctum of Nodens's temple at Lydney, who would have interpreted such visions and instructed pilgrims to pursue such paths.

Bargaining with the gods

'I have given to the goddess Sulis the six silver coins which I have lost. It is for the goddess to exact them from the names written below: Senicianus and Saturninus and Anniola. The written page has been copied out.
Anniola
Senicianus
Saturninus'[41]

This is the inscription written on one of the curse tablets found in the spring-reservoir at Bath. Like others from the site, the person with the grievance adopts a curt and peremptory tone with the goddess; basically, the message is, 'you get them, you keep them'. But there is more: it seems to have been important for the efficacy of the curse for the accused to be named not once, but twice. Identity is wrapped up in names, and presumably by naming the thieves, the curse was perceived to carry more potency, for the goddess's avenging arm could be directed straight at them. It is interesting, too, that the victim was less concerned to get his property back than to 'finger' those responsible. One of the accused in this curse bore the name Senicianus. It would be rather wonderful were he to have been that same villain who stole Silvianus's ring from the Lydney temple.

The 'coin curse' exemplifies an aspect of the relationship between deity and person in the context of healing rituals. In Chapter 3 the idea of asking and thanking prayers (the *nuncupatio* and the *solutio*) was introduced. In rogation invocations, the supplicant would often make a vow offering a gift to the divinity if the request was granted and, if the god gave a positive response, the result might be an altar mentioning that the devotee was fulfilling the pledge as promised. Underpinning all this was the rather pragmatic principle of reciprocity: a boon for a boon. The supplicant entered into a contractual relationship with whichever deity was seen to be the most likely to grant a particular request.

Offerings to the gods, in both asking and thanking rituals, could take many forms: altars, brooches, bronze statues, finger-rings. A particular form of votive took the form of miniature tools, weapons or other implements.[42] A good example of a Romano-British shrine containing many of these is Woodeaton in Oxfordshire, a sanctuary that bordered the powerful tribes of the Dobunni and the Catuvellauni. The most common type of model here (and, indeed, generally within the province) was the model axe, but six tiny copper-alloy spears were also deposited at the shrine, of which three had been bent double. This practice was by no means confined to Woodeaton. Pilgrims visiting the great shrine to Mercury at Uley in the Gloucestershire Cotswolds also brought offerings of miniature spears. Most are of iron, but a much costlier and more ornate example was made of silver. The blade had been pierced, as if for suspension, and it was twisted back on itself before being placed in the temple. Why offer

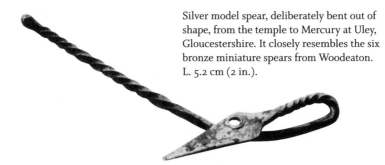

Silver model spear, deliberately bent out of shape, from the temple to Mercury at Uley, Gloucestershire. It closely resembles the six bronze miniature spears from Woodeaton. L. 5.2 cm (2 in.).

models to the gods? A cynic might be inclined to suspect that offering a small substitute of a grander item was a cost-cutting tactic. But could miniaturization itself have been symbolic, a way of rendering an object unusable, like the damaging of full-size weapons in the Iron Age or of the miniature spears at Woodeaton? This seems a more plausible interpretation. Deliberate breaking and shrinking both render objects unusable and therefore serve to remove them from the world of the mundane, thus symbolically 'killing' them (much as happens with an animal or human sacrifice). The objects are thus transformed in order to enable their reception by the gods.

The principle of reciprocity seems to have been central in healing cults, for at curative sanctuaries, offerings frequently fell into the category of 'bodily exchange': a sick pilgrim would visit a curative shrine and dedicate a model replica of the diseased organ or limb in the hope and expectation that, in return, the presiding spirit would grant the ailing supplicant a healed and whole body-part in exchange. The anatomical votive habit was common across ancient Greece, Italy and Gaul. The god Asklepios (Roman Aesculapius) appears to have had a particular reputation for curing deafness, for many of the offerings made at his shrine at Epidaurus were of model ears or ears carved on altars.[43] But we need to be careful in making such a unilateral correlation. When Asklepios revealed himself to a supplicant named Aelius Aristides at Pergamum, the god gave him specific instructions to go barefoot.[44] So it might be that at Epidaurus, the ears did not reflect diseased ears but the need to make sure the god's commands were heard, heeded and acted upon.

At Ponte di Nona, near Rome, a Republican healing shrine was visited by hosts of sick pilgrims who brought large numbers of 'health' offerings in the form of clay models depicting bare feet, hands, female breasts, penises and what may be a uterus.[45] The model sex organs might have reflected prayers associated with love and fertility, but perhaps also sometimes depicted diseased organs: Catherine Johns has suggested[46] that the model phalluses were offered by men suffering from phimosis (tight foreskins), a condition that can cause both discomfort and, if left untreated, infertility. The potters who turned out these offerings perhaps made deliberately ambiguous models that could stand for a range of health issues: so a model breast might be purchased by women who wanted children, who struggled to breast-feed or who had breast-disease.

Models of body-parts in wood and stone from the sanctuary of Sequana at *Fontes Sequanae* were just as varied as those from Ponte di Nona, and included arms, hands, feet, eyes, heads, torsos, genitalia and even whole bodies of pilgrims. The site is of particular interest because of its geography and the divergence of offerings within the sacred space. The wooden images were grouped around the sacred pool and marshy ground at the foot of a low cliff, away from the temple-buildings, while the stone models and statues were placed inside the sacred precinct. It is possible that the materials chosen reflected the different states of being outside and inside the temple; impermanent wooden offerings might have represented the instability of the human condition, while the permanence of stone within the sanctuary perhaps acknowledged the transformation of pilgrim-supplicants after they had visited Sequana's sacred pool. According to this theory, when they had bathed in or drunk from it, the sick supplicants crossed the threshold to the goddess's

Miniature bronze leg from South Cerney, Gloucestershire. The polish and finish of the top surface indicates that it was cast as a votive leg, not broken from a statuette. Ht 3.7 cm (1½ in.).

Pair of miniature gold eyes, probably offered to a healer-
deity, from Wroxeter, Shropshire. Numerous other model
eyes, fashioned from painted wall-plaster, have been
found in the Roman town. W. 6.3 cm (2½ in.).

'power-house', having been possessed by the healer-spirit, and their new
transcendent state might have been depicted by the use of stone.[47]

Roman Britain has produced no sanctuaries whose anatomical votive
offerings compare – in either numbers or variety – to those from the great
Gallic healing sanctuaries such as *Fontes Sequanae* and Chamalières. But
reference has already been made to the little bronze arm with its diseased
fingers from Lydney and the pairs of model breasts from Bath, one of which
was made of ivory, and may have been worn as an amulet. The little pair
of sheet-gold eyes from Wroxeter[48] may have been the gift of a pilgrim to
an unknown healer-deity: the use of gold suggests the thank-offering of
a grateful suppliant.

This religious habit of placing anatomical votive offerings in curative
sanctuaries has been an incredibly tenacious one, common throughout the
Classical world but continuing to the present in Mediterranean Catholic
churches and monasteries. In my own travels, I have happened upon two
shrines dedicated to the Virgin Mary that function as curative centres
and involve the donation of anatomical models. At Mellieha Bay on Malta
an ancient rock-cut cavern whose rough walls are festooned with model
body-parts is filled with motorcycle crash-helmets, crutches, discarded
plaster-casts and baby clothes. They are offerings to the Virgin Mary who
here, as in numerous other Roman Catholic countries, has an enduring
reputation for her healing powers (Lourdes, of course, being a case-in-
point). I visited Mellieha in the 1980s and learnt the legend of the place.

For centuries, a statue of Mary stood outside the eight-hundred-year-old shrine. Two hundred years ago, the community built a new brick church on the hill above, and re-erected the statue outside the entrance. But every morning, the image was found back at its old site outside the cave. This mysterious overnight phenomenon repeated itself so many times that, in the end, the locals gave up and left Mary in her original position.[49] Not only did the Maltese Virgin have the gift of healing, so did her original sanctuary.

The second curative sanctuary to Mary that I have encountered is at Fátima in Portugal. This is very different, founded only in 1917 after local shepherd children repeatedly saw visions of the Virgin, who first appeared to them on 13 May of that year. The apparitions from Heaven began to visit more and more of the townspeople, and now there is a huge and magnificent centre of pilgrimage at Fátima that attracts many thousands of pilgrims and where, on Mary's festival day, the visitor can hardly move for the crowds that pour in from near and far. But the relevance of Fátima to ancient Gallo-British healing-cults is the custom there of purchasing model body-parts in a reciprocal therapeutic ritual. The Portuguese models are made of wax, and when modern pilgrims visit, they purchase a replica of the anatomical part they wish to be cured. They then progress, many on their knees, to a long trough of flames into which they cast the wax model; the belief is that as the wax melts, so the Virgin accepts the offering. The constant recycling of the wax, recovered in molten form from the fire and reused when solid, serves to intensify the efficacy of the offerings.[50]

Cursing rituals: walking on the dark side

'Germanicus had a relapse – aggravated by his belief that Piso had poisoned him. Examination of the floor and walls of his bedroom revealed the remains of human bodies, spells, curses, lead tablets inscribed with the patient's name, charred and bloody ashes, and other malignant objects which are supposed to consign souls to the powers of the tomb.' TACITUS[51]

All over Roman Gaul and on fewer but significant sites in Britannia, people consulted the gods for positive as well as negative reasons. I want now to give this 'dark side' more detailed consideration, partly because of the British deities from whom vengeance and retribution were demanded. This practice is particularly noteworthy at Bath, where the presiding goddess Sulis Minerva's primary function was supposedly that of a healer. Curse tablets, or *defixiones*, were employed all over the Classical world for the divine settling of grievances, and the cursing-habit was eagerly embraced in the western provinces too.[52] In the quotation above, Tacitus tells of the dark magic used to get rid of Germanicus in AD 18, allegedly perpetrated by Piso on the orders of the emperor Tiberius, who was determined to stamp out any possible rival claims to the imperial title – including that of the unfortunate Germanicus..

In the Roman world, curses were traditionally written in cursive script on sheets of lead – a heavy, base metal that was believed to have a particularly strong connection to the underworld. In Latin such a tablet was a *defixio*, something literally 'fixed' so that the potentially unstable spell could only travel in one direction and not rebound on the curser. So each curse tablet would be transfixed with a nail into position on a door or wall of a shrine or other building. Such tablets frequently appear at Bath, where the curative goddess Sulis was called upon to reverse her powers for ill rather than good. The other major shrine to have produced multiple curse tablets is the temple to Mercury at Uley in the Gloucestershire Cotswolds (see pp. 192–93).[53] And it is clear from examination of the two deposits that some of the scribes who worked at one temple were also employed at the other. Why should such curses appear at sanctuaries in Britain where the presiding deities were essentially beneficent healers, dispensers of good health or prosperity?

These two sanctuaries appear to have embraced contradictory powers (those of helping and harming) but, upon reflection, perhaps this is not so strange. Sulis was a goddess of both fire and water: both elements have the capacity to give and take life. Her solar energy is complemented by its dark side, the moon. Mercury's character is equally complex: his main emblem, the *caduceus*, is made up of a serpent-entwined staff, a motif still used in the medical world today as a symbol of healing. Mercury's *caduceus* acted as his herald's wand, to beckon the gods and (like another of his images, the cockerel) to welcome the new day. But Mercury had a darker role, too, for he was a 'psychopomp', a leader of souls to the Otherworld, so perhaps the aggrieved saw him as a deity who would willingly wreak vengeance on transgressors. This may account for another group of cult-objects found at Uley: a collection of miniature spearheads, like those from Woodeaton but made from iron, except for one of silver,[54] most of which had been deliberately bent or twisted, perhaps to symbolize the damage that could be done by *defixiones*.

Blood and blindness

'Docimedis has lost two gloves. He asks that the person who has stolen them should lose his mind and his eyes in the temple where she appoints...'[55]

'The person who has lifted my bronze vessel is utterly accursed. I give him to the temple of Sulis, whether woman or man, whether slave or free, whether boy or girl, and let him who has done this spill his own blood into the vessel itself...'[56]

It is notable that so many of the curse tablets from Bath contain messages to the healer-goddess Sulis asking that she deny health to malefactors, the very reverse of what we should expect of curative deities. In a sense, the aggrieved party was demanding that the thief be 'excommunicated', excluded from Sulis's beneficence; perhaps the curse went far beyond the physical illness wished on the 'defendant' and struck at the very roots of his or her personhood and access to divine aid. By cursing an individual in this manner, the curser was sending the ill-doer beyond the pale of civilized society. It is striking that the curses request ill-health for the miscreant in the form of blindness and anything to do with bodily fluids – blood, semen or urine. Blindness and fluid-related curses may be linked with Sulis's role as a goddess associated with heat and light, like the sun (the British word 'Sul/is', cognate with the Latin 'Sol', being associated with solar energy) and the flow of spring-water. So the curses might directly reflect the perceived powers and responsibilities of the goddess.

Most of the curse tablets from Bath were tightly rolled up, presumably to keep their contents secret, for the eyes of the goddess alone. Maybe their efficacy depended upon their exclusivity and a belief that exposing them to the light and to the gaze of others would dilute their potency and interrupt the connection between the aggrieved person and petitioned deity. There is a possible – and tragic – parallel in today's Britain, a shocking incident surrounding a Middle Eastern ritual whose outward manifestation is curiously similar to the treatment of curse tablets by Roman Britons at Bath.[57] In February 2016 a seventy-one-year-old imam named Jalal Uddin was beaten to death by two young fellow Muslims in Rochdale, ostensibly for engaging in 'black magic'. Uddin had been practising an Islamic healing ritual called *ruqya*, which involves writing a series of 'magical formulae' on pieces of paper that are then rolled up and placed in a small container to be worn on the body by a sick person as an amulet, or *taweez*, in order to repel the evil spirit causing the sufferer's ill-health. Because *ruqya* attracts criticism from some Islamic quarters, the *taweez* is often kept hidden by being sewn into clothing. The attack on Jalal Uddin was very particular: his face, and particularly his mouth, was the main target of his assailants, and this is likely to have been because of the 'magical incantations' used in the practice of *ruqya*. The 'link' between this Islamic ritual and the use of *defixiones* in Roman Britain is the outward signature of secrecy, the rolling up of the sacred messages. But what befell a quiet, peaceful healer in present-day England serves as a reminder of possible prejudices against magic in the far-removed context of ancient Britannia. Uddin's magic was positive 'white magic'. The *defixiones* were far from that, yet both rituals were associated with the healing art, the one for good, the other for its opposite: retribution.

Subverting Symbols
Heads, horns and seeing triple

'And Philip arose and went: and behold, a man of Ethiopia, a eunuch
of great authority under Candace, queen of the Ethiopians, who had the
charge of all her treasure, and had come to Jerusalem to worship'[1]

Between 40 and 10 BC, Queen Amanirenas (the biblical Candace) ruled
over the ancient African kingdom of Meroë, just to the south of the Roman
Empire's southernmost border. Meroë occupied a part of what is now
North Sudan, covering the region of the Nile Valley between Berber and
Khartoum. The empire flourished between the 6th century BC and the
4th century AD. Queen Amanirenas regularly led raids from her Sudanese
kingdom into southern Egypt, and on one of these sorties, in 25 BC, she
captured the bronze statue of Augustus that stood in the town of Syene and
beheaded it. Amanirenas carried the severed head of the imperial image
back to Meroë in triumph and ceremonially buried it underneath the steps
of her temple of Victory. This was a powerful act of subversion, for the
head's position meant that all the pilgrims who visited the sanctuary would
trample the emperor's face underfoot on their way to worship. The head
is preserved in the Greco-Roman collection of the British Museum, and
the tiny grains of sand forced into the bronze face by the feet of ancient
Meroitic worshippers can still be discerned.[2]

What Queen Amanirenas did was not so different from the treatment
meted out to the statue of Claudius at Colchester by Boudica's maraud-
ing army (see pp. 44–45). For the head of Augustus in the African desert,
the ultimate humiliation was being trampled underfoot. But the fate of
Claudius's head in faraway Britain was somewhat different, for casting it

into a nearby river was perhaps a multifaceted act: on the one hand it was drowned, but on the other it was appropriated and turned into a British sacred symbol, that of the severed head.

Talking heads

'They cut off the heads of enemies slain in battle and attach them to the necks of their horses. They nail up these "first fruits" upon their houses... They embalm in cedar-oil the heads of the most distinguished enemies and preserve them carefully in a chest, and display them with pride to strangers, saying that for this head...the man refused the offer of a large sum of money from the enemy's family. Some of them boast that they refused the weight of the head in gold.' DIODORUS SICULUS[3]

In this passage, Diodorus Siculus describes a Gallic custom central to which was the perception that human heads were special, full of meaning and power. Other authors speak of the display of heads in Gallic temples. Archaeological corroboration of this habit is particu-
larly evident in the Lower Rhône Valley, at Iron Age Saluvian[4] shrines such as Roquepertuse and Entremont.[5] All over Gaul and Britannia, real heads and images appear to have pos-sessed a particularly compelling meaning.[6] Human skulls from the disued grain silos at Iron Age Danebury and similar sites, and the careful defleshing of the adolescent boy's skull and its ritual disposal in a shaft outside a Romano-British temple at Verulamium (see pp. 17–18, 81), exemplify similar special treat-ment of disembodied heads. In late Iron Age and Roman-period iconography, once again, the significance of heads is demonstrated both by the depiction of heads without bodies and the modifica-tion of human-body presentation to exaggerate them.

Stone head found reused in a wall at Bryn y Môr Farm, Anglesey. Ht c. 40 cm (16 in.).

Two sculptures from Roman Caerwent clearly display the importance of head-symbolism for the local tribe of the Silures.[7] Both were carved out of local sandstone and, although each was found in a different chronological context from the other, certain similarities in style and craftsmanship raise the possibility that they were made at the same time by the same stonemason and that the 'earlier' one was curated for a time before its final deposition. The treatment of the facial features in both sculptures has much in common: the circular eyes, in which the right is more deeply carved than the left (suggesting that the left eye was closed), the wedge-shaped nose and, most tellingly of all, the deeply-drilled open mouth.[8] The first Caerwent sculpture was deliberately carved as a disembodied head, rather than being part of a broken statue, for the neck is cleanly finished off, as if the object were designed to sit on a plinth. The second image is that of a female figure seated in a high-backed chair. She sits staring straight ahead at the viewer; her hooded head is huge in relation to her body with its diminutive limbs, and she holds what might be interpreted as a frond of yew and an 'aril' (a yew berry), perhaps symbols of longevity or the afterlife.[9] Both carvings were found in sacred contexts: the dis-embodied head found standing on a platform within a *fanum* (a private shrine) in the backyard of a substantial late Roman house; the 'goddess' at the bottom of a deep pit near the Romano-Celtic temple adjacent to the *forum-basilica* (the market and civic hall) in the centre of the town. The head comes from a 4th-century context but the yew-bearer was associated

Stone disembodied head (ht *c.* 22 cm/8 in.) and statuette of seated female (ht *c.* 27 cm/10 in.) from Caerwent.

with material dating at least a century earlier.[10] If they were the work of a single sculptor, the only way this can be explained is if the severed head was kept somewhere, perhaps on display in another sacred place, before being hidden in the garden of a wealthy person whose house contained a mosaic hinting at his or her Christian affiliation.[11]

So, if the chronological divergence can be explained, is it too far-fetched to suggest that the images of the head and the female statuette represent the same religious entity? I wonder whether both might have been 'oracle stones', somewhat like the *palantíri* of Tolkien's *The Lord of the Rings*, spiritually charged prophetic stones that glowed and became translucent when touched, allowing the viewer to gaze into them and see the future. Were the Caerwent stones used like the *palantíri* or the Sibyls of Classical antiquity, as mouthpieces for the words of the gods, and could they have been manipulated by priests who spoke 'through' them in divinatory rituals? Their open mouths would seem to suggest as much. If the two stones are synchronous, might they have represented the same entity, whether a priest, sacred oracle or deity? And what was the significance of their eventual resting places? The statuette was placed deep underground, while the head was hidden away in a secluded place, both implying a certain sense of secrecy. The Cumaean Sibyl, who features in the Augustan poet Virgil's *Aeneid* as Apollo's Oracle, lived deep in a dark cavern[12] and caves are 'thin' places, regarded by many traditional societies as gateways to the world of the spirits.

Horn-bearers and shape-shifters: masks and masquerades

'And then Math took up his magic wand and struck Gilfaethwy, so
that he became a good-sized hind, and he seized Gwydion quickly
and struck him with the same magic wand, so that he became a stag…'
FROM THE MABINOGION[13]

The medieval Welsh myths contain numerous references to 'skin-turning', the ability to morph between human and animal form. In this mythology, as demonstrated in this passage, transformation of people into animals was often a punishment for transgressing human rules of conduct. In this legend, the two brothers Gwydion and Gilfaethwy had raped a virgin called Goewin, who belonged to Math, the lord of Gwynedd in North Wales. Goewin had occupied the bizarre position of 'footholder' to the king[14] but once raped, she could no longer maintain this role. In his fury at his nephews' perfidy, let alone for their outrageous violation of Goewin, Math changed them into mating pairs of wild creatures for three consecutive years. In Irish mythology, conversely, shape-changing was more often the voluntary action of divine beings. For instance, in the Ulster prose tale the *Táin Bó Cúailnge* (*The Cattle Raid of Cooley*), the fearsome battle-fury known as the Badbh or the Morrigán spent a lot of her time morphing at will from young girl to old crone to crow.[15]

Stag-people: wearing the wild

Religious beliefs in Roman Britain and Gaul included the notion that gods were not perceived just in human form but could present themselves with animal characteristics, particularly horns. In Chapter 3, reference was made to the little sandstone relief of a horned warrior-god from the Roman fort of Maryport in Cumbria, perhaps the fusion of a local deity with the Roman Mars; he is one of several horned images from northern Britain.[16] One sculpture of an antlered deity from Cirencester is of particular note because of the intensity and multiple nature of the shape-shifting: both the deity and his animal-companions are hybrid creations. This crouching naked figure with vestigial antlers on its head grasps in each hand a large serpent with a ram's head, and by each snake/ ram's open mouth is an open bag of coins, fruit or grain.[17] The most

Stone relief-carving of an antlered deity clutching ram-headed serpents from Cirencester. Ht c. 23 cm (9 in.).

obvious explanation of this double divergence from 'real' beings is that the meaning of the sculpture was more important than sticking to the 'norms' of nature.

This image's significance lies not only in its intrinsic symbolism, but also in its affiliation to a widely distributed group of cognate images not just in neighbouring Gaul but in faraway Denmark, notably the human head sprouting antlers, the cross-legged seating position, the torcs and the ram-horned/headed snakes; such iconography had its roots in the Iron Age. Depictions of an antlered 'human' on rock-carvings dating as far back as the 4th century BC are known from Val Camonica in northern Italy.[18] To find a name for this being we need to go to Paris, to a complex stone monument dedicated by a guild of boatmen plying their trade on the river Seine at Paris in AD 26. One of the several divine images on this great stone pillar is the head and shoulders of a bearded god wearing antlers, suspended from which are two torcs. Inscribed above his head is the Gaulish word '[C]ernunno', 'to Cernunnos' – or 'the horned one'.[19] It is not certain whether this was a name meant to represent a single spirit-entity, or whether it was a generic term used to address a variety of divine beings.

The appearance in Roman Cirencester of an antlered god in company with the even more idiosyncratic mixed-up snakes evidently derives from a widely shared sacred story or myth, for the same combination occurs on one of the inner plates on the great silver cauldron found in a marsh at Gundestrup in Jutland, Denmark, probably made in the 1st century BC.[20] The peculiar ram-headed snakes appear on a number of Gallo-Roman

Inner plate depicting antlered human figure clasping a ram-headed serpent, and accompanied by a stag, from the gilded silver cauldron found at Gundestrup, Denmark. W. *c.* 40 cm (16 in.).

images, including a bronze figurine of a seated man with removable antlers from Savigny in Burgundy.[21] His detachable antlers may have been intended to represent the stag's annual cycle of antler-growth and -shedding, perhaps to tie into different seasonal festivals. In about AD 10, just before the Roman conquest of Britain, a silver coin was minted and lost at Petersfield in Hampshire. On one side is the depiction of a human head with antlers sprouting from it.[22]

Cat-faces at Caerleon: god, myth or shaman?

'Thus was Cairbre the cruel
who seized Ireland south and north
two cats' ears on his fair head
a cat's fur through his ears'[23]

Before delving a little deeper into the thinking behind hybrid iconography, I want to consider another human-animal image, this time from a military context: the Roman legionary fortress of Caerleon. For while the tribal capital of the Dobunni at Cirencester was clearly 'owned' by Britons, albeit exposed to strong Roman influences, Caerleon was inhabited largely by Roman citizen-soldiers. Having said this, it is only right to point out that by the time the fortress was established, in the later 1st century AD, the Roman army was itself a hybrid creature, with recruits from all corners of the Empire, including Britain's nearest neighbour, Gaul (see Chapter 3). Caerleon has produced a number of triangular clay roofing-tiles (*antefixa*) that display human heads, a few possessing feline elements: cat-ears with fur between them.[24] The passage quoted above is from a medieval Irish poem, and the person mentioned was Cairbre of the Cat Head. Was it this man's reputation for cruelty or hunting prowess that gave

Clay roofing-tile (*antefix*) displaying a human head with cats' ears, from Caerleon. W. of base *c.* 20 cm (8 in.).

him such a title? Or could it be a veiled reference to something to do with ritual? It is well established that Irish (and Welsh) myths had deep pagan roots, despite their codification by medieval Christian clerics.[25] Cairbre's cat persona perhaps contained a 'back-story' of pre-Christian 'shamanic' ceremonial activity that involved dressing up in animal-costume in order to enter the world of the spirits.[26] Could it be that the images of the cat-eared heads on the Caerleon *antefixa* represented the kind of shape-shifting that later blossomed into early medieval mythic storytelling?

Fedelma's speckled cloak

'They saw a young grown girl in front of them. She had yellow hair. She wore a speckled cloak fastened around her with a gold pin, a red-embroidered hooded tunic and sandals with gold clasps. Her brow was broad, her jaw narrow, her two eyebrows pitch black, with delicate dark lashes…She had hair in three tresses…Her eyes had triple irises. She held a light gold weaving-rod in her hand, with gold inlay. Two black horses drew her chariot, and she was armed' TÁIN BÓ CÚAILNGE[27]

This passage from the early medieval Irish epic prose tale of the legendary war between the kingdoms of Ulster and Connaught introduces a young prophetess called Fedelma. The storyteller employed powerful word-painting, full of deliberate shocks and contrasts. She had fair hair but dark brows; she wore a bi-coloured cloak; her clothes were decorated in red (symbolic of the underworld); she gazed at the world through strange threefold eyes; and she carried the peaceful, domestic symbol of the spindle alongside the aggressive motifs of war-chariot and arms. She prophesied to Queen Medbh of Connaught that the young Ulster champion Cú Chulainn – a half-human, half-divine hero – would bring about her downfall.

The oppositional imagery employed by the Irish storyteller in his presentation of Fedelma appears to reflect her identity as a 'two-spirit' person – a shaman – who moved freely between the layers of the cosmos, acting as a mouthpiece for the spirits and as a conduit between earth-bound humans and the gods. Speckling is a typical mark of a shaman, and

Fedelma's bi-coloured garment thus signifies the shaman's soul-journeys through the worlds of the humans and the spirits. The triplism displayed in her hair and her eyes recalls a persistent magical symbol in Irish and Welsh mythology: the sacred nature of the number three. We will return to this theme in the context of Romano-British iconography. But the image of Fedelma may also serve as a lens through which to examine some of the hybrid imagery already met, the half-people, half-beasts who we may interpret as shamanistic beings, their unstable, shifting position in the double world of the material and the spirit reflected in their dual physicality. In many traditional societies, such as Amerindia and Siberia, where shamanism is still active, particular individuals within their communities are able to communicate with the world beyond in order to foretell the will of the divine and to heal (see Chapter 6). They do this by achieving out-of-body trance-states, sometimes attained through music, chanting, sensory deprivation, hyperventilation or the ingestion of narcotics, and also by donning animal-skins, painting their faces with whiskers or wearing horns or antlers on their heads.[28]

Many of the hybrid human-animal images that have been discovered from Iron Age and Roman Britain might in fact represent people dressed as animals, rather than 'genuine' hybrid beings; indeed, such ritual regalia has been discovered by archaeological excavations. Dressing up was clearly a tradition among officiants at certain religious ceremonies. In 1886, the Stone Age scholars John and Arthur Evans came across an assemblage of Iron Age material found in a gravel pit at Aylesford in Kent.[29] They had been searching the pit for Palaeolithic artefacts, but they immediately recognized the importance of this later group of objects, which turned out to belong to a late Iron Age cemetery. One rich cremation grave of the late 1st century BC produced a wooden bucket clad in sheet-bronze, the uppermost band decorated in repoussé,[30] with ornamental La Tène designs, including swirls and whirligigs, but also a rather significant motif: a pair of mad-looking 'pantomime' horses whose human lips and back legs betray their identity as costumed people (see pp. xii–xiii).[31] The sacral character of the decoration on this funerary vessel is enhanced by the two escutcheons on its rim, in the form of human heads wearing elaborate crowns. Buckets like these were made for holding large quantities of locally brewed liquor (ale, fermented berry-juice or mead); in the European and British Iron Age, drink was closely associated with affirmations of status, power, social relationships, politics and religious ceremony. It also arguably played a role in attaining altered states of consciousness during shamanic ritual.[32] So the people dancing opposite each other in their horse-costumes on the Aylesford bucket may represent religious specialists taking part in the funerary rites of the deceased, helping his spirit, freed from the body, to cross into the world of the ancestors.

Close scrutiny of the antlered man depicted on the Gundestrup cauldron reveals that he may be wearing an animal headdress, rather than being a true hybrid creature, for antler-headdresses are known in Britain as early as the Mesolithic (around ten thousand years ago): red-deer antlers modified for human wear have been found at Star Carr in Yorkshire,[33] where people were heavily exploiting the red-deer population not just for meat but also for antler as a material for making implements. But something similar was apparently going on eight thousand years later in Roman Britain, for a similarly modified pair of red-deer antlers comes from a pit at Hook's Cross in Hertfordshire, found in association with pottery dating to the 2nd century AD.[34] So there is a body of evidence, from iconography and liturgical regalia, that fits the shamanistic model and supports the theory that in late Iron Age and Roman Britain certain individuals assumed alternative personae in order to signify their unstable oscillations between the upper and lower layers of the cosmos, the realm of the spirits and the mundane material world.

Ravens and 'bird-men'

'Conare took his sling and stepped from his chariot and followed the great
  speckled birds until he reached the ocean. The birds went on the waves,
  but he overtook them. The birds left their feather hoods and turned on him
  with spears and swords; one bird protected him, however, saying, "I am
  Nemglan, king of your father's bird troop. You are forbidden to cast at birds,
  for, by reason of your birth, every bird is natural to you."'[35]

Nemglan appears in Irish mythology as a 'bird-man', probably a shaman who assumed an animal-persona, the better to communicate with the spirit world. The speckling of his and his fellow birds' plumage is telling for, as we have seen in the description of the future-telling Fedelma, dappling was the signature of a 'two-spirit' being. Nemglan's fellow bird-man was a blind Druid named Mog Ruith whose physical incapacity allowed his inner sight to flourish and to be used to see into the future.[36] The 'prohibition' placed upon Conare by Nemglan resonates with the doctrine of bodily rebirth mentioned by Classical chroniclers as preached by Gallic Druids (see Chapter 10).

The Aylesford 'horse-people' wore elaborate headdresses that look as if they were made from feathers. There is some circumstantial evidence for the use of plumage for ceremonial headgear too, from Iron Age ritual deposits at hillforts in southern England. The practice of reusing decommissioned grain silos as foci for votive offerings has long been known at sites such as Danebury and Winklebury.[37] Deposits often include the entire or partial bodies of humans and animals, and by far the most common of the latter belonged to domestic species: cattle, sheep and pigs, kept as livestock, plus significant numbers of horses and dogs, often found together. But the only wild creature to occur in any quantity is the raven, and this has been explained in terms of its underworld connotations, based on its blackness and its carrion-feeding habits.

Recent research on Iron Age and Romano-British bird-burials, including the Danebury burials and a group of corvids found in shafts in the centre of Roman Dorchester,[38] has suggested another explanation for the presence of ravens in these pit-deposits, proposing that these creatures might have been exploited for their feathers, perhaps for use in religious ceremonies.[39] The reason for proposing this stems partly from their singling out for special, arguably ritual, deposition in deep underground locations, but the most compelling argument for such a thesis is the revelation that some ravens had their wings and feathers removed after they had been killed, but were otherwise left intact. The selection of ravens for such treatment might be because of the large, glossy feathers that would make ideal and striking headdresses, but also because of the raven's distinctive 'voice', one that can mimic and learn simple human speech, its longevity, its memory and its reputation for being able to foretell the future (this last perhaps because they were quick to spot bloodshed and fly to the scene to scavenge). Moreover, ravens are frequently considered to have an affinity with people, because of their particular intelligence – they have been witnessed counting, figuring out solutions to problems and using tools, and are known to be adept at deception.[40]

Gallo-Roman relief-carving of a raven-god from Moux in Burgundy. W. 27 cm (10½ in.).

Two images of ravens serve to symbolize this 'special relationship' between ravens and people: an Iron Age warhelmet and a Gallo-Roman relief-carving. The helmet comes from a warrior's grave at Ciumeşti in Romania, and dates to the 3rd or 2nd century BC.[41] It was fashioned with bronze ravens' wings, one on each side, hinged so that they would flap up and down (and probably screech as they did so) when the wearer charged into battle. This was a piece of visual and auditory psychological warfare, designed to unnerve the enemy, and it is no surprise that the large, carrion-hungry raven was chosen for the purpose.

The Roman-period sculpture conveys a very different message, one of peaceful communication between a god (or a shaman) and two ravens. It comes from Moux in Burgundy and depicts a bearded man dressed in Gallic breeches and a cloak, a gnarled stave in his right hand, an open bag of fruit (or possibly oak-apples) in the crook of his left arm and a billhook in his left hand. By his side sits a large hound and on each of his shoulders sits a raven, its beak pointing towards him as if conversing with him.[42] The raven-images on both the Romanian helmet and the Burgundian carving exhibit the close connections that people felt with these large carrion birds. One conveys war; the other intimate 'conversation'. But in each case, the raven's presence may signify the birds' perceived role as advisor, helper or prophet to humans.

The sacred power of three

'As Conare was making along Slige Chúaland, he perceived three horsemen
up ahead making for the house. Red tunics and red mantles they wore, and
red shields and spears were in their hands; they rode red horses, and their
heads were red. They were entirely red, teeth and hair, horses and men.'[43]

This excerpt from a medieval Irish myth – the tale of a luckless king,
Conare Mor, who disobeys a *geis* or sacred prohibition and is condemned
by the gods – communicates vividly the Celtic preoccupation with the
colour red. For the Celts, red was a colour belonging to the Otherworld,
and the three red horsemen were thus harbingers of Conare's impending
doom. The horsemen's special status is also conferred by their triplicate
coming; three is a constantly recurring number in Irish and Welsh mythic
literature, signifying magic and mysticism. The description of the Irish
prophetess Fedelma contained reference to her triple tresses and the
triple irises of her eyes, and the Welsh brothers Gwydion and Gilfaethwy
were punished in a cycle of three forms. Its special significance can be
traced back much earlier, first in Iron Age art and into Romano-British
iconography. The 'triskele', or three-armed whirligig, design is a persistent
motif particularly in Welsh Iron Age La Tène art, as illustrated by the
decorative bronze plaques from Moel Hiraddug and Llyn Cerrig Bach in
North Wales.[44]

But it is in Roman Britain (and Gaul)[45] that triplistic imagery blossomed;
it is such a feature of religious sculpture of this period that it must have
possessed an especial spiritual resonance. Some Gallo-British deities, such
as Epona, were rarely multiplied but others, such as the mother-goddesses
and the little hooded gods known as *Genii cucullati* (see Chapter 4), were
typically depicted as triads. Sculptures of disembodied heads, too, were
often grouped in threes. Wroxeter (Viroconium Cornoviorum, the 'settlement of Virico of the Cornovii tribe'[46]) appears to have been the centre
of one such 'head-cult', for in the remains of one of its temples fragments
of deliberately defleshed human skulls, and one of a horse or cow, were
recovered during excavations. One of the human crania had been scalped,

and coated or steeped in vegetable oil. Another had clearly reposed for a time on a bronze plate or sheet, for it was stained with the green colour that comes from copper. And a column from one of the buildings in the forum (the central market-place) was once decorated with a strange, native-looking threefold male head, each with luxuriant curly hair.[47] A more complete triple disembodied head with curly hair, full moustache and beard comes from the Roman city of Lugdunum (Lyon) in Gaul, but the carving differs from the British stone in that it represents a single head with three distinct faces.[48] And unlike the Wroxeter stone, where the three faces stare, more or less, straight ahead, the faces on the Gallic image gaze at the world at right-angles to one another. Although some elements of *romanitas* can be distinguished in the modelling of these triple heads, the three-faced Iron Age stone head from Corleck (County Cavan) in Ireland,[49] beyond the western frontier of the Roman Empire, serves as a reminder that the roots of the motif lay in the indigenous traditions of the west. All these threefold heads have in common a slight but perceptible differentiation between each face and an air of power, and perhaps even of threat. In his description of the Corleck head, Barry Raftery aptly refers to 'the stern and brooding presence of an Otherworld being'.[50] The same may be said of the triple head from Wroxeter, whose half-shut eyes and grim expression give the faces an air of malevolence.

In Roman Britain, the power of three was represented not simply by disembodied heads but, more often, by triple beings whose entire bodies are replicated. Earlier chapters have already touched on the two most common forms of Gallo-British cult-images treated in this manner: the

Monumental stone triple-faced male head from the Roman forum at Wroxeter, Shropshire.

mother-goddesses and their frequent companions the *Genii cucullati*, small, non-gender-specific figures shrouded in the long hooded cloak known as the *birrus Britannicus*. Such garments were robust woollen coats designed to withstand the cold wet weather that is so much more prevalent in Britain and northern Gaul than in southern Europe. One aspect of the hoods worn by these triple 'godlets' is their capacity to shroud faces. Was the choice to depict them hooded designed to demonstrate hidden or obscured identity?

The Cotswolds around Cirencester seem to have been a particular focus for triplistic imagery and, while threeness occurs in varying forms and combinations, it was a persistent and clearly significant symbol for the Dobunni. Even 'unlikely' Cotswold deities were triplicated, like the 'Mars' or native warrior-god found in a well at Lower Slaughter.[51] What is particularly striking is the way in which sculptors played with the triplism

Stone figure of a goddess with three apples in her lap, from Ashcroft, Cirencester. Ht *c.* 42 cm (16 in.).

associated with the mother-goddesses. In Chapter 4, the carvings of three goddesses were introduced. But even when the goddesses were presented alone, triplism was referenced in associated imagery. So, for example, a solo mother-goddess from Ashcroft (a site identified as a likely temple for mother-goddess worship) sits in a chair with three apples in her lap;[52] and a once-lost but rediscovered relief found at Stratton, near the Dobunnic capital, depicts another single seated woman, with a large round object in her lap, facing a processional trio of *cucullati* who approach her, each carrying a goblet of liquor.[53] These two carvings illustrate the primary importance of threeness, over and above other features within these carvings. But the Stratton carving

Small stone relief of three cloaked standing figures
(*Genii cucullati*) and a seated woman, all deliberately
decapitated, from Stratton, Gloucestershire.

has additional interest in that, sometime in antiquity, the three *genii* and
the goddess were deliberately 'beheaded', thus emphasizing the triplism
even more, without the viewers' gaze being distracted by the individual-
ity conferred by heads and faces.[54] This was not iconoclasm but a careful
modification that took place some years later than the date the stone was
carved, a statement of purposeful and religious intent. There is no sign
of what happened to the severed heads: perhaps they were considered no
longer necessary to the carving's meaning, or maybe they were reused in
other 'head-centred' ritual events, or received a dignified and respectful
burial somewhere nearby.

So why was triplism so significant and so persistent in Romano-British
cult-imagery? What did 'threeness' mean to the Britons? We need to be
very careful in ascribing meaning without much tangible evidence. In
Llandaff Cathedral there is a 19th-century stone corbel depicting a three-
faced head representing the Holy Trinity whose iconography is remarkably
similar, in visual terms, to the Lugdunum triple-head mentioned earlier.[55]
It serves as a warning that meaning is entirely context-dependent, and
no written sources reveal any clues as to what triadism represented in
the western Roman Empire. But there is no harm in indulging in some
mild speculation. A clue may present itself in a particular form of triple
image from Roman Gaul, a group of sculptures from Nuits-Saint-Georges

in Burgundy depicting goddesses of varying ages: youth, middle age and old age.[56] Here, at least, triplistic imagery is associated with the 'three stages' of humankind – birth and childhood, adolescence, and old age and death. Perhaps such images were meant to warn human worshippers of the brevity of life, a reminder of the inexorability of time and that the vital thread might be cut whenever the gods willed it. Other alternatives suggest themselves for the meaning behind such a persistent and widely distributed tradition: past, present and future, perhaps. Triadism might have been connected to spatial perceptions of a triple-fold cosmic structure, in which the uppermost level was deemed to be inhabited by the spirits, 'middle-earth' by people and other living beings, and the underworld, the land of the dead. The triple-layered cosmos has wide currency in traditional societies where shamanism plays a prominent role.[57] These layers are permeable for the shaman, whose soul has the power to move between worlds to liaise with the spirits and the dead, to negotiate with them on behalf of the living communities dwelling on the central, mate-rial level. Some of these individuals might also be able to cause time to become fluid, to segue between temporal layers and manipulate the past and the future by tapping into the will of the gods. Whatever perceptions lay behind the 'triple habit' in Roman Britain and its Gallic neighbour, what is clear is that, like horns, disembodied or exaggerated heads and other reality-bending iconography, triplism fed into a broad tradition of 'otherness', of presenting divine forms outside the 'normal' template of the human or animal image.

Being different: the surreality of spirits

In this chapter we have seen how the world of the spirit was expressed in iconographic traditions that thought outside the parameter of the natural. In the Classical world, the gods were perceived as beings who were essentially superhuman versions of people, despite their exalted status as immortal deities. Certainly, the world of Classical mythology allowed for monsters, like the Gorgon or the Hydra, but Zeus, Mars, Venus and Mercury were recognizably human. In Gallo-British communities, the gods were not always imagined like this. For religious officials, artists and worshippers, the spirit world was demonstrably different from that experienced by humans, and sometimes this difference was represented by crossing the boundaries between realism and surrealism. This predilection for twisting real life to create other canons of being can be traced back to the Iron Age artistic tradition known as La Tène,[58] which produced a rich array of fantastical creatures, from human-headed horses to nightmare human faces with bulging eyes and animal-ears or enormous leaf-shaped headdresses, as well as stylized leaf-designs whose tendrils end in birds' heads, hybrid bull-horned horses and cats' faces that morph into owls as you look at them. This is two-thousand-year-old surrealism, what Ernst Gombrich called 'the ambiguity of shapes, the game of "rabbit or duck?"',[59] the desire to escape earthbound reality and get beyond it to truer truths.

It is possible to use early 20th-century surrealism as a lens through which to consider some of the images that are the subject of this chapter. There is one other iconographic custom in Roman Britain with which to conclude, namely the 'schematic habit'. Alongside the three-dimensional moulding of the human form in religious imagery, there marched a tradition that stripped back form to its very essence, deliberately eschewing detail to create mere outlines. This is not, as some purist Roman scholars would suggest, simply 'bad art', the failure of British sculptors to master the art of realistic sculpture, but an attempt to express alternative ways of seeing, a 'schematic shorthand'[60] where all that mattered was the message. For it is almost certain that the school of figure-carving that was so active in the Dobunnic Cotswolds, with its centre almost certainly in Cirencester, produced sculptors capable of creating both realistic and shorthand images, probably depending upon the choice of their clientele. One carving is sufficient to demonstrate minimalism at its most evocative: the little plaque from Cirencester depicting the three *Genii cucullati*, or hooded spirits,[61] whose slanting legs depict them scurrying off to the viewer's right, one behind the other. The body of each figure is represented by a simple triangle, the only detail of the heads being the side-projection of the hood. But all the essentials are present: threeness, hoodedness and movement. The power of the image is in its spare economy of line, where

Highly schematized
relief-carving of three
scurrying *Genii cucullati*
from Cirencester.
Ht *c.* 23 cm (9 in.).

the interplay of shape, contour and light can be appreciated without the
clutter of unnecessary detail.

At the very end of his life, when he was in his nineties, Michelangelo
sculpted the last of his three images of the Pietà,[62] the Virgin Mary cra-
dling the dead Christ in her arms, in an attitude of deep mourning. The
fine detail of the first two exhibit the artist's breathtaking mastery over
his medium of marble; his final piece represents an entirely new artistic
direction. Here, the minutiae of detail are subordinated to shape, form and
the all-consuming image of grief. The two figures, mother and son, seemingly merge into a single ululation of sorrow. The sculpture is all the more
potent because Michelangelo died before finishing it; its incompleteness
allows for the viewer's own interpretation to contribute to its message.
Confrontation with a minimalist image allows for active and personal
engagement on the part of those who gaze at it. It is immersive, wrapping
the spectator in a private and organic dialogue that permits fluidity and
interactivity, so that each individual can connect to a sculpted figure in a
meaningful, highly personal way. The schematic *cucullati* from Corinium
present just such a 'blank canvas', upon which every worshipper had the
capacity for their own endowment of meaning. Despite the presentation of
movement in these three little figures, there is about them – and many of
their fellow carvings – a kind of 'robust tranquillity',[63] a muscular stillness
that greatly enhances their power to draw the gaze and to invite people
to ponder on the nature of the divine.

CHAPTER EIGHT

Candles in the Dark and Spice from the Orient: *Mystery cults*

'But what a small part of our dregs
Is Greek! Long ago the wide
Orontes of Syria poured into the Tiber
And brought
With its lingo and morals its flutes
And harps...' JUVENAL[1]

Rome did not sit entirely happily with the East. In the 1st century AD, the memories of the notorious Egyptian queen Cleopatra, whose seduction of both Julius Caesar and Mark Antony had such a devastating effect upon Roman politics late in the previous century, were still fresh and raw. There was prejudice against the perceived effeteness and decadence of the painted and perfumed 'Oriental'. In his *Satires*, Juvenal poked fun at Eastern customs and religion.[2] In the particularly scornful verse quoted at the beginning of this chapter he probably echoed the prejudices of many of his contemporaries. But the traditions of the East did undoubtedly penetrate the Roman Empire, even as far to the north as Britain. These exotic religions arrived here with army units recruited in the eastern provinces, like Anatolia and Syria, and with merchants, oriental entrepreneurs who sought new markets for their wares. So it is unsurprising that archaeological evidence for these cults is clustered in large entrepôts like London and, above all, on military sites, particularly on Hadrian's Wall.

New research taking place in London is shedding light on the multicultural nature of the city's population, demonstrating the presence of people from all over the Empire relatively early after its establishment as a major Roman port. To appreciate how important Roman London was as a hub of commerce, we need look no further than the recent finds of wooden tablets preserved in the waters of the river Walbrook. The most ancient of these tablets dated to the first decade of Roman rule, between AD 43 and 55. It 'reveals that the city was a snake pit for financiers twenty centuries before the stock market crash caused by the collapse of sub-prime mortgages',[3] and that the city recovered incredibly quickly from the ravages of the Boudican revolt in AD 60 to flourish as the financial capital of Britannia for the next three hundred years.

The analysis of Roman skeletons recently undertaken by Rebecca Redfern at the Museum of London has demonstrated the cosmopolitan nature of the city. Study of the DNA from the bones and teeth of people buried in its cemeteries enabled Dr Redfern to trace their ethnic origins, and her results prove that some ancient Londoners came from northern and eastern Europe and North Africa. Most astoundingly of all, two individuals, buried in a cemetery in Southwark, were of Chinese origin.[4] They are quite likely to have been traders in silk, for the penchant for this exotic fabric is well documented in Roman literary sources from the 1st century AD onwards.[5] Given Roman London's multiculturalism, the importance of international trade and the ethnic mixture of the Roman army, the presence of eastern cults in Britain is easy to comprehend.

Only good men allowed: Mithras the Persian God

'Mithras, God of the Midnight, here where the great bull dies,
Look on thy children in darkness. Oh take our sacrifice!
Many roads Thou hast fashioned, all of them lead to the Light,
Mithras, also a soldier, teach us to die aright.' KIPLING [6]

Rudyard Kipling's poem is about the most prominent of the new oriental religious movements to be established in Britain, the cult of the Persian god Mithras, an exclusively male cult. Not only that, his followers had to be of good character. Mithraism was an exacting religion that accepted only those capable of the kind of physical stamina and endurance that Mithras himself demonstrated in his wrestle with a great bull. Mithras was sent to earth as the emissary of the great Iranian creator-god, Ahura Mazda, to hunt and slay the divine bull so that its life-blood would revital-ize the earth and humankind; he was a guider of souls, teaching people the right path, that of goodness.[7] So, unlike most other religions in the Roman Empire, it was a cult whose adherents were required to live a life of merit, and furthermore to undergo a complicated series of seven initia-tion rites. The Christian leader and writer Saint Jerome wrote in the early 4th century AD of 'the monstrous images there by which worshippers were initiated as Raven, Bridegroom, Soldier, Lion, Perseus, Sun Runner and Father'.[8] Jerome was born in c. AD 348 in Dalmatia,[9] but taken to Rome early in his life, to be taught by the greatest theologians of the time. As an ardent and outspoken Christian leader, he was both appalled by and scornful of Mithraism, which seemed to him to represent a twisted and wicked travesty of monotheism that set itself up to rival Christianity.

The fundamental basis of the Mithraic cult was dualism, the cease-less struggle between right and wrong, light and darkness; but the dark forces were perceived as necessary for the existence of good, to enable it to triumph and flourish. Central to the 'dark side' was Ahriman, lord of chaos and the clouds of disorder, and even Mithras himself contains contradictory aspects. He represented the great Persian god of light and the cosmos, but was born deep in a lightless cave, as if sprung from the forces of primeval chaos. Mithraea (sanctuaries to Mithras) were gener-ally sunk into the ground, in acknowledgment of Mithras's subterranean birth, and worship took place in the dark, the shrines lit only by oil-lamps, torches and candles flickering in the blackness. The most visible focus in Mithraic temples was the tauroctony, the bull-slaying scene that formed the *reredos*, or high altar, of the sanctuary, which would have been specially lit for dramatic and theatrical effect. Wealth may have been a factor in the acceptance of novices for training and initiation, for it was a cult whose devotees came mostly from the officer ranks of the army and prosperous merchants, and they gave generously to the upkeep of their temples and to the honour of the god.

North and south: the Mithraea in London, Carrawburgh and Inveresk

'To the Unconquered Mithras, Lucius Antonius Proculus, Prefect of the
First Cohort of Batavians, willingly and deservedly fulfilled his vow.'[10]

This inscription comes from an altar, one of three, set up in the early 3rd
century AD in front of the apse behind which the bull-slaying scene would
have been mounted in the Carrawburgh Mithraeum. Several temples to
Mithras existed in the cities and military installations of Roman Britain; it
was essential to the rituals that the sites chosen had access to a stream or
spring, which as we have seen was also a consideration in the location of military bases, as, for example, Coventina's Well at Carrawburgh and the temple
to Sulis at Bath (see Chapter 5).[11] Lustration (purification by water) was a key
element in oriental cults, such as Mithraism and the worship of Cybele (see p.
166). The Mithraea in London and on the Hadrian's Wall fort of Carrawburgh
are among the best preserved, allowing some appreciation of what it
must have been like to worship there. The temples' construction followed

a set architectural formula.
The sanctuary buildings consisted of a small entrance-hall
or narthex, through which the
devotee progressed down a
flight of steps to the nave,
flanked by two side-aisles, in
which altars and images were
displayed (see p. xiv, bottom).
At the end of the nave nearest

The stone foundations of the
Carrawburgh Mithraeum. The
shrine is semi-subterranean,
divided into a central nave with
side-aisles. Three altars can be
seen at the far end.

the narthex stood two images of Cautes and Cautopates, keepers of the sacred flame. Cautes was depicted holding an upright torch, while Cautopates's torch was inverted, between them representing the dualism of light and dark in Mithraic doctrine. At the far end an apse framed the sculpture of the bull-slaying scene, subtly but dramatically lit so as to reveal Mithras astride his victim, wearing his soft, 'Phrygian' cap (a form of soft, conical hat that originated in ancient Phrygia, now Turkey), his knife plunged into the bull's neck, the figures picked out in bold colours.

The diverse sculptures from the London Mithraeum reveal that devotees of other cults were welcomed to the shrine: the Egyptian god Serapis was represented here, as were the Roman Bacchus and Minerva. Some were depicted in exquisite marble carvings, others less well executed in oolitic limestone, probably from the Cotswolds.[12] Coin evidence suggests that the sanctuary was erected in the 2nd century AD and went through a number of phases before falling out of use sometime in the 4th century. During its lifetime, there were at least two events that involved the deliberate burial of some of the sculptures, perhaps in attempts to prevent their desecration by early Christian persecutors.[13] Little can be discerned about the ritual practices that went on in the London Mithraeum, but some of the finds provide tantalizing clues: broken cups for libations or votive offerings, and the food-remains of sacred feasts;

Marble relief of Mithras astride and slaying the sacred bull, from the Walbrook Mithraeum, London. The torchbearers, Cautes and Cautopates, flank the bull. Ht c. 43 cm (17 in.).

Gilded silver canister and strainer from the Walbrook Mithraeum, London. Ht 6.35 cm (2½ in.).

lustral basins that would once have held water for purifying supplicants; and candlesticks that would have glowed in the gloom of the sanctuary and dramatically illuminated the sculptures. The most exceptional small find was a gilded silver canister decorated with scenes of hunting and combat, inside which was a strainer. This was almost certainly used for the preparation and keeping of the secret fluids that had a part in Mithraic ceremonies.[14] The vessel's iconography has a strongly oriental flavour: people wearing Phrygian caps, exotic-looking trees and animals such as lions, hippopotamuses and elephants. It was probably made at a workshop somewhere in the eastern Mediterranean in the late 3rd or early 4th century AD, towards the end of the temple's life.

The Mithraeum belonging to the fort at Carrawburgh on Hadrian's Wall was a smaller, more modest affair than the great, lavishly furnished Walbrook shrine in London, but it was of similar basilical design, and contained a feature whose presence hints at the enactment of initiation rituals there: a trench sunk into the floor with a flagstone lid. Guy de la Bédoyère is almost certainly correct in interpreting this structure as 'some kind of endurance pit for an initiation exercise',[15] designed to test the physical and psychological stamina of would-be Mithraists before their admittance into the mysteries of the cult. Here, perhaps, the confined initiate struggled with the pain of hunger and thirst and with solitude and darkness before being released and judged by those already accepted into the inner circle of cult-adherents. The epigraphic evidence from the Carrawburgh Mithraeum indicates that, here at least, Mithras, god of light, was equated with Sol Invictus, the Unconquered Sun, whose cult, which was of Syrian origin, became popular during the reign of the emperor Aurelian in the 3rd century AD.[16] One of the three altars ranged in front of the *reredos* at the far end of the Mithraeum depicts Sol-Mithras clad in a cloak, carrying a whip, the solar rays sprouting from his head pierced so as to allow back-lighting to illuminate it, in a wonderfully theatrical statement of the god's celestial power.[17] This altar was deliberately damaged in antiquity, perhaps by devotees of a rival cult.

The dramatic visual effects of Mithraic rites at Carrawburgh were replicated further north, at the Roman fort of Inveresk in East Lothian, Scotland, where in 2010 excavators uncovered part of a Mithraeum just east of the fort itself. The discovery is particularly exciting because it is the first to have been found in Scotland and because of its secure date in the mid-2nd century AD, when the Antonine Wall was built and garrisoned.[18] The shrine was of typical form, rectangular and sunk into the ground. At one end, two altars had been deliberately buried face-down, one dedicated to Mithras, the other to Sol, the sun-god, both bearing rich cult-iconography. As at Carrawburgh, the image of Sol was lit from behind to illuminate his facial features, but at Inveresk, Sol's nose had also had an iron rod at the back, perhaps in order to manipulate the god's face and introduce sound effects, like breathing or speech. So we can imagine the rituals here, on the very northern edge of the known Roman world, of a cult far from home but displaying all the flamboyance, theatre and spectacle of a sophisticated sanctuary in London, Rome or an eastern city.

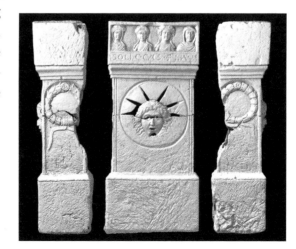

Stone altar to Sol-Mithras from the Inveresk Mithraeum on the Antonine Wall, Scotland. Ht. *c.* 125 cm (49 in.).

New light on Mithraic Wales

Mithras was venerated by army units stationed at forts and fortresses in both North and South Wales. The Mithraeum excavated at Segontium (Caernarfon) was founded in the mid-2nd century AD and probably went out of use by about AD 350, with some evidence for deliberate destruction. It conformed to type, with a narthex, nave, aisles and an apsidal recess for the bull-slaying *reredos*, and its temple furniture included small altars, lamps and – unusually – a free-standing portable candelabrum,[19] perhaps designed to be moved from altar to altar during ceremonies, or to illuminate the faces of would-be initiates as, one by one, they presented themselves to the presiding officers in the temple. No Mithraeum has been discovered in Wales's principal legionary fortress at Caerleon, but an inscribed dedication to 'the Invincible Mithras' erected in the fortress by a devotee called Justus from the 2nd Augustan Legion formed part of a circular base, perhaps for a statue of the god.[20]

In 2007, the local Monmouth Archaeology unit discovered some exciting new evidence for the cult of Mithras at Caerleon while undertaking an archaeological evaluation of some land on the Bulmore Road, just over the river Usk from the legionary fortress and near to the *vicus* (the extramural settlement) and to major Roman cemeteries for soldiers, veterans and the civilians living in the *vicus*. The finds were part of the liturgical furniture, almost certainly for the Caerleon Mithraeum, and take the form of fragmentary ceramic altars and sacrificial tables (*mensae*), some pieces pierced with holes for the insertion of candles or torches and showing signs of burning. These objects were made of local clay, probably by army potters. During two episodes in the life of the temple (one in the later 2nd century AD, the second in the later 3rd or 4th century), some of these portable clay tables and altars were deliberately smashed by being hit hard by a heavy object at their centres, and then recycled to form part of a drainage channel for a nearby Roman building. The debris of ritual feasting, including the burnt and butchered bones of sheep or goats, was placed inside this channel and covered with a capstone.

On some of the surfaces of this sacrificial material are fragmentary inscriptions that do not, by themselves, convey any useful information revealing the rites performed. However, one of the pieces, part of a 'box' altar, bears decoration that ties it directly to sacrificial rites: palm-branch garlands for decorating the animal before its slaughter, and the main instruments for despatching animal-offerings: a pole-axe for stunning the beast, and a knife for cutting its throat. What is more, a hole was deliberately bored into the clay in the space between the garlands and the axe, possibly as a receptacle for real palm-fronds.[21]

So far, their intrinsic form and decoration serve to link these ceramic finds firmly into the context of sacred rites. But what is the rationale behind their possible connection with Mithras? Although ceramic altars are rare, they do occur in Romano-British temples whose cults were nothing to do with the Persian cult, an example being the fragments of a 'box' altar from the temple to Mercury at Uley.[22] But research by Mark Lewis of the Roman Legionary Museum at Caerleon[23] has put together a persuasive assemblage of evidence that points strongly to a Mithraic role for the Caerleon ceramic temple furniture, particularly the sacrificial *mensae*. There is a close parallel between the examples from South Wales and similar fragments from the Tummel Platz Mithraeum at Linz on the Danube frontier in Austria, the coin-evidence indicating that the sanctuary was built in about AD 275. The *mensa* from this Danubian Mithraeum bore an inscription that confirms the shrine's dedication to Mithras. Lewis also draws attention to a series of monumental stone altars dedicated to the Persian god at Tummel Platz. These, like the clay ones from Caerleon, were

Fragments of clay 'table' altars, with holes for candles, probably from a Mithraeum, found at Caerleon, South Wales.

pierced with candle-holes. Comparable Mithraic temple-furniture has also been found in the Roman military establishment at Dura Europos, on the eastern bank of the river Euphrates in Syria.

The inscribed stone dedicated to Mithras at Caerleon indicates his worship at the legionary fortress. Although the evidence of the clay altars from the Bulmore site is largely circumstantial, based on parallels with other Mithraic liturgical equipment from elsewhere in the Empire, it is reasonable to make the connection between these ceramic altars and the Persian deity, and to suggest the presence of a small Mithraeum placed deliberately near the Bulmore cemetery in the 2nd century AD. These altars show signs of (possibly iconoclastic) destruction, as did the Segontium Mithraeum. What is particularly special about these recent discoveries in Caerleon is the emphasis on light in the darkness: the candles. These finds help us to visualize the physical experience of entering a dim, shadowy sanctuary whose gloom was dramatically pierced with subtle, carefully controlled illumination that shone on sculptures, inscriptions, priests and supplicants as desired by the bearers of the flame, while keeping the mysteries secret in the artificial, cave-like night of the shrine.

Fertility and castration: Cybele and Atys

'Of Cybele it is a shame to speak: unable to satisfy the affections of her luckless lover – for mothering of many gods had made her plain and old – she could not allure him to lust and castrated him, so as to make a god, no less, a eunuch, and in deference to this fable her *galli* priests worship her by inflicting the same mutilation on their own bodies. Such practices are not sacred rites but tortures.' MINUCIUS FELIX[24]

Sometime during the earlier 3rd century AD, the North African Christian writer Minucius Felix constructed a fictitious dialogue between a Christian whom he called Octavius and a man called Caecilius Natalis from Cirta (in what is now Libya) in the province of Numidia. This 'dialogue' presented arguments that held up pagan rites to ridicule, while at the same time defending Christians from allegations that their Eucharistic rituals involved cannibalism.[25] In this passage, Felix is poking fun at the cult of the *Magna*

Mater, the Great Mother goddess of Phrygia in Anatolia (today part of Turkey). She was, in origin, a nature-goddess, sometimes known as 'Our Lady of the Animals', and in many of her images, she is depicted flanked by lions or panthers.[26] Hers was one of the earliest and most enduring of the oriental cults to be absorbed into mainstream Roman religion. It was imported to Rome around 205 BC, in response to a prophecy that the Carthaginian armies under Hannibal would be defeated only if Cybele's sacred stone from Ida in Anatolia was brought into the city. The worship of Cybele lasted until finally ousted by Christianity in the late 4th century AD under the emperor Theodosius.[27]

Our Lady of the Animals

'Eunuchs will march and thump their hollow drums, and cymbals clashed on cymbals will give out their tinkling notes; seated on the unmanly necks of her attendants, the goddess herself will be borne with howls through the streets in the city's midst.'[28]

'The Virgin in her heavenly place rides upon the Lion; bearer of corn, inventor of law, founder of cities, by whose gifts it is mans' good lot to know the gods...'[29]

The first passage quoted comes from the Augustan poet Ovid's poetical calendar of the Roman religious year, the *Fasti* (or 'correct days'). Like his compatriot Juvenal, Ovid shows scant respect for this exotic, and somewhat unrestrained and over-emotional cult, whose flamboyant processions probably rather shocked the senate fathers, particularly at a time when Augustus was trying so hard to impose an austerity regime on Rome.[30] The second quote is part of a stone panel dedicated to Cybele in the late 2nd or early 3rd century AD by the military tribune Marcus Caecilius Donatianus at Carvoran on Hadrian's Wall. It is the opening of a poem or hymn in honour of the goddess, and the paean goes on to link her with the cult of Julia Domna, the Syrian wife of the African emperor Septimius Severus (r. AD 193–211), who was often referred to with the honorific title 'The Virgin'.

The myth underpinning the cult of Cybele was based upon jealousy and infidelity. Cybele was in love with a young shepherd called Atys and, catching him *in flagrante delicto*, she drove him insane, bending his mind so that he castrated himself beneath a pine tree and bled to death. Built upon this myth was a cult founded upon the rhythm of the year: the winter of mourning for Cybele's dead lover (the ceremony of the *tristitia*) was followed by the joy of the spring of his rebirth and the renewal of the earth's fecundity (the *hilaria*). In the annual re-enactment of Atys's funeral ceremony, cult officials known as *dendrophori* ('tree-bearers') paraded through the towns and cities carrying pine trees, in deference to the tree under which the young god died. Felix was correct in his description of the Great Mother's religious attendants, for initiates to the priesthood had, like Atys, to undergo castration, and ceremonies involved the ingestion of mind-altering substances, trance-dancing in ecstasy, self-flagellation and the enactment of the *taurobolium*, the bull-sacrifice, in which the blood of the animal poured through a grille set into the ground into an excavated space where initiates were bathed in the gore, as part of their trial-rites.[31] Because of its reputation for orgiastic rites and general wildness, the cult was strictly controlled in the Roman Republic, when no Roman citizen was allowed near it, but the emperor Claudius relaxed the rule and the cult of Cybele and Atys became 'respectable' and even a Roman State Religion,[32] with the eunuch celebrants (*galli*) and their high priest (the *archigallus*) fully absorbed as Romans, with Latin names.[33]

Cybele and her unfortunate consort, Atys, were – like Mithras – worshipped in cities, where foreign

Stone head of Atys from a Roman cemetery at Caerleon. Ht *c.* 48 cm (19 in.).

merchants plied their wares, and on army bases, such as Carvoran and Corbridge on or near Hadrian's Wall, where regiments from the eastern provinces were stationed. The specialist auxiliary cohort of Syrian archers, *Cohors I Hamiorum*, was deployed from Carvoran, and here the Anatolian Cybele seems to have been merged with the Syrian goddess Caelestis or Dea Syria.[34] There must have been a temple (called a Metroon) to Cybele at Corbridge, just south of the Wall, for here, in the 3rd century AD, army personnel set up an altar to the Anatolian goddess under the name Dea Panthea; on each lateral surface of the stone a figure of Atys in mourning is depicted, wearing a Phrygian cap and cloak.[35] A disembodied head of Atys from here[36] may have belonged to the same temple.

London was clearly an important centre for the cult of Cybele, for several small figurines of Atys have been found in the city, as well as two more significant objects: an altar (alas now lost) and a curious piece of liturgical equipment. The altar was rich in iconographical detail: on one surface was carved the figure of Cybele holding pomegranates and a small wine-flask, flanked by two of her *galli* (priests); another face depicts the funeral of Atys, with his bier carried in procession by clergy (with a basket and pine branches said to represent the dedication of the unfortunate youth's genitals to the jealous goddess).[37] The ceremonial bronze object mentioned earlier has gained much notoriety for its identification as a 'castration clamp' for gelding the would-be priests of Cybele. It comes from the river Thames near London Bridge and comprises a hinged pair of 'forceps', serrated on the inside and decorated on the outer surfaces with busts of Cybele, Atys

Bronze 'castration clamp', used in the rites of Cybele, from the river Thames, London. Ht c. 29 cm (11 in.).

and other deities, with the terminals ending in the heads of lions.[38] The object may have been thrown into the water as a sacrificial act or, perhaps just as likely, to avoid its despoliation by a rival cult, maybe that of Christ. It wasn't intentionally broken, for the hinges seem to have decayed naturally, and the two arms, though separate, were found close together. It may have been a purely ceremonial object, symbolizing Atys's own castration, but it is not impossible that such an instrument was actually used in the initiation rituals for Cybele's eunuch priests, a rather gruesome thought.

Mountains, smiths and double-axes: Jupiter of Doliche

'By order of Jupiter Optimus Maximus Dolichenus Eternal, for the preserver of the firmament and for the pre-eminent divinity, invincible provider, Lucius Tertius Hermes, Roman knight, candidate and patron of this place, for the welfare of himself, his wife Aurelia Restituta, his daughter Tertia Pannuchia and his family, and his dearest brother Aurelius Lampadus, and for the welfare of the priests and candidates and worshippers of this place: he presented a marble plaque.... Jupiter Optimus Maximus Dolichenus chose the following to serve him: Marcus Aurelius Oenopio Onesimus as recorder...'[39]

The above is part of a long inscription from the Dolichenum on the Aventine Hill in Rome. The plaque was dedicated by a high-ranking Roman citizen in the mid-3rd century AD, and the passage quoted goes on to list the religious officials according to their status within the religious community. Oenopio's name is Greek, and his role as 'recorder' may relate to his role in initiation of candidates to the Dolichene sect. Inscriptions like these demonstrate the high degree of the cult's organization. The text goes on to list the names of those aspiring to acceptance to the ritual hierarchy: the 'father' of the candidates, their 'patrons' and 'brothers', the 'leaders' of the sanctuary, the 'guardian' of the temple, priests and the god's litter-bearers (presumably these carried the images of Dolichenus in processions). Doliche was in the north of the Roman province of Syria and from this small town emanated an eastern cult that enjoyed high prominence and popularity within the Roman State religious system. Dolichenus achieved his elevated profile by being linked with Jupiter Best and Greatest, the head of the Roman pantheon, father of the gods and lord of the heavens. Sanctuaries were built for his worship all over the Roman world, from Dura Europos on the Euphrates to Corbridge in northern Britain.

So who exactly was Dolichenus, and what was his role as a Syrian deity in the Roman world? He was essentially a mountain-god, the personification of Mount Commagene, and presided over the sky and storms, but he was also a god of iron, responsible for mining, smelting and smithing. Frequently, he is depicted wearing the conical hat typical of a smith-god, and wielding a double-axe, probably a thunderbolt-symbol. He was worshipped in Britain, particularly in military regions and, while his cult may have been imported through Syrian-raised army units, the evidence from the great Dolichene sanctuary on the Aventine Hill in Rome demonstrates what a mainstream 'Roman' deity he had become by the early 3rd century AD. He enjoyed a particular spike in popularity during the reign of Septimius Severus.[40]

A number of Dolichena (temples to Dolichenus) may have been built for the worship of the Romano-Syrian hill-deity[41] in Britain, and his worshippers seem to have come almost exclusively from the frontier regions. One shrine is known for certain, though no surviving structure has been identified: a dedication-slab from Bewcastle, an outpost-fort 6 miles (10 km) north of Hadrian's Wall, records the building of a temple 'to Jupiter Best and Greatest Dolichenus, this temple from its foundations...'.[42] A stone frieze, richly ornamented with sacred images, and a temple-pediment may well come from a Dolichenum at Corbridge, where a centurion of the 6th Legion dedicated an altar to Jupiter Dolichenus and his Syrian consort Caelestis.[43] Here, her Syrian name was twinned with that most British of goddesses, Brigantia, the guardian-goddess of the great north British hegemony of the Brigantes. The stone bull from Corbridge,[44] sawn in half in antiquity and the surviving portion reused as a threshold stone, may well have come from a temple, for Dolichenus's animal was the bull. He is often depicted standing on a bull's back, perhaps because its bellowing roar evoked the god's power as a thunder-god.[45]

Potsherd from a slip-decorated ceramic vessel depicting the Syrian god Jupiter Dolichenus, with his distinctive conical smith's hat and double-axe, from Sawtry, Cambridgeshire.

The popularity of Dolichenus is shown by the widespread distribution of his cult: he was venerated as far apart as the legionary fortress at Caerleon in South Wales[46] and the auxiliary fort at Birrens in Dumfriesshire.[47] But perhaps the most poignant symbol of his cult is a small, personal object far away from the military frontier: a fragment of painted ceramic Castorware from Sawtry, in the vicinity of the potteries, depicting the head and shoulders of Dolichenus, bearded, with his tell-tale conical hat, brandishing his double-axe.[48] Because this Eastern god was mainly worshipped among the military and in cities, to find his image on a Romano-British pot in the Cambridgeshire countryside is true testament to his dedicated following.

Cleopatra's gods

'Lo I Isis am at hand, moved by your prayers, Lucius, I the parent of the nature of things, mistress of all the elements, initial begetter of the ages, supreme of divine powers, queen of the shades of the dead, first of heavenly beings, the uniform countenance of gods and goddesses. I who control at my will the luminous points of the sky, the salubrious breezes of the sea and the lamented silences of the underworld…' APULEIUS[49]

Lucius Apuleius was born in about AD 123 into a wealthy family at Madaurus in North Africa. His education took him to Carthage, then to Athens and

Rome. His quasi-autobiographical novel, *The Golden Ass*, is about a fictional character, Lucius, who meddles in black magic and is turned into an ass, meets a range of deities (including the Gallic horse-goddess Epona) and people and has all sorts of adventures until the Egyptian goddess Isis rescues him and returns him to human form.[50]

The mystery cult of Isis in the Roman Empire was a legacy from Pharaonic Egypt. Despite the opprobrium that Egypt attracted in the late 1st century BC for the behaviour of Cleopatra, first luring Julius Caesar, then Mark Antony, into her bed and her politics, Isis was popular in the west, particularly in Rome itself. The emperor Domitian, who ruled from AD 86 to 91, was an adherent of the goddess: the writer of court gossip Suetonius gives an enthusiastic description of how he escaped from the warfare between Vespasian and Vitellius in AD 69 by taking refuge with the priests of Isis, even donning their garb as a disguise.[51] So when he became emperor, he fostered the cult, and became its powerful patron. From Apuleius and from wall-paintings surviving in Pompeii,[52] it is possible to get a smattering of information about the rituals and beliefs associated with the cult, although some of it was quite secret. Behind all this was the essential triadic myth of Isis the mother-goddess, her husband Serapis, and their son Harpocrates (originally Osiris and Horus respectively). Serapis was destroyed by Seth, god of evil, avenged by his son and then brought back to life by Isis.[53] So she had power over creation, nurture and the ability to resurrect the dead. The rites of Isis were built upon this myth.

Apuleius speaks of his initiation: it involved lustration (purification by washing), fasting, the reception of secret instructions concerning the liturgy for several days before the initiate was brought into the temple, and the 'meeting of the goddess' in the inner sanctum of Isis's temple. Once received by the divine one, the new adherent would be dressed in special garments and his or her transformed self would be presented to devotees, who welcomed and feasted the newly initiated, as someone reborn,[54] like the god Serapis himself. Because of the secret rituals associated with the cult of Isis and her divine family, the cult had a sub-religious aspect: that of magic. Charms were worn by people who sought to invoke Isis as a guardian against evil forces. Martin Henig[55] cites an amulet made of red haematite from the vicinity of the Roman villa at Welwyn in Hertfordshire that he thinks must have been the property of someone from the east, perhaps a slave-girl. The message on the charm beseeches the goddess to protect her from the dangers of childbirth, a hazardous business in the ancient world. The blood-red colour of the stone surely added to the potency of the magic. The owner of the amulet may well have kept it hidden on her person, beneath her clothing, so that only she knew of it resting against her skin, wrapping her in a symbolic cloak of protection. The theme of quiet secrecy occurs on other Isiac objects too, for images of her son Harpocrates typically show him as a small child with his finger to his lips.[56] A silver-washed bronze figurine of the divine child from London depicts him in company with a watchful dog and a silent snake.[57]

Isis had her adherents in Roman London, where there is evidence for at least two temples built for her worship, as well as the possession by devotees of small portable objects, such as figurines. In the 3rd century AD, a Roman governor called Marcus Martiannius Pulcher set up an altar recording the restoration of a temple to the goddess.[58] There may be a back-story here: did the original temple fall into disrepair, or was it targeted by zealots from a rival cult? Martiannius's Iseum may have been the home of another major find: a pottery flagon, dated by its fabric and form to the 2nd century AD, that bears a graffito scratched on with a sharp pointed instrument, like a *stylus*: 'in London, by the temple of Isis'. The vessel comes from Southwark and may originally have been used to hold water in the goddess's lustration rites. But its undamaged condition may reflect either that it was reused as part of funerary furnishings or, perhaps more likely, that it was placed in a ritual pit[59] outside the Iseum. If the latter was the case, the inference is that for some reason it was deemed no longer fit for use, maybe because it had somehow been defiled.

In the 2nd century AD, there were no fewer than forty-two temples to Isis's consort Serapis in his Egyptian homeland. He was particularly popular because he was perceived as a gentle and forgiving god, a less dominating deity than Isis, and his worship continued until the very end

Ceramic flagon with scratched inscription referring
to a temple of Isis in London, from Southwark,
London. Ht 25.4 cm (10 in.).

of the 4th century AD, despite the growing influence of Christianity.[60] Temples were also built for Serapis in Roman Britain. One of the most outstanding marble sculptures from London's Walbrook Mithraeum was a magnificent head of the god, wearing a *modius* or corn measure, which has a hole at the top to hold real ears of corn.[61] Like other carvings from this temple, it had been deliberately buried sometime during the life of the sanctuary. A Serapeum at York is recorded on an inscription by an officer of Legion VI Victrix, in the late 2nd or early 3rd century AD.[62] As a born-again god, rescued from the dead, Serapis must have held particular appeal for soldiers, who hoped that if they perished in battle, they would, like the deity they worshipped, live again in the afterlife.

The appeal of the oriental cults

The oriental religions offered something that those of 'undiluted' *romanitas* did not. Their exoticness, their secrecy and their fraternities brought with them a flavour of the mysterious East, demanding passion, emotion, stamina and loyalty (to each other as well as to the divine). These cults involved the initiation of the chosen, based on physical and psychological tests of endurance, on fasting and feasting and on secret formulae of prayer and ritual. Mithraism offered worshippers a discipline, a rule of conduct that, if followed faithfully, promised rewards based on merit. The myths and rituals that underpinned these foreign religions offered the excitement of theatre: dramatic lighting in dark sacred spaces, the offering of their manhood by priests of Cybele, the ordeals of sensory deprivation, the initiation ceremonies and pledges of faith, all of which meant that worshippers felt truly and actively involved in their chosen cult. Isis beckoned with the hope of rebirth. For the most part, the cults that came out of Asia were 'thinking' religions that attracted the educated classes and satisfied their intellectual curiosity. But in saying that, we should remember the girl from Welwyn, perhaps an immigrant eastern slave, homesick for her sunny homeland, whose most precious possession might have been the little amulet that she wore so that Isis would protect her from harm.

Head of Serapis, Egyptian god of death and rebirth, from the Walbrook Mithraeum, London. Ht c. 43 cm (17 in.).

The Coming of Christ
From many gods to one

'Whether pagan or Christian, whosoever, whether man or woman,
whether boy or girl, whether slave or free, has stolen from me, Annianus
son of Matutina, six silver coins from my purse, you, lady Goddess,
are to exact them from him...but reckon as the blood of him who
has invoked this upon me...' *DEFIXIO* FROM BATH[1]

Of more than a hundred lead curse tablets found in the sacred spring at
Sulis's temple in Bath, this is the only one to mention Christians. The piece
has been dated to the later 4th century AD, by which time silver coinage
was circulating reasonably regularly in Britannia. Although the text is
written in Roman (rather than British) script, the entire text is written
backwards. While such a technique is not unique to curse tablets, it is
comparatively rare, and leads to speculation as to the need for secrecy
surrounding these supplications and, perhaps, to the particular desire to
hide the allusion to Christianity.

This chapter examines the way in which Christianity was introduced
into Britain, at first secretly, and then practised more openly from the time
the emperor Constantine himself embraced the new faith and elevated it
to the State Religion of the Empire in AD 314. We will not journey much
further forward in time from this cataclysmic religious event, because
our main interest is the relationship between paganism and Christianity
and, in particular, the manner in which certain cult-objects from the
early 4th century clearly indicate an attempt to woo pagans to Christian
monotheism using material culture that resonated with the old belief-
systems. Early Christianity in Britain, as elsewhere in the Empire, was by
no means a fully formed and coherent belief-system, and it is likely that

Reproduction of Christian curse tablet from the sacred
reservoir at Bath. Ht 6 cm (2¼ in.).

many converts, including Constantine himself, did not entirely shed the
pagan mantle when adopting the cloak of Christ.

Christianity probably began to trickle into Britain during the late 2nd
or early 3rd century AD. At the beginning of the 3rd century, the North
African Christian convert Tertullian wrote, in a text attacking the Jews,
that even people living in remote places such as Britannia were beginning to learn about Christ.[2] Because it was a monotheistic cult, unlike
the pagan mystery religions, Christianity faced huge opposition from the
Roman imperial establishment, not so much because its followers denied
the Roman gods but – far more importantly – because Christians turned
their back on the Imperial Cult itself, and so struck at the very roots of
fealty to the Empire and its ruler. Any group of people who challenged
the worship of the emperor was immediately suspect, potentially seditious
and dangerous. There is a telling moment in the epic film *Barabbas*, where
the eponymous 'hero' (the man whom the Jews chose to be pardoned
in place of Christ), a convicted slave condemned to the deadly sulphur
mines of Sicily, is persuaded by his companion-worker to convert to the
Christian faith. Barabbas allows his friend to scratch the sign of the cross
on his identity disc but, when challenged by the Roman overseer, Barabbas
hastily denies he is a Christian and the official dramatically erases the
hated symbol with his dagger.

From the time of Christ's life and death in the early 1st century AD, Roman emperors strove to eradicate the disturbing new religion. Strong waves of imperial persecution affected Britannia, particularly in the mid- to late 3rd century AD. Diocletian, who ruled from 284 to 305, is often 'credited' with the martyrdom of Britons, because of comments to this effect by the fiery and irascible 6th-century Welsh monk Gildas in his excoriating book *De Excidio Britanniae (The Ruin of Britain)*.[3] But it is perhaps more likely that these people died by the hands of earlier emperors, such as Decius or Valerian in the 250s.[4] Among several martyrs who died in Britain during reigns of terror, the names of three are recorded: one from Verulamium (St Albans) and two from Caerleon, the 'City of the Legions'.

A trio of martyrs

'Saint Alban suffered on the twenty-second day of June near the city of Verulamium...When the peace of Christian times was restored, a beautiful church worthy of his martyrdom was built, where sick folk are healed and frequent miracles take place to this day. In the same persecution suffered Aaron and Julius, citizens of the City of the Legions, and many others of both sexes throughout the land...' BEDE[5]

Significantly, perhaps, all three of the men to whom the Venerable Bede refers were murdered in the amphitheatres attached to major cities and legionary fortresses, huge arenas whose public displays attracted enormous gatherings. The slaughter of these three martyrs in the mid-3rd century AD sent a clear message: 'don't mess with the Imperial Cult; venerate it or be damned!'

It is Saint Alban of Verulamium (the city later renamed after him) about whom we know most, because of Bede's full account, some of which was derived from that of Gildas. Alban was a pagan, but offered shelter to a Christian priest fleeing persecution. Observing the fugitive's manner and devotion, Alban became a convert, turning his back on 'the darkness of idolatry'.[6] When the priest's pursuers tracked him down, Alban put on the man's clothes and pretended that he was the refugee they sought.

Artist's reconstruction of the amphitheatre at Caerleon, where early Christian martyrs were executed.

The judge to whom Alban was presented recognized him and tried to force him back to pagan worship, which he refused to do. He was then flogged and tortured in the vain hope that he would renounce his new faith; he would not yield, so he was brought to the arena beyond the town's walls and the order was given that he should be decapitated. But the soldier chosen as his executioner could not bring himself to wield the axe, and begged to be allowed to die in his place, as a Christian martyr. Alban climbed a hill, asked God for water and a spring immediately flowed at his feet. He was then executed, but his murderer was cursed by God; as Bede put it, 'he was not permitted to boast of his deed, for as the martyr's head fell, his eyes dropped out onto the ground'.[7]

Little is known of Alban's fellow martyrs Julius and Aaron, said to have died at Caerleon at roughly the same time. But their names are intriguing: while Julius is a common Roman name, well attested in Roman Britain, Aaron is Jewish,[8] so he may have originated in Judaea or have adopted a Judeo-Christian name at the time of his conversion. The record of their martyrdom seems to suggest that they were comrades, perhaps fellow-converts who worshipped together and died together.

Constantine and his conversion

'We forbid soothsayers and priests and persons accustomed to serve that
rite to approach a private home or under pretext of friendship to cross the
threshold of another; and punishment will threaten them if they disregard
that statute. You, however, who thinks this profits you, go to the public
altars and shrines and celebrate the ceremonies of your custom; for we do
not forbid the services of a bygone usage to be conducted in public view.'[9]

The passage quoted contains the emperor Constantine's 'take' on the continuing practice of pagan rites after Christianity was officially adopted as
the Roman State Religion. Constantine was hailed as the new emperor in
AD 306, but his succession was by no means straightforward, and it was
not until 324, after he had beaten off a number of rivals and engaged in
several civil wars, that he finally emerged as undisputed ruler. He enjoyed
a 'special relationship' with Britain, having visited the province more
than once before his elevation, and it was the Roman army stationed at
York who first proclaimed Constantine as their Augustus.[10] But in AD 312,
Constantine underwent a dramatic conversion to Christianity, when he,

Coin of the emperor Constantine: his head
is on the obverse (front), and an image of
his army's standard, showing the chi-rho
Christian monogram, is on the reverse.

with his army behind him, confronted Maxentius, a rival contender for the purple, at the Milvian Bridge outside Rome. Different chroniclers of this event have presented varied accounts of Constantine's experience, but in all versions he saw a vision, in the form of a shining cross and the words '*in hoc signo vince*' ('in this Sign, conquer').[11] He commanded his soldiers to put the sign on their shields, and his consequent victory over his rival convinced Constantine that Christ had intervened.[12] Two years later, in AD 314, Christianity became the official State Religion of the western Empire. The emblem Constantine adopted, based on his visionary experience at the Milvian Bridge, was the 'chi-rho' monogram, a diagonal cross (the Greek letter 'chi': χ) together with a vertical ascender with a closed loop at the top (the Greek letter 'rho': ρ): these are the first two letters of Christ's name in Greek. His army wore this sign as its insignia, and the chi-rho monogram became widely used in shrines, houses, pottery and church plate as a Christian symbol.[13]

It is by no means the case that even the emperor himself thereafter eschewed all other cults – far from it; but Christianity became firmly established from this period onwards, despite attempts by later rulers, such as Julian the Apostate in the mid-4th century, to resurrect paganism in its place. The passage quoted at the beginning of this section clearly states Constantine's ambivalence towards paganism, though interestingly what made him uneasy was the private pursuance of pagan rites and practices, not its public presence, which he condoned. This may be because in the early 4th century many Romano-British Christians appear to have conducted their liturgies in 'house-churches', shrines set up within their own homes. But Constantine himself continued to have a foot in both camps until his 'deathbed baptism'.[14] Before the Milvian Bridge episode, Constantine commissioned a great coin series depicting the 'Sol Invictus', the Unconquered Sun, a cult closely associated with Mithraism, and these coins continued to be minted and circulated long after AD 312. Gradually, Christ himself came to be worshipped as the great solar creator-god; John Ferguson[15] draws attention to the proclamation, made in AD 321, of 'Sunday as a day of rest...precisely because it was a Sun-day'.

Archaeological traces of Christianity in Roman Britain

'When this storm of persecution came to an end, faithful Christians [in Britain], who during times of danger had taken refuge in woods, deserted places, and caves, came into the open, and rebuilt the ruined churches. Everywhere the Faith advanced victoriously; the shrines of the martyrs were built and endowed, the festivals of the Church were observed, and its rites performed reverently and sincerely.' BEDE[16]

The evidence for Christianity in early 4th-century Britannia consists of small private sanctuaries, mainly within Roman villas, and portable objects marked with Christian symbols. What is clear from the material culture is that the new religion was taken up by wealthy and high-ranking Romano-Britons, who may have been more receptive to the monotheistic idea than 'ordinary' people. This seems to mirror the demographic of other oriental 'saviour' cults, like Mithraism. But the evidence may, of course, be skewed in favour of the rich finds, such as mosaics, wall-paintings and liturgical equipment. Poorer British Christians may have marked their adherence to their faith in less visible ways that have not survived: on wooden objects, domestic pots or other ephemera that have left no record of their presence.

Church plate

'Those who devote their service to this holy worship – those who are customarily named clerics – shall once and for all be kept completely exempt from all compulsory public services. They shall not be dragged away from the worship due the Divinity through any mistake or irreverent error, nor shall they be disturbed in any way from devoting themselves completely to serving their own law.' EUSEBIUS[17]

The Palestinian-born Eusebius became Bishop of Caesarea in AD 314, two years after Constantine's conversion to Christianity. This passage comes from a letter probably written in 313 to Anulinus, proconsul of the Roman province of Africa, and is relevant to the story of early Christianity in Roman Britain because it underlines both the presence and the importance of organized clergy even before the faith achieved official paramount status within the Roman State.

Whether they conducted worship in established churches or in private houses, early Christian clergy mentioned by Eusebius in the quotation would have used special plates, bowls, chalices and utensils for the celebration of the sacrament from at least the early 4th century AD.[18] This liturgical equipment might comprise splendid gilded silverware, but sometimes people made use of much humbler, more sentimental objects, like a small pewter bowl from Caerwent. This seems to have begun life as a utilitarian vessel, but during the period of its use, someone took a sharp-pointed tool and scratched a chi-rho monogram on the inside of its base.[19] This is interesting enough but what happened at the end of its life was also significant, for it was carefully hidden, sealed in a large jar within a house, presumably because the owners feared persecution or some other threat to them or the precious bowl itself. There were probably other early Romano-British Christians living here; the person in whose garden reposed a little shrine containing a disembodied pagan stone head may well have been a Christian, if the mosaics that decorated his house are anything to go by.[20] And we must not forget the two martyrs – Julius and Aaron – who had met their deaths at nearby Caerleon. While there is no evidence for a purpose-built early Christian church at Roman Caerwent, a suite of rooms in one of the houses seems to have been adapted for use as a house-church.[21]

At the other end of the scale from the modest little pewter bowl modified by a roughly scratched Christian symbol is the magnificent set of silver church plate from Water Newton in Cambridgeshire, close to the Roman town of Durobrivae, almost certainly representing 'the communal property of an *ecclesia* or Christian community',[22] so markedly different from the individually owned pewter bowl from Caerwent. Many of the twenty-eight precious-metal objects (twenty-seven of silver and a small plaque made of gold) from Water Newton were marked with the chi-rho symbol, and significantly the form of the monogram belonging to the reign of Constantine.[23] The assemblage thus represents the earliest known collection of Christian liturgical plate from the Roman Empire.[24] Bowls, chalices and an ornate jug formed the 'sacramental' part of the assemblage and one piece, a hanging-bowl,[25] bears an inscription that reads 'O Lord, I Publianus, relying on you, honour your holy sanctuary'.[26] The hoard, perhaps deliberately concealed to avoid looting at a time of instability, was found accidentally during ploughing in February 1975. Sadly, less is known about its context than should have been the case, owing to metal-detectorists' actions at the site.

Notwithstanding the splendour of the silver vessels, the most exciting of the finds are the nearly twenty feather-shaped plaques from the Water Newton hoard, all marked with the Christian chi-rho, of which some also bear the further Christian symbols, the Greek alpha (α) and omega (Ω).[27] What makes them so significant is that these distinctive objects repre-sent a kind of 'halfway-house' between paganism and Christianity. Their triangular, feathered (or leaf-shaped) form and their manufacture from sheet-metal speak to their origin as objects associated with pagan worship. They are found in votive contexts all over the Roman Empire, sometimes blank but often bearing images of deities and/or inscribed dedications, and they were brought to shrines by devout pilgrims, and laid on the altar in homage to their chosen god or goddess.

The hoard of early Christian silver church plate, including a chalice, flagon, bowls, a platter (used in sacramental liturgy) and 'feather' plaques, found at Water Newton, Cambridgeshire.

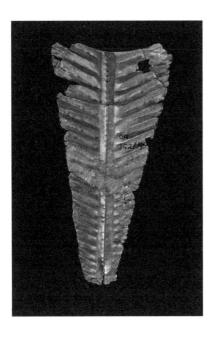

Silver 'feather' plaques from
Water Newton: a plain one (left)
and another marked with the
Christian chi-rho symbol.

Many pagan feathered plaques have been found in Roman Britain, including a rectangular silver example with feathering round the edges from London, bearing an image of the triple mother-goddesses.[28] The hoard of votive material found in 1789, concealed in a large pot at Stony Stratford, Buckinghamshire, provides a rich religious context for such plaques; alongside several inscribed silver and bronze sheets was a priest's head-dress. Two of the pieces were dedicated to Mars, and the most complete one to Jupiter and Vulcan, to whom the dedicant, one Vassinus, pledged six *denarii* if they saw him safely home from a journey.[29] Like curse tablets (see Chapter 6), these objects were used as a means of invoking the gods, but in a more positive, rogatory way than the vengeful messages written on the lead *defixiones*. But how interesting it is that such ritual material should have been the agents for displaying and disseminating Christian worship at Water Newton in the early 4th century. The presence of these overtly Christian feather-plaques, boldly marked with the chi-rho and other symbols of the faith, seems to indicate a strong desire to beckon pagans towards Christ using comfortably familiar liturgical pieces in an inclusive rather than a threatening or combative, manner.[30]

House-churches

In the 4th century AD, people began to worship Christ in their own homes, and this is particularly evident in a few large and prosperous villas in the countryside. Two great mosaic floors, at Frampton and at Hinton St Mary in Dorset, clearly demonstrate the Christian affiliation of the villa-owner. One of the rooms at Hinton St Mary contains a mosaic that actually depicts the head and upper body of Christ himself, as a young, beardless, robed man with fair hair and large dark eyes, standing in front of a large chi-rho monogram (see p. xv, bottom).[31] This portrait represents one of the very earliest depictions of Christ, certainly in the west of the Empire, but, as Charles Thomas has pointed out,[32] the iconography presents a conundrum in so far as its position, on a floor, suggests that it was meant to be stepped on, surely a rather sacrilegious thing to do. So, perhaps the roundel that surrounded the image was marked off in some way, signifying holy ground so that the villa's inhabitants and their visitors could walk round it and look down upon it.

The mosaic in the villa at Frampton bears no portrait of Christ, but it is decorated with a large chi-rho monogram, clearly demonstrating that its owner belonged to the Christian faith. This motif is associated with that of a chalice, which surely references the Eucharist. The same mosaic is rich with the symbolism of Neptune, the Roman god of the sea, whose head appears in conjunction with an inscription that reads: 'The head of Neptune to whose lot fell the kingdom of the sea scoured by the winds is figured here, his deep-blue brow girt by a pair of dolphins'.[33] According to the great Roman art-historian Jocelyn Toynbee, the juxtaposition of overtly Christian and pagan imagery does not present an irreconcilable clash of ideologies. She argues that the villa-owner probably used the Neptune symbolism as an allegory of death, rebirth and heaven, sentiments that would sit equally well within a pagan or Christian context.[34] So the person who commissioned the pavement showed an erudition in his knowledge of Greek and Roman mythology that in no way detracted from his adherence to the Christian faith. Indeed, such imagery enhanced the mosaic's message by adding the familiar to the new and strange and

Reconstruction of the mosaic floor from the house-church at Frampton
Roman villa, Dorset. The apsidal extension contains a depiction of a
sacramental chalice and a large chi-rho monogram.

thus, perhaps, giving its owner's guests a gentle introduction to his chosen
cult. A person who owned such an establishment would have been educated and sophisticated, and one could imagine how, at dinner parties,
the mosaic would have been a talking point, the centre of intellectual,
philosophical and theological discussions about the place of humans in
the material and spiritual worlds.

Christianity in Roman Britain possessed an idiosyncrasy all its own,
not least in its inclusion of the images of Christ. Early Christian writers,
such as Tertullian, strongly disapproved of such depictions as blasphemous
idolatry, so the owner of the Hinton St Mary villa, with the likeness of
Christ on its floor, would have been condemned to eternal damnation
if Tertullian were to have his way. The person who inhabited a villa at
Lullingstone, Kent, in the 4th century might have been equally frowned
upon by the early Christian fathers of the Roman Empire. Lullingstone[35]
had a long life, beginning with a house built close to the arterial road

of Watling Street in the later 1st century AD, with easy access to major towns and cities, including London and the other southern ports. The establishment underwent a huge programme of expansion and refurbishment around AD 150, and there is speculation that it may even have been the equivalent of 'Chequers' (the official country retreat of British prime ministers), for use by the Roman governor of Britannia. Further phases of building took place in the 3rd and 4th centuries, but finally – whether by accident or arson – the house was burnt to the ground early in the 5th century.

At some point in the life of Lullingstone, its owner built a pagan shrine to water-deities in one room and, in the 3rd century, the focus of devotion was altered, perhaps to become a sanctuary for the worship of the villa-owner's ancestors and household gods, a theory founded on the discovery of two marble busts of middle-aged men, of the kind often made as portraits of the dead. In the 4th century, the room above this domestic temple was made into a Christian house-church, with elaborate frescoes unique to Britain and virtually so for the entire Empire (see pp. xiv–xv, top).[36] It is likely that, for some time, the pagan and Christian shrines co-existed, one above the other, either for the same person, who – reluctant to abandon his old ancestor-gods – sought to embrace both traditions or, perhaps, for members of his family or his staff.[37]

The wall-paintings recovered from the house-church at Lullingstone are remarkable both in terms of their content and their quality. On one wall of an anteroom was an ornate chi-rho monogram, encircled by a wreath, the intersection of the diagonal chi flanked by an alpha (α) and omega (Ω); other chi-rho decoration was also present. But even more significant is the depiction of a row of robed figures in the attitude of *orantes*, people in the act of prayer, their hands uplifted in supplication.[38] At least one of these worshippers was a woman, and another of the figures especially stands out: a young man with flaming red hair, his lustrous eyes bring to mind the Christ-figure on the Hinton mosaic. Unlike the others, whose hands are extended in prayer, his fingers bend inwards. It has been suggested that this figure represents one of the family ancestors.[39] But might it not have been intended to represent Christ himself?

Holy water

> 'All who are convinced and believe that what is taught and said by us is true,
> and promise that they are able to live accordingly, are taught to pray and
> with fasting to ask forgiveness of God for their former sins; and we pray
> and fast with them. Then they are brought by us to where there is water,
> and they are reborn in the same manner as we ourselves were reborn. For
> in the name of God, the Father and Lord of the universe, and of our Saviour
> Jesus Christ, and of the Holy Ghost, they then are washed in the water...'
> JUSTIN MARTYR[40]

Justin Martyr was born in AD 100 and died for his faith in Rome sixty-three
years later. His two *Apologiae* were written in defence of Christianity;
in this section he describes the rite of baptism and the centrality of
blessed water to the sacrament. As we have seen, water also played a key
role in many pagan rites and practices in Roman Britain and beyond. It
was the focus of active worship at healing sanctuaries such as Bath and
Coventina's Well, and equally prominent in the lustration-rituals of the
Eastern mystery cults, such as those of Mithras and Cybele. From its beginnings in the earlier 1st century AD, a central focus for Christians was the
cleansing of their sins by baptism, which wiped their souls clean of both
inherited ('original') sins and those that they had acquired in life. So it
is not surprising that in late Roman Britain, there is material evidence
for the practice of baptism and its association with water. A large lead
tank found at Icklingham in Suffolk[41] was marked with a chi-rho, flanked
by capital alpha and omega symbols, dating to the 4th century AD (and
probably the reign of Constantine). In all likelihood this vessel acted as an
early baptismal font, and it is worth noting that a later Christian church
was built here, on pagan temple-land, one of several such foundations.[42]

A different kind of font may have existed in the 4th century at the great
Roman villa-estate at Chedworth in the Gloucestershire Cotswolds. The
house possessed an extensive suite of bathrooms and so required a good
water supply. This came from a spring, whose water was conducted to a
reservoir contained in an octagonal stone basin. The building was almost

Small chi-rho symbol scratched on one
of the slabs around the Nymphaeum
basin at Chedworth Roman villa.

certainly a Nymphaeum (a shrine to the spring-spirits) but sometime, probably in the early 4th century, three of the stone slabs around the basin were
inscribed with small chi-rho monograms.[43] So at a point late in the great
villa's history, its owners appear to have been Christian, and converted the
spring's sanctity from that of a pagan water-spirit to a Christian font. It is
a rather nice thought that those same spring-waters originally personified
as a Nymph came to be used to cleanse a Christian's sins. Of course, it is
necessary to be careful in the interpretation of these markings. The most
sceptical view is that the symbols scratched onto the stones were merely
doodles, engraved in an idle moment by someone who had seen them
elsewhere without fully grasping their meaning, but it seems certainly
plausible that the owners of Chedworth deliberately built a baptismal font
around their spring and that the house itself became a place of Christian
worship, like Hinton St Mary, Frampton and Lullingstone.

Pagan shrines and Christian churches

The religious events that took place in Britannia during the later 4th
and 5th centuries AD are beyond the remit of this volume, but it is worth

considering the way that early Christians 'accommodated' paganism, not only in terms of objects and the juxtaposition of pagan and Christian imagery but also in sacred architecture. We have seen how the hoard of early church plate from Water Newton contained objects that were deliberately chosen for their resonance as pagan ritual objects, but boldly marked with Christian symbols. Did something similar happen in sacred architecture? It is certainly the case that early churches were sometimes founded on the site of pagan temples. This appropriation can be regarded in one of two ways: it was either a confrontational act of defiance to replace a polytheistic sanctuary with a Christian structure, or it represented a less oppositional attitude, one of wishing to entice pagans to the new religion by means of the familiar.

The site at West Hill, Uley, in Gloucestershire, presents a complex relationship between paganism and Christianity. There was an Iron Age hillfort here and, as often occurred, a Roman temple was built inside it, perhaps both to reference the past and to utilize a dominant position in the landscape.[44] Uley is special because it was a cult site that maintained its sacred nature, in one form or another, for more than six centuries. Indeed, there is even evidence to suggest that many thousands of years earlier a Neolithic community chose this place to erect a monumental ceremonial enclosure. Certainly in the late Iron Age, in the early 1st century BC, local people marked out a special space, with palisades round it, to create a *temenos*, or sacred boundary, inside which two wooden shrines were built. Ritual activity at this period included the sinking of deep pits to receive votive deposits, along with pottery and weapons that were 'sacrificed' to an unknown deity, probably a war-god. In the 2nd century AD, a temple of Romano-Celtic form (see Chapter 4) was constructed in stone. It was a popular sanctuary, judging by the finds, and seems to have been an important focus of pilgrimage. Iconography and epigraphy reveal that the temple was dedicated to Mercury, and offerings included the animals particularly sacred to him: goats or sheep, and cockerels.[45] Supplicants not only brought gifts to the god but also, using lead curse tablets similar to those from Bath, implored him to wreak vengeance on those who had wronged them.

Stone head of Mercury
from the cult-statue
at the temple at Uley,
Gloucestershire, possibly
'recycled' as an image of
the young Christ when the
early church was built here.
Ht c. 35 cm (14 in.).

The Romano-British shrine at Uley went through a number of modifications during its life, but early in the 5th century the temple was deliberately deconstructed, the building levelled, its cult-statue broken up and its furnishings and sacred objects removed and sometimes buried. A new sacred building was erected in its place, a basilican timber church, later replaced by one of stone. But the spirituality lingering from the previous pagan shrine appears to have been acknowledged by the Roman colonizers, for some of the ancient iconography and altars were repurposed in these new buildings and, what is more, the life-sized stone head of Mercury, from the great cult-statue that had stood in the centre of his temple, seems to have been carefully reburied, upright. Perhaps the young, curly-haired deity was 'reborn' as an image of Christ.[46]

Earliest Christian burial rites

According to pagan funerary practice, a reasonably well-to-do Romano-Briton would expect the observance of particular obsequies when he or she died. Depending on fashion and century, the deceased might be laid in a tomb with grave-goods, including personal possessions, or be cremated and the burnt remains collected and buried in an urn within a cemetery (see Chapter 10). The grave would be marked with an inscribed tombstone, giving at least the person's name and age (to the day), and often including tribal affiliation, occupation and rank (if an official or a soldier). Early Christian burials were different: the precise age at death was not mentioned because it was considered unimportant; there were few, if any, grave-goods, because the soul would not need them in the afterlife; and the deceased were usually oriented east–west, because of the belief that Christ would welcome them from the east. The funerary site at Poundbury outside the Roman city of Dorchester, Dorset, contained both pagan and Christian tombs. It is our best-recorded early Christian cemetery, and some of the dead interred here were placed in simple stone or wooden coffins, some packed with gypsum, perhaps in an attempt to preserve the bodies inside. Given the belief that the mortal body would not be necessary in heaven, this is both interesting and puzzling. More telling still is that rank still counted for something, for a few of the dead had little mausolea erected over their graves, some decorated with painted wall-plaster.[47] Evidently the new Christian beliefs did not entirely eradicate the old religion; it is not impossible to imagine that some newly converted Christians were cautious about letting go entirely of the beliefs that their ancestors had held for half a millennium or more.

Britannia Christiana

'We are but of yesterday, and we have filled everything of yours – cities, islands, forts, towns, public meeting places, even the camps, tribes, courts, palace, senate, forum. We have left you only the temples…' TERTULLIAN[48]

So wrote the Christian writer from Carthage in the late 2nd or early 3rd century AD.

Literary sources record that in AD 314, just after Constantine's conversion, three British bishops from the dioceses of London, York and Lincoln attended the Ecclesiastical Council at Arles in Provence.[49] If the texts are to be believed, the mention of these three prelates means that as soon as Christianity became the Roman State Religion, bishoprics were already in place, and so hierarchical Church structures must have been in existence for some time prior to the date of the Council, at a period between the martyrdoms of Alban, Aaron and Julius in the mid-3rd century (or even before) and the second decade of the 4th.

But it should not be assumed that the adoption of the new monotheistic faith in Britain was a one-way street; far from it. Paganism persisted

Reconstruction painting by Alan Sorrell of the late Romano-Celtic
temple complex, near the forum and basilica (market and
town hall) at Caerwent, South Wales.

alongside the worship of Christ and, in the reign of one mid-4th-century
emperor, Julian the Apostate, many of the Empire's provinces witnessed
a resurgence of paganism. Britannia was no exception; there was a wave
of pagan temple refurbishment, particularly in the southwest, and some
new sanctuaries sprang up, too. A Romano-Celtic temple was constructed
at the Roman town of Caerwent, tribal capital of the Silures, in about
AD 330. It is not known to whom the shrine was dedicated, but it might have
been a local god, Mars Ocelus Lenus Vellaunus, whose name is recorded
on inscriptions from the town, or – perhaps – the mother-goddess whose
statuette was found buried deep in a pit near the temple.[50] And across the
river Severn, sanctuaries such as the great Classically styled temple to the
British healer-hunter-god Nodens (see Chapter 4) flourished at this time,
long after Constantine's edict concerning the status of Christianity in the
Empire. Paganism died hard, and was periodically resurrected in Britain
for many centuries to come.

CHAPTER TEN

Journey into Avernus
Death, burial and perceptions of afterlife

'A deep, deep cave there was, its mouth enormously gaping,
Shingly, protected by the dark lake and the forest gloom:
Above it, no winged creatures could ever wing their way
With impunity, so lethal was the miasma which
Went fuming up from its black throat to the vault of heaven:
Wherefore the Greeks called it Avernus, the Birdless Place.' VIRGIL[1]

The 6th Book of Virgil's epic poem, written to glorify the emperor Augustus, is wholly concerned with the journey made by the eponymous hero Aeneas to find his dead father Anchises in the underworld. Not only does Virgil paint a vivid picture of Classical attitudes to death and the afterlife, he also describes funerary ceremonies in great detail: the building of the pyre to consume the body after its cleansing and anointing, the prayers said for the dead and the need for the mourners to undertake the correct ritual in order to enable the dead to progress to the happy Otherworld of Elysium. Although a work of poetry, and therefore loaded with dramatic and imaginative writing, this text demonstrates the importance of mortuary rituals and the belief among Romans and Greeks that death did not mean oblivion. February 2017 saw the publication of George Saunders's novel *Lincoln in the Bardo*.[2] Its theme is an exploration of limbo, the term for the liminal space occupied by the newly dead who wait in purgatory for the expiation of their sins before admittance to heaven. The book tells the story of Abraham Lincoln's visit to see the body of his dead son Willie, who succumbed to typhoid in 1862 when he was eleven years old. Willie's corpse lay in the crypt of the Georgetown Cemetery in Washington DC and, while Lincoln kept vigil with the body, a myriad of spirits thronged limbo, perhaps waiting to welcome the newly dead. The interesting thing about these dead souls is their perception of what has happened to them. They do not fully accept their deceased status; to them, the living world is an exclusive club from which they have been expelled and to which they aspire to return. There are aspects of Saunders's treatment of death and the afterlife that resonate with Virgil and with the documentary and archaeological testimony concerning ancient perceptions of death, including ideas about reincarnation. Roman attitudes to the dead appear to have been somewhat ambivalent. Alongside the elaborate rituals attending some funerals and the expensive tombstones erected by families or colleagues in commemoration of the deceased, corpses were sometimes treated not with respect but with dismissive contempt. While the honourable dead received a commensurately careful burial, the fate of the poor was less certain. Despite the long-standing rule that the dead could only be interred outside the city walls,[3] body-dumping was a persistent problem in the city of Rome, and legislation had to be brought in to prevent the 'fly-tipping' of corpses. In his *Life of Nero*, the author Suetonius recounts how, when the disgraced emperor was fleeing from Rome, his horse stopped dead, terrified by the sight of a dead body that had been left in the street to rot.[4]

The ambiguity with which the Romans regarded the human dead is reflected not just in the treatment of bodies but also of the people whose job it was to manage them, the undertakers. Both corpses and those who handled the dead and dealt with the physical aspect of their disposal were imbued with the miasma of pollution that hung about them like a toxic cloud. The death-industry involved the morticians, the cremation-teams, the grave-diggers and – for certain high-ranking dead – the embalmers. These people were regarded as deeply polluted, and undertakers were required to be tattooed in a way that marked out their profession and allowed people to avoid having physical contact with them.[5] Virgil makes it clear that the unclean properties of the dead themselves could have a disastrous effect upon the living. When advising Aeneas as to what he must do in order to see his father, the Sibyl (the Oracle of Cumae) reminded him that no progress could be made until his dead friend Misenus had been cremated, because an unburied corpse polluted the hero and all his companions.[6] I wonder, then, whether even those whose task it was to produce tombstones and the *scriptores* who inscribed them might also have been subject to prohibitions simply because of their association with the dead.

Contemporary texts tell us about attitudes to the dead in Rome and Italy, but virtually no documentation reveals to what extent such views were adopted in far-flung provinces such as Britannia and Gaul. But, for the latter at least, we do possess some informative documents about how the afterlife was perceived. Most importantly, several authors refer to the belief in rebirth. For some writers, rebirth appears to have meant bodily resurrection itself, involving actual reincarnation (or the renewal of the physical person); for others, it was the spirit (or the soul) that was reborn.

Recycling the dead: reincarnation and rebirth

> 'The Druids hold that the soul of a dead man does not descend to the silent, sunless world of Hades, but becomes reincarnate elsewhere; if they are right, death is merely a point of change in perpetual existence. These Northerners are most fortunate to believe in a doctrine which frees them from that besetting terror of mankind: fear of extinction.' LUCAN[7]

> 'The belief of Pythagoras is strong in the Gauls, that the souls of men are immortal, and that after a definite number of years they live a second life when the soul passes into another body. This is the reason why some people at the burial of the dead cast upon the pyre letters written to their dead relatives, thinking that the dead will be able to read them.'
> DIODORUS SICULUS[8]

Both Lucan and Diodorus were commenting on customs they had heard about as practised in Gaul, not Britannia. However, as the Druids (active in both regions) were heavily involved in religious doctrinal matters, it is likely that Britons and Gauls shared many of their attitudes to the dead. The Greek geographer Strabo reinforced the observations of both Lucan and Diodorus in his remarks that Druidic doctrine included the belief that the souls of people never perished.[9] For the Romans, the afterlife was a mixture of heaven and hell and where the dead ended up – according to Virgil at any rate – depended at least in part upon how they had conducted themselves in life, how they died and whether they had been given proper burial rites. The situation with regard to Britain and Gaul pre-conquest is, of course, less clear because of the pre-literate nature of society in these lands. And once they became part of the Roman Empire, the scanty textual references to such matters are bound to be tinged with notions that belonged to mainstream Roman views of death.

Burying the dead

One archaeological clue to how pre-Roman Iron Age Britons regarded death and the afterlife lies in the ways in which the dead were treated. In the hundred or so years leading up to the Claudian invasion, people practised several methods of body-disposal. Both cremation and inhumation were employed, but the scarcity of formal interments in urns or coffins suggests that other, less visible means of dealing with the dead were also used, including the scattering of cremated bone and ash in rivers or on land and excarnation, the exposure of bodies in the open air for wild animals and birds to feed on, followed by the disposal (or dispersal) of the bones. It is possible that some of the enigmatic four-post structures excavated at the Iron Age fortified settlement of Danebury are the remains of excarnation platforms. It could even be that the complete skeletons and body-parts interred in the disused grain silos here represent the final act of disposal for selected individuals.[10] The archaeological 'evidence' for the practice of excarnation in Iron Age Britain is circumstantial, but two Classical writers make specific reference to this funerary ritual in Celtiberia: Aelian and Silius Italicus, both of whom describe the selective rite of body-exposure. According to their testimony, only the valiant dead – those who had perished in battle – were granted this honour; the religious thinking behind the excarnated corpses involved the belief that their consumption by vultures allowed the souls of the honourable dead to ascend straight to heaven. For Celtiberians, vultures were sacred to the celestial gods, so they were considered a fail-safe way of fast-tracking the chosen ones to the happy afterworld.[11] It is difficult to interpret beliefs surrounding death and the survival (or otherwise) of corporeal and spiritual existence from archaeological evidence alone. But the placing of grave-goods with the bodies of certain individuals, as if to accompany them to the next world, hints at the prevailing understanding of death and the afterlife. This funerary ritual was practised in Britannia both before and after the Roman conquest of AD 43. In the British Iron Age, the corpses of some people were treated with elaborate ceremony and their tombs might be richly furnished with precious objects: jewelry, weapons, food and liquor. A special grave of a woman aged about thirty-five, who died in the late 4th or early 3rd century BC, was found at Wetwang in East Yorkshire (see p. xvi). It provides a wealth of information about her life through the funerary rituals accorded her. She was given a chariot-burial, an honour more often accorded to British Iron Age men, the mode of interment so named because of the placement of an entire or disassembled two-wheeled vehicle in the tomb.[12] The mourners and religious practitioners who attended her funeral had laid her body on the floor of the tomb, carefully placed joints of pork and her mirror on it, and then covered her with part of the chariot. She was a distinguished person, both physically and in terms of rank, and the two may have been linked. Forensic examination of the woman's skull revealed that she had a large, bright-red growth by the side of her nose that would have pushed her features out of shape. Far from being a source of shame and ridicule, it appears that her community revered her disfigurement, for many of her grave-goods were liberally decorated with red coral, as if to celebrate her difference. And the chariot, mirror and meat all suggest that she was a person of no mean consequence.[13] The Wetwang 'coral' woman's high rank – and perhaps her physical distinctiveness – was reflected in her funeral rites and tomb-furniture.

Very different but equally special was the burial of an infant who probably died in the 2nd century AD and was interred in a lead coffin at Arrington in Cambridgeshire.[14] Although babies seem often not to have been accorded formal burial rites in Roman Britain, there were exceptions, of which the Arrington child is one. He was about nine months old when he died; his vastly enlarged cranium indicates that he suffered from hydrocephalus. His coffin was evidently not custom-built for him, being adult-sized, but he was interred with care, wrapped in expensively dyed red and blue cloth. Around his head were traces of aromatic resin, perhaps a gesture to ensure the healing of his condition when he reached the afterlife, and white pipe-clay figurines were placed in a box near his body to join him on his journey to the next world. These statuettes comprised images of people and animals: rams and a bullock. Two human images took the form of a baby and an older child, and they may represent the hoped-for life-journey of the dead child.

The most striking object in the Arrington child's grave was a small clay figure of what appears to be a mother-goddess, seated in a high-backed chair and wearing a cloak clasped with a brooch. On her lap is a basket or plate of fruit, and she wears a massive circular 'beehive' headdress. This last identifies her not as a British *Mater* but as one of the Germanic *Matronae Aufaniae* whose worship was centred in the Rhineland. It is very likely, therefore, that the infant's parents came from this region, as foreign migrants or visitors, bringing their own gods with them. We can imagine that they would have chosen a nurturing goddess from their homeland as a fitting guide or divine 'chaperone' for their dead son's spirit on its perilous journey to the unknown. Indeed, it may well be that the child was singled out for special burial precisely because of a perceived need to compensate him for his dramatically

Pipe-clay figurine of a Rhenish mother-goddess, made in the earlier 2nd century AD, found in a baby's lead-lined oak coffin at Arrington, Cambridgeshire. She wears a lunate amulet at her throat, perhaps a symbol of her role as a bearer of light in the darkness of death. Ht c. 15 cm (6 in.).

short time on earth and a hope that his sojourn in the Otherworld would be blessed by the companions he took with him; the images of domestic animals might have been present as surrogate sacrificial beasts, to ease his passage and provide payment for his conferral to Elysium. Of course, it is possible these little figures were simply his toys, but it is tempting to think that the grieving mother saw the goddess as a surrogate for her own loving care for her child. The Arrington child is by no means the only infant to have been provided with a spiritual guide on his travels to the underworld; in 2011, excavations in a Roman cemetery at Bridges Garage in Corinium revealed the remains of a child buried with an enamel-decorated copper-alloy figurine of a cockerel.[15] This bird was sacred to Mercury, one of whose roles was that of a 'psychopomp', a leader of souls to the afterlife.

The dead and the living

The many Roman-period cemeteries that have been discovered across Britain provide clues not just about the dead and the mortuary rituals associated with their passing, but also about the living.[16] Two examples are particularly noteworthy: Dunstable in Bedfordshire, and Lankhills, Winchester in Hampshire. The Dunstable cemetery exhibits idiosyncrasies associated both with groups of burials and with individuals.[17] In the 4th century AD, one sector of the burial ground seems to have been set aside for a specific and favoured community, as the mean age at death of these individuals far exceeds the average in the other areas. It has been suggested that the longevity of this particular group might have been due to their special status in life – they may have had access to better, and more abundant, food, and have enjoyed a less rigorous lifestyle than the general population. Could these people have belonged to a protected sub-set of society, maybe even a religious community, perhaps thereby avoiding the hazards of warfare or hard manual labour and, for women, the dangers of childbirth? The second unusual feature of the Dunstable cemetery is the treatment of certain individuals: several corpses were decapitated, a practice not uncommon in late Roman inhumation, while others had dismembered limbs, and at least one woman's face was deliberately obliterated before her head was removed and placed next to her body.[18]

The late Roman cemetery at Lankhills, Winchester, displays similar (mis)treatment of the dead to the patterns of mortuary behaviour at Dunstable. In the 4th century, certain elderly women's bodies were beheaded, and their severed heads carefully placed by their knees. Equally bizarrely, one of the decapitated corpses buried here was accompanied by two dogs, itself quite unusual, but even more so because one of them had been subjected to extreme post-mortem (it is to be hoped) violence: its limbs were severed and both ends of its backbone bent together and tied in that position.[19] These peculiar burial practices at Dunstable and Lankhills were not unique, but did not represent 'normative' rites. The treatment of elderly females at Lankhills bears marked resemblances to some odd interments at Kimmeridge in Dorset where, in the 3rd century AD, a group of mature women were interred with their heads taken off and placed by their feet, with a spindle whorl by each body.[20] Such objects might have signified their work as weavers, but a more sinister interpretation may be equally feasible. Like the Roman Fates, who spun the thread of people's lives and cut it off at will, might these women have been thought to have power over the destinies of those within their communities?

The disfigurement and mutilation carried out on certain bodies at Dunstable and Lankhills is likely to have had something to do with who these people were in life. Were the beheaded women 'scolds', or witches, whose powers of incantation had to be firmly and ritually curtailed? What about the woman whose face was removed? And why chop the limbs off cadavers? Was it necessary for the defaced person to have her very identity stripped away, because of some shameful episode in her past? Was the dismemberment meted out to the bodies of particularly disruptive individuals done in order to stop them walking back to their community? And was the mutilated dog treated in this manner because of its own persona, or that of its human companion? We can but speculate on these possibilities, because the context has been lost. But it is legitimate to speculate in a general way; clearly unusual death-rites had some motivation, a purpose designed to reach beyond the end of human life into the world beyond, and the probability is that communities felt the need – sometimes – to take steps to protect themselves from the unquiet dead.

Interrupting death: freeze-framed bodies

In about 441 BC, the ancient Greek dramatist Sophocles published his play *Antigone*, an overtly political drama whose central theme is tyranny. Antigone, daughter of Oedipus and Jocasta, falls foul of her uncle Creon, dictator of Athens, by flouting his will concerning the denial by him of proper burial rites to his enemy, and her brother, Polynices. While Creon is adamant that the body should lie unshriven and unburied, Antigone is equally determined that her brother should be accorded the funeral rites that would allow his spirit access to the afterworld. So she secretly visits the body and sprinkles earth upon it, thereby releasing Polynices's shade to cross over between worlds.[21]

The funerary rituals considered in this chapter are not only expressions of grief, but also acknowledgment of some kind of existence after death. But there were special and unusual circumstances in Britannia and elsewhere in northwest Europe where there appears to have been a deliberate intention to deny the natural processes of dissolution and soul-release. The phenomenon of the bog-bodies has been touched upon already, in Chapter 1, where Lindow Man was considered in the context of human sacrifice. The two people whose preserved bodies were found in the Cheshire marshlands in the 1980s also represent the Iron Age practice whereby certain individuals were selected for violent killing and disposal specifically in an environment that prevented bodily decay. The active preservative agent in raised bogs is *sphagnum* moss. Bogs containing this marsh plant act like fridges, eternally keeping organic material (including human corpses) fresh and whole until, when disinterred, the natural process of dissolution is triggered. It is debatable whether those responsible for the despatch of these bodies were deliberately trying to keep them intact but I think this is entirely feasible, at least in part because there is evidence that Iron Age people purposely placed foodstuffs, such as butter and meat, in bogs in order to keep them fresh, so were well aware of their preservative properties. The Lindow bodies belong to a large group of Iron Age and Roman-period bog-people, whose remains have been found for the most part in Ireland, Denmark, North Germany and the Drenthe region of the northern Netherlands.[22] It seems possible, even likely, that the persons chosen for this kind of death and watery interment were considered special within their communities and that, for whatever reason, it was deemed essential that they met particular deaths and that their bodies were prevented from disintegrating in decay. The victims not only met untimely and highly ritualized – sometimes extremely violent – deaths, but they were also denied 'proper' burial and, by inference, entry to the next world or to the realm of the ancestors. We can only ponder why both the deaths and the special disposal happened. Surely the mode of death and the post-mortem treatment were linked. Were both to do with ultimate humiliation, a shame that reached beyond the grave? Or were the spirits of these ritually murdered people considered too dangerous to be allowed to haunt the living?[23] One further possibility is that the bogs themselves were considered liminal spaces, not quite land nor water, and so were perceived as gateways between the world of mortals and the underworld spirits. If so, then might the bog-people have been 'gatekeepers',[24] whose role after death was to help patrol these dangerous boundaries and keep the dark powers from interfering with the living?

Dark forces: the gods of the underworld

'In this, this enchantment of women, the enchantment of the seeress of this binding curse. O Adsagsona, look twice upon Severa Tertionicna, their diviner, their restrainer, so that she shall commit the enchantment when they are bound by malediction.'[25]

This somewhat abstruse passage comes from a long inscription on a lead sheet, written in Gaulish, as a *defixio* (curse) or *duscelinata* (evil death-song), the recipients being pairs of women, foster-mothers and foster-daughters. Everything about the 'song' concerns women: Adsagsona appears to be a goddess of death and vengeance; the diviner is a seeress.

The curse tablet was found in 1983 during archaeological excavation of a Gallo-Roman cemetery at Larzac in southern France. The lead sheet had been deliberately snapped in two and placed as a lid over the mouth of a funerary urn whose surface was inscribed with the name Gemma, the woman whose burnt remains were contained within the urn.[26] The whole thing hints at a dark story, and it was no accident that the broken tablet was positioned so as to engage directly with the dead. It is as if it was thought that the curse would find a quick way to the underworld if it 'hitched a ride' on Gemma's grave.

Larzac is a fair way from Britannia, which has produced nothing as dramatically evocative as the Severa Tertionicna's *duscelinata*. But a similarly dark message to the underworld spirits may be discerned in human remains found in an Iron Age settlement at Great Houghton in Northamptonshire. In the 4th century BC, a woman's body was interred in a pit here.[27] Her arms and legs had been bound, probably before she died, but the most striking thing about her was that she wore a lead torc that had been carefully placed around her neck back to front. The metal used for this necklet is highly unusual: torcs are usually of gold, silver or bronze, occasionally of iron. Its positioning, too, with the terminals at the back of the neck, is contrary to the way that torcs were donned and worn in life, with the opening under the chin. The burial in a pit (like

The Iron Age woman from Great Houghton,
Northamptonshire (left), her lead torc in position
round her neck; and the broken lead torc (right).

rubbish), the restraints, the use of lead for the torc and its back-to-front position all point to a complex raft of symbols apparently designed to convey an intense message of shameful death and the desire to consign this woman to outer darkness.

So do we know anything about the deities who might have been the intended recipients of *duscelinatae* or tenebrous burials? The evidence from both Larzac and Great Houghton seems to acknowledge not the happy Otherworld of Elysium but hell. However, there is literary evidence to suggest that Gauls and Britons did not always perceive darkness as cognate with evil and death. In speaking of Gallic beliefs, Julius Caesar commented on the Druidic doctrine that the Gauls were descended from Dis Pater (the Roman god of the dead); he goes on to remark that this lineage caused them to calculate elapses of time by nights rather than days.[28] And there is an enigmatic inscribed bronze calendar from Coligny,

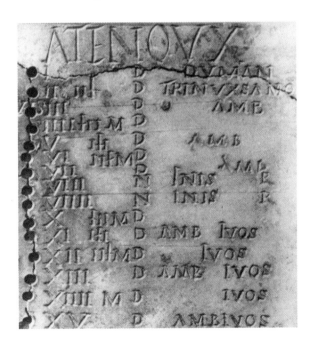

Part of the Gallo-Roman ritual calendar, written in Gaulish, from Coligny, near Bourg, France, showing the word 'Atenoux' ('returning night') to mark the start of the moon's waning fortnight.

near Bourg in Central Gaul, which lists the months and seasons using the Gaulish language, though the calendar dates to the early Roman period.[29] Its purpose was to mark the correct timing for religious events, and it is clear that the reckoning was done by nights. Indeed, each month was divided into fortnights according to the waxing and waning of the moon, by the Gaulish word 'atenoux' ('returning night').

One find, from a Romano-British context at Upper Deal in Kent, might depict an underworld divinity. It is a simple human image made of chalk, with schematic facial features and a rectangular block for a torso; no limbs are depicted. By itself, the figurine tells us little, but its context is intriguing, for it was found in a small chamber at the bottom

Chalk figurine from a Romano-British underground 'shrine' at Upper Deal, Kent. Ht c. 18 cm (7 in.).

Early Iron Age bronze
figurine of a woman
with ornate headdress in
the shape of a crescent
moon, from Culver Hole
Cave, Gower, South Wales
(see p. 99). Ht c. 10 cm
(4 in.).

OPPOSITE ABOVE The temple-pediment at the entrance to the sanctuary of Sulis Minerva at Bath, showing the great frowning head of a composite male Medusa-sun/water deity (see pp. 111–15).

OPPOSITE BELOW The great bath at the temple of Sulis Minerva at Bath. A close look at the water reveals the swirl of the springs that fed it, and the steam given off by the heat.

ABOVE Gilded bronze head from the cult-statue of Sulis Minerva from Bath. The head was deliberately hacked from the body in antiquity, and the face shows cut-marks. Ht 24 cm (9¾ in.).

The wooden, bronze-clad bucket found in a high-status
late Iron Age grave at Aylesford, Kent. To the right
are details of one of the two crowned human heads
forming the handle-escutcheons (top) and the people
dressed up in horse-costumes (bottom) (see p. 147).
Diam. 27.6 cm (10¾ in.).

ABOVE Reconstructed wall-painting from the 4th-century Christian chapel at Lullingstone, Kent, showing a frieze of *orantes* (praying figures) (see p. 189).

LEFT Reconstruction of part of the Carrawburgh Mithraeum, showing Mithras slaying the bull above three altars inscribed with dedications to the 'Invincible god Mithras'. The one to the viewer's left shows Mithras identified with the sun god Sol (see pp. 162–63).

RIGHT The head of Christ in front of a chi-rho symbol, on the 4th-century Christian house-church mosaic from Hinton St Mary, Dorset (see p. 187).

FOLLOWING PAGE The 'red lady' of Wetwang. Iron Age chariot-burial of a high-ranking woman from Wetwang, East Yorkshire. Her rich grave-goods included her war-chariot and many objects decorated with red coral. It is thought that the colour might have been chosen specially in reference (and perhaps deference) to the woman's bright red facial tumour (see p. 200).

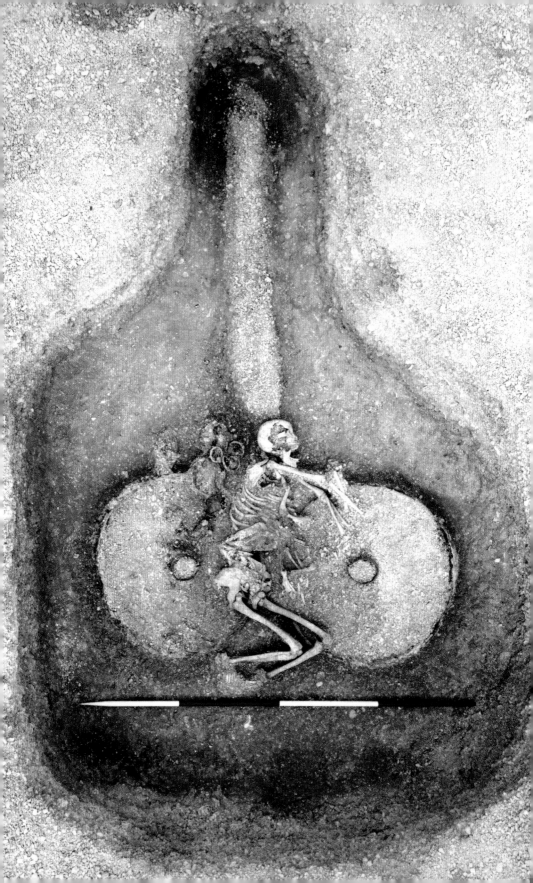

of a shaft dug 2.5 m (8 ft) into the chalk, within a native Romano-British settlement.[30] The image had clearly been dislodged from a niche carved into the wall of the chamber. But what was it doing deep in a dark pit where nobody would see it? Did it represent a god of the underworld, or was the white chalk figure instead meant as a gleaming light shining in the darkness, designed to combat the forces of darkness rather than to honour them?

Remembering the dead: tombstones along the way

'To the spirits of the departed; Mercatilla, freedwoman and foster-daughter of Magnius, lived 1 year, 6 months, 12 days'[31]

This inscription is typical of the epitaphs on tombstones from Roman Bath, which provided important details about the dead and those who mourned them. There is tenderness in the precise record of Mercatilla's age, even to the very day of her passing, poignant testimony to the

Tombstone of an eighteen-month-old girl
Mercatilla, from Bath. Ht 61 cm (24 in.).

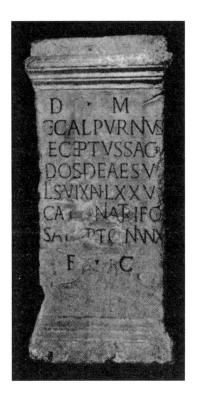

Tombstone of Calpurnius Receptus,
priest of Sulis, from Bath.
Ht 134.5 cm (53 in.).

sadness of a life cut off almost before it had begun, The inclusion of the age at death is common on Roman tombstones because details about the deceased were deemed important for the dead soul's sojourn in the afterworld.[32] What happened to Mercatilla in her short life? Despite her extreme youth, her status as a 'freedwoman' (an ex-slave) is described, as well as her relationship with her foster-father. Her mother is not mentioned. It is likely that she was (or had been) the freedwoman and, probably, the wife of Magnius, who adopted her daughter when they married. Mercatilla would have had the same status as her mother. Fosterage was common in the Roman world; even adults could be fostered or adopted.[33] The pairs of foster-mothers and foster-daughters who were the targets of the Larzac curse, too, serve as a reminder that fosterage was probably a regular part of Gallo-British society. Marriage between free citizens and their ex-slaves was by no means rare in the Roman world. Calpurnius Receptus, a priest of Sulis, married his freedwoman, Calpurnia Trifosa. Another such marriage was that of a Syrian called Barathes, who came from Palmyra. He set up a tombstone to his British freedwoman-wife, Regina, a Catuvellaunian woman from southeast England.[34]

Other tombstones from Bath are interesting, too, for the personal details they reveal. Gaius Calpurnius Receptus lived, worked and died close to the great sanctuary of Sulis, where he was a cult-official. His *trianomina* suggest that he was a Roman citizen, probably a Briton, and he clearly enjoyed high status as the priest of one of the most prestigious cult-centres in Britain. The tombstone of Aventina, a tribeswoman of the Mediomatrici, aged fifty-eight, indicates that she hailed from eastern Gaul, and she may well have died while on pilgrimage to Bath, appealing to Sulis to cure her of disease. If this were so, her plea was not heeded and she may well have died without her family around her. Her principal mourner, Sestius, was named as her heir, though not her son. These epitaphs are brief, but hint at life stories, grief, loss and the need to remember, as well as the committal of the dead to the 'spirits of the departed'.

Disposal of the dead, in Britain as elsewhere in the Empire, was either by inhumation – the interment of the entire corpse – or by cremation. Graves were often placed within designated cemeteries, outside towns or other settlements, but tombstones were frequently not with the grave itself but ranged along the roadsides. Such positioning seems to have represented a perceived need for the dead person to be remembered by people as they went about their everyday lives. However, there was also the factor of show: the better and more expensive your loved one's memorial stone, the better you, as the bereaved, displayed your wealth and status within your community. Fashions changed over time, both in burial practices and in the design of tombstones. In general, cremation was the more favoured means of body-disposal in the earlier centuries of Roman provincial rule, with an increasing trend towards inhumation later on, though that was by no means a hard-and-fast rule. But the selection of burial practice may well have been influenced by religious beliefs: cremated bone and ash rise up towards the sky, while an inhumed body decomposes and its remains sink into the earth. So the choice of cremation or burial may have been governed by differing beliefs concerning death, life after death and the gods responsible for the dead.

The need to provide corpses with nourishment after death seems to have been a serious concern to those left behind. Sometimes the bereaved actually fed the deceased: after one death at the legionary fortress of Caerleon, mourners placed the cremated remains of their dead in a lead canister, which they connected to a leaden pipe up to ground-level. In a similar burial, found in the 18th century, the pipe gave onto an elaborately sculpted stone funerary table, presumably piled with food and drink to be shared between the living and the dead. Martin Henig graphically describes how wine would have been poured down the pipe for consumption by the dead person.[35] The theme of feasting is also represented in a popular form of tombstone, which depicts a funerary banquet: a good example is an elaborate pedimented stone from Chester, which depicts the dead person reclining as if at dinner; and several tomb-reliefs from York portray families sharing a meal.[36] Other grave-sculptures consist of portraits of the dead, as they wished to be remembered when alive, like the tombstone of Facilis at Colchester, who stands staring out at the viewer, dressed in full legionary uniform,[37] and those of the Corinium calvarymen Dannicus and Genialis (see p. 41).[38] More sombre are the tomb-images that depict

Tombstone of Julia Velva, a fifty-year-old woman from York (left, ht 160 cm/63 in.), who is depicted reclining on a couch, cup in hand, at the centre of a banqueting scene, surrounded by her family; and the tombstone of Marcus Favonius Facilis (right, ht 183 cm/72 in.), a centurion of the 20th Legion at the time of the Boudican rebellion. His cremated remains were found in a lead container nearby.

The Colchester sphinx (left, ht 84 cm/33 in.) and the
Corbridge lion (right, ht 86 cm/34 in.), both monumental
funerary images depicting the ravages of death.

death as a ravening wild beast like the lions from Cowbridge,[39] in the Vale
of Glamorgan, and the better-known one from Corbridge, near Hadrian's
Wall and the sphinx from Colchester.[40] These dark images served to remind
the living of the grimness of death, a very different message from the
cheerful feasting scenes chosen by other mourners.

Living, dying and afterwards

Elizabeth Jennings's 'A poem for Lazarus Saturday'[41] takes as its theme the
New Testament episode in which Jesus raised his friend Lazarus from the
dead,[42] and explores, with great insight, the problem of earthly resurrection: the recomposition of the stinking, decaying body of Lazarus; the way
that, even brought back to life, the smell of death still clung to him, his
refusal to speak to his sisters and onlookers when brought out of the tomb
at Christ's summons, and his clear reluctance to be torn from heaven and
forced to re-enter the material world. But the poem begins with something
wonderful: the dazzling whiteness of Lazarus's shroud, as if lit from within,
testament to the fact that his soul had been touched by God. The process

of bringing Lazarus back to life was a painful one, not just for the dead man but for everyone, because it reversed time, interrupting the 'norm'. There is always something disturbing about death but the resurrection of Lazarus brought an earthquake-like shock to those who witnessed it.

Exploration of Romano-British burial practices provides some clues as to how communities regarded death and what came afterwards. The rituals involved clearly indicate a threefold dimension to personhood: one's past, the present moment and the future. It is this last, the future, wherein lies the key to why people treated the dead as they did. For Romano-Britons, as for so many people, past and present, who possess religious beliefs, the future of an individual does not end when they die but reaches out into a perceived afterworld, however that may be imagined. Burial practices in Roman Britannia, and in its immediate Iron Age prequel, embrace endearing traits, as in the placing of sentimental, comforting things in a baby's grave, or the tender message on a tombstone. But they also show elements of violence that remain foreign to our scrutiny. All these ritual practices appear to convey something in common: an expectation that the dead were capable of having a post-death existence, whether in body or body and spirit, and a consonant need for the living to undertake what was necessary for that afterlife to be manifest or – in rare instances – curtailed. The Lazarus story, and Elizabeth Jennings's poetic presentation of the event, provides an evocative exploration of the threefold nature of being, and particularly the complicated and disturbing nature of the transitions between life, death and its aftermath.

Worshipping Together
Acceptance, integration and antagonism

'All the faiths clung on to the old religion during the Communist years,
and they sprang straight back to life afterwards'[1]

'This holy spot, wrecked by insolent hands and cleansed afresh,
Gaius Severius Emeritus, centurion in charge of the region,
has restored to the Virtue and Deity of the Emperor'[2]

Val McDermid's *The Skeleton Road*, a tense psychological crime novel
focused on Croatia and other former Soviet-bloc satellite countries, makes
the very valid point that religion is a conservative business; while old
indigenous beliefs may have perforce to take a back seat during colonial
oppression, they are often not dead but hibernat-
ing, biding their time on the sidelines until the
tyrannous regime is ended. Is such a model
relevant to a Roman province like Britannia,
given the Roman Empire's apparently lenient
attitude to provincial religions? To what extent
did such indigenous systems adapt and assert
themselves under Roman rule?

The second quotation comes from an altar
found in 1753 at Roman Bath. Its date is uncertain, but it may have been carved during the

Altar set up by the centurion Gaius Severius
Emeritus to mark the restoration of a desecrated
holy place, Bath. Ht 89 cm (35 in.).

3rd century AD. The stark message of the inscription both gives and with-holds a good deal of information. The 'insolent hands' are likely to have been those of an impious individual (or group) whose hostility to a particular faith or deity caused them to destroy a shrine, a sacred image or an altar. This particular stone was found very close to two others, one of which was dedicated to the Treveran divine couple Loucetius Mars and Nemetona,[3] and the other, a statue-base, to the Suleviae,[4] a trio of goddesses whose name links them closely to Sulis, goddess of the town's hot springs. Could that lost statue have been the victim of counter-religious bigotry, smashed by adherents of a rival cult? There is further suggestion of intolerance at Bath, in the evidence for an assault on the gilded bronze cult-statue of Sulis Minerva herself. At some point in antiquity, her life-sized, Classically styled head was hacked from its body and the face sustained knife-cuts, as if an attempt was made to desecrate and disfigure it.[5]

The myth of tolerance: tension, opposition and entrenchment

'Moreover, the temple erected to the divine Claudius was a blatant stronghold of alien rule, and its observances were a pretext to make the natives appointed as its priests drain the whole country dry....When all else had been ravaged or burnt, the [Roman] garrison concentrated itself in the temple. After two days' siege, it fell by storm.' TACITUS[6]

In this passage, Tacitus describes the build-up to the rebellion of Boudica in AD 60, a cataclysmic event for Rome that almost cost it the province of Britannia. Soon after the initial Claudian invasion of AD 43, the Trinovantes' tribal capital of Camulodunum was turned into the veteran legionary garrison town of Colchester (see p. 43–44). Retired soldiers were given parcels of land seized from the local inhabitants and right in the middle of the new city a gleaming new Roman stone temple was built, a stark reminder and affront to the people of Camulodunum that a foreign power was in charge. To add insult to injury, the temple and its upkeep was to be paid for by the Trinovantes themselves, out of the pockets of its Roman-appointed priests, the *seviri Augustales*.[7] What happened at Camulodunum was an unhappy mix of politics, religion, ideology and muscle-flexing on the part of the conquering colonists. No wonder that the Trinovantian uprising was centred on the blight on its landscape that was the temple to the cult of Claudius the invader.

In a recent lecture at the University of Edinburgh, Jane Webster addressed the issue of religion along Hadrian's Wall. She referred to the Wall's situation 'at the crossroads of multiple diasporas', a colonial landscape in which the whole of the Roman Empire was represented in microcosm.[8] Like so many parts of the world today, the Wall was home to a multitude of migrants, who were, in Webster's words, 'natally alienated' persons. Alongside these military incomers were the native populations, socially displaced people whose world had been turned upside down by the Roman occupation of their lands. The upheaval caused to the Wall region can be mapped not only in terms of people but also their gods. The deities soldiers brought with them on their garrison duty formed an integral part of the diaspora scene, and the divine immigrants had to find a *modus vivendi* with the deities and rituals that were already in residence. If this diaspora model is true for Hadrian's Wall, then it may also be applied to the rest of Roman Britain.

It is often iterated and reiterated that Roman society was tolerant of other faiths and cults. There is a somewhat cosy assumption that because Roman religion embraced polytheism, there was therefore no problem with the continual absorption of foreign beliefs and divinities. But the reality has to have been far more complex and problematic than this picture of easy acceptance. In addition to the well-documented hostility of the Roman state to the intransigently monotheistic Christian religion, there is abundant literary testimony to Roman antipathy towards the Druids of Gaul and Britain, not least because of their nationalistic, seditious influence on the newly annexed provinces. We have seen, too, that there existed lively prejudices against pagan oriental cults, particularly their percolation to Rome.

But there is a more fundamental issue at work within any colonial system, of which the Roman Empire is no exception: the beliefs and cults of the conquering power will always take precedence over those of subjugated peoples. In the particular case of *romanitas*, such apparent asymmetry is reinforced by the nature of the surviving evidence for provincial religion. The Romans not only brought to Britain a fully formalized, hierarchical religious system, based largely on that of the Greeks, they also introduced what Webster has termed 'new technologies of worship': image-making on an industrial scale, and epigraphy.[9]

If we are to try to understand the multiple religious systems coexisting within Roman Britannia, it is worth viewing such 'pluralism' through a modern lens. Over the past few decades, Britain and Europe have seen the growth of Islam in ways that have encompassed both peaceful and aggressive relationships between it, Christianity and the cultures within which they are, broadly speaking, respectively followed. In February 2008, the then Archbishop of Canterbury, Rowan Williams, caused a storm of controversy when he made a public statement advocating the formal adoption of some aspects of Sharia Law within the British legal system,[10] arguing its necessity within modern Britain in order to safeguard social harmony.[11] Dr Williams's comment is important, for it presents the case for religious, or moral, relativism. According to such a principle, all religions have equal virtue, value and validity within any given cultural context, whether such faiths are 'home-grown', like Christianity in modern Britain, or not. The argument for such relativism has to be seen in the context of the need to break down barriers between modern British communities, rather than to build or reinforce them. With respect to Christianity and Islam, it is crucial to remember that the same God is worshipped by the followers of both. It is the manner of human conduct within each faith where the gulf between the two may yawn wide.

If we apply such a model to the Roman past, 'religious relativism' would mean that the Roman pantheon, as introduced to Britannia by the occupying colonial forces, was accorded no more or less weight than the cults of the indigenous Britons or foreign religions that came in with soldiers recruited from the provinces. But this, evidently, was not the case within Roman society, because of the inextricable link between the highest Roman cults – those of Jupiter Optimus Maximus (Best and

Greatest) and of the emperor – and fealty to Rome. However inclusive *romanitas* was in its attitude to foreign religious systems, there was little doubt that, within the Empire, the gods and goddesses of Rome took precedence, at least officially.

The complexity of the relationship between *romanitas* and 'Britishness' in terms of religion and its expression is demonstrable in a range of cult-objects from Britannia. Along and in the vicinity of Hadrian's Wall, a plethora of apparently local and non-Roman gods sprouted under the stimulus of the Roman military presence. A fine example is the martial deity Cocidius, 'the red god'.[12] Cocidius appears to have been worshipped particularly in the Irthing Valley, centred on Bewcastle, a northern military outpost of Hadrian's Wall. Two rare embossed silver plaques from Bewcastle bear both images of and inscribed dedications to the god; each depicts Cocidius fully armed, and rendered in highly schematized 'shorthand' manner.[13] This form of schematic depiction reflects British divergence from the true-to-life representation so central to Greco-Roman figurative art. The images of Cocidius (like his distinctively British name) suggest that the god represented was of native (or at any rate Gallo-British) rather than Roman origin. Who was worshipping Cocidius? One plaque identifies the devotee as a man called Aventinus, which is not much help, but stone altars from the site provide interest-

Two silver embossed plaques dedicated to Cocidius, from Bewcastle, Cumbria. Ht of larger plaque *c.* 8 cm (3 in.).

ing information. Far from being a god whose worshippers were humble Britons or low-ranking soldiers, the epigraphic testimony indicates that Cocidius's cult attracted high-status military officers. One, Aurunceius Felicessimus, was a tribune, who had been promoted after having been an *evocatus* (a veteran soldier who had volunteered for re-enlistment). Another cult-follower of Cocidius was of even higher rank: Quintus Peltrasius Maximus was a member of the Praetorian Guard, an elite corps of imperial bodyguards, and so his loyalty to the emperor was beyond question (you don't get much more 'Roman' than the Guard).[14] So were gods like Cocidius, and so many other 'Wall-deities', such as Belatucadrus, Coventina and Antenociticus, British or not?

Perhaps soldiers stationed in the military frontier-zone simply invented gods at need. If so, then was it important to them that such divinities be endowed with a British identity? Did this somehow improve their spiritual efficacy, through stronger ties with – and therefore influence over – the lands that the Romans were seizing? It is possible that such 'new gods' had less of a genuinely indigenous voice than is suggested by their local names. Britishness *may* have been manipulated (perhaps even with a degree of cynicism) by the Roman military. But an equally valid alternative is that Roman soldiers serving along Hadrian's Wall felt a religious need to identify with, and give a voice to, the spirits already residing here.

The case for iconoclasm: religious hatred in action?

'It was certainly a deliberate and calculated act by which the work of art, once dedicated by a shoemaker and a stonemason, perished, and it was not the only such act to affect the cult inventory of the temple. The sculpture of Mithras born out of the rock was beheaded, and so was the image of Mithras as a bowman...'[15]

This account relates the vicious treatment of the superb collection of religious iconography that once adorned the Mithraeum at Dieburg in southern Germany, until it was targeted by a group of people hostile to the cult, possibly foreign Germanic tribesmen or Christian communities.

While much of the evidence for Persian Mithraism gives the impression of a somewhat exclusive cult, the preserve of high-status military men and entrepreneurs, the Mithraeum at Dieburg in the Roman province of Upper Germany had more humble origins.[16] Sometime during the later 2nd or early 3rd century AD, a family of artisans set up an elaborate stone carving in honour of Mithras here. The relief was double-sided and could be rotated by a device so that, during the dark, mysterious lamp-lit ceremonies, devotees could view both the 'front' and 'reverse' surfaces, both richly decorated with images and epigraphy. The dedicants were a stonemason called Silvestrius Silvinus, his brother, a cobbler, Silvestrius Perpetus, and the shoemaker's grandson, Aurelius. Despite their modest professions, the iconography shows a high level of knowledge about Mithraism and its mythology, as well as of the broader corpus of Classical cult systems and stories. The Mithraeum attracted other cults and icons to the site, the largest of the latter being that of Mercury.

In AD 233, the Alemanni, a powerful Germanic tribe, invaded the region and thereafter its inhabitants struggled to maintain its *romanitas*. Sometime during the 3rd century, a hostile group targeted the Dieburg Mithraeum for wanton and systematic destruction that seems to have been fuelled by a desire not just to smash, but to signify utter rejection of the religious beliefs and practices associated with the Mithraic sanctuary. The central Mithraic relief dedicated by the Silvestrius brothers was damaged by savage blows from a broad-bladed chisel-like tool; blows not seeking random destruction, but deliberately 'killing' the hunting Mithras by targeting the figure's head. Likewise, other images from the shrine were decapitated, as if in acts of capital punishment, and the great statue of Mercury was smashed to smithereens.[17] The destruction meted out to these sacred stones indicates more than mere vandalism; it represents a fanatical religious hatred. So who was responsible? Was it the Alemanni, or perhaps a group of zealous Christians? One possible clue is that a lot of the violence of the Dieburg iconoclasts appears to have focused on the naked or near-naked male images within the shrine, particularly their genitals; this may be why Mercury attracted special attention.[18] The culprits might, therefore, have been Christians, repelled by what they might see as the indecent nudity displayed on the carvings. Fellow pagans did not generally harbour such hang-ups about naked depictions. But if such pagans were foreigners – like the Alemanni – the destruction of the Dieburg iconography was probably carried out for reasons of enmity rather than religious scruple. But we will never know for certain who perpetrated such vandalism upon the Mithraeum's sacred stones.

Dieburg is a long way from Britannia, but the religious hatred directed at its Mithraeum evidences the turbulence and hostilities that could exist in the Roman provinces. There are tantalizing glimpses of tensions at Bath, as we have seen. And what about the row of deliberately broken stones re-erected outside a late Roman shop in Cirencester (see pp. 82–83) that may have been rescued, along with the cults they reflected, and brought back to life after a period of iconoclasm? Conversely, other sacred stone sculptures from the town were deliberately and sometimes carefully beheaded, as if to rob them of their sanctity, or at least to change their identity.[19] One such figure, depicting Fortuna, the Roman goddess of Chance, was carefully stowed away in a flue inside the stoking room of a bath-building, but not before her head had been removed.[20] We saw in Chapter 8 that sometime during the life of the London Mithraeum, sacred images were deliberately buried, as if to prevent their desecration and destruction, perhaps by Christians, by adherents to a rival cult, or simply by vandals.

The violence meted out to the sacred sculptures at Dieburg appears to represent extreme reactions of an aggressive counter-religious movement not, alas, dissimilar to what is happening to ancient religious images and temples, like that at Palmyra in Syria, at the hands of Islamic State today.[21] But iconoclasm can be a complicated issue, particularly when applied to the remote past,[22] without adequate written records to confirm the intent of apparent destruction. Of course, the destruction of a sacred monument does not necessarily destroy the relationship it has with its believers. T.S. Eliot speaks of 'prayers to broken stone' in his poem 'The Hollow Men';[23] even fragmentary images should be treated as potentially significant elements in sacred practice.

The evidence from one temple in Roman Britain exemplifies the dilemma of how to interpret 'broken stone': the sanctuary to Mercury at

Uley in the Gloucestershire Cotswolds, discussed in Chapter 9. That the shrine was an important centre for the worship of Mercury in the region is obvious from the many votive objects dedicated to him placed there by pilgrims, but more so on account of the great stone cult-statue erected to the god.[24] Mercury was an influential god in the western provinces, including Britannia. He was not only a god of commercial prosperity (hence his emblem of a purse), but also led souls to the Otherworld, so he looked after people in life and in death. By no means all of the sculpture at Uley survives, as it was systematically broken up some while after its production in the mid-2nd century AD, and all that the excavators found were parts of limbs, the god's accompanying animals (a ram and a cockerel) and an exceptionally finely carved head of the young god that had been deliberately severed from the body in antiquity. This head is virtually undamaged, apart from the tip of the nose, and it is clear that trouble was taken to keep it intact; it was evidently curated and then given a careful burial in the post-Roman period.[25] If, as I suggested in Chapter 9, Mercury was morphed into Christ, we are witnessing the very antithesis of iconoclasm.

Twinning and connecting: the two-way street of *interpretatio romana*

'The god the Gauls worship most is Mercury, and they have very many images of him. They regard him as the inventor of all the arts, the guide of all their roads and journeys, and the god who has greatest power for trading and moneymaking. After Mercury they worship Apollo, Mars, Jupiter, and Minerva, having almost the same ideas about these gods as other peoples do: Apollo averts diseases, Minerva teaches the first principles of industry and crafts. Jupiter has supremacy among the gods, and Mars controls warfare.' CAESAR [26]

Just what was Caesar saying here? Given that he was writing in the 50s BC while on campaign in Gaul and before that region had become absorbed into the Roman Empire, it is somewhat curious that he presented the Roman pantheon as a fully established part of the Gaulish religious system. There is no way that this could have been the reality. It is true that the Roman deities were present in Gaul, brought there by Caesar's army, and that the long-standing trading links between Gaul and the Classical world might have led to a basic familiarity with Roman cult-systems among the native tribes. But for Caesar to speak so emphatically about the Gaulish adoption of Roman gods was surely a literary device rather than accurate reporting. Given that his comments were situated in a campaign report (or war diary) designed to be read to the Senate in Rome, one explanation of his 'Gaulish pantheon' is simply that he was trying to make his report comprehensible to people who were unfamiliar with Gaul, by describing in Roman terms foreign deities whose function accorded with his own gods. But another possibility is that he was kept in the dark about Gaulish divinities, only being told what the Druids or other local religious officials considered fitting for him – as a foreign conqueror – to know.

In equating the principal Roman gods with what he may have seen as Gaulish equivalents, Caesar was invoking the principle of *interpretatio romana*, a phrase first used by Tacitus in his description of the religious beliefs held by an obscure German tribe called the Naharvali, who lived far beyond the frontiers of the Roman Empire.[27] Like Caesar, Tacitus sought to equate a pair of German gods, the Alci, with the only divine Classical twins with whom he was familiar: Castor and Pollux. While Caesar did not attempt to give the Gaulish-equivalent names, Tacitus did so and, what is more, he actually used the term *interpretatio romana* to describe what he was doing. Both chroniclers, Caesar in the mid-1st century BC and Tacitus more than a hundred years later, were recording religious beliefs outside Britannia. Archaeological evidence, particularly from epigraphy, demonstrates that pairing between deities with Roman and Gallo-British names did indeed occur in Roman Britain; but the more nuanced testimony of material culture shows that *interpretatio* was not a one-way street. The equivalence between divinities of two cultures can be seen to have involved both the interpretation of indigenous god-names through a Roman lens and the reverse: the perception among indigenous people that 'Roman' deities had original British identities.

We can observe the mutual exchange of *interpretatio* in action. It encompasses multiple variations but the two main categories consist of a single spirit being endowed with a double-name, one British (or Gallic or German) and the other Roman, and the phenomenon of divine couples of whom one (generally the female) may have a local (or at any rate non-Classical) name and whose partner usually carried a Roman name or a double Roman/British one. Rarely – as occurred with the Gaulish couple Sucellus and Nantosuelta – both male and female deities bore only indigenous names. We have already met some of these in earlier chapters. A good example of the former group is Sulis Minerva, the personified spirit of the hot springs at Bath. The surviving bronze head of her cult-statue closely resembles Minerva, even down to the helmet she once wore. Yet, the vast majority of inscribed dedications to her – whether in stone or on the prolific lead curse tablets invoking her as a goddess of retribution – name her Sulis Minerva (the British element almost always coming first) or simply as Sulis. What are we to make of that? Who was driving the notion of pairedness? Did Sulis exist as a British water-goddess before the Romans arrived or was she – according to Jane Webster's model of god-invention at need[28] – newly created by the Roman army in order to ground their worship within the local community? We need to be careful not to allow the new technologies of devotion (iconography and epigraphy), introduced under the Roman occupation of Britannia, to cloud our judgment. Just because Iron Age Britons rarely depicted their gods with visibly set identities that does not mean that these deities were not firm entities within Britannia's pre-Roman consciousness. It is just that their voices were silent and their footprints barely discernible. In the case of Sulis at Bath, we should remember the scattering of Iron Age silver coins from the sacred spring,[29] which might indicate her veneration before the monumentalization of her sanctuary, although it is always possible that they were deposited early in the Roman period.

To explore the phenomenon of gendered divine couples, in terms of the degrees of *romanitas* (or its absence) shown by their epigraphy and iconography, I want to look at three that occur in Roman Britain: Mercury and Rosmerta, Loucetius Mars and Nemetona and Sucellus and Nantosuelta, for each represents a particular and graded manner of cultural presentation. The first reflects a pattern of overt *romanitas* in the case of the male deity and Gallo-Britishness for the female; in the second, the female once again has a totally un-Roman name while her male companion possesses a double-name, one Roman, one not; and the third represents total epigraphic avoidance of adherence to the Roman pantheon.

I will begin in reverse order, with an image unique to Britain but a frequent occurrence in Burgundy and southern Gaul: that of Sucellus and Nantosuelta.[30] On a rare relief-carving from Sarrebourg, near Metz, the tribal capital of the eastern Gaulish tribe the Mediomatrici, the pair is depicted with an accompanying dedication that names them.[31] Usually, though, the images and inscriptions do not appear together. The key identifying elements of their imagery are the long-shafted hammer and small pot or goblet held by Sucellus, and varying symbols associated with hearth, home and well-being carried by his companion. In Britannia, Sucellus's name appears on a few objects but the only image of the couple so far to be identified comes from East Stoke in Nottinghamshire, in the tribal territory of the Corieltauvi.[32] The names have been interpreted as Gallo-British titles: 'the good striker' (Sucellus) and 'winding brook' (Nantosuelta). Neither the epithets nor the images conform to *romanitas* except in the fact of their physical naming on inscriptions and their presentation as 'human' images. Indeed, there seems to have been a conscious desire to emphasize the independent, non-Romanness of these deities.

A settler or a wandering pilgrim from the land of the Treveri in the Moselle Valley set up an altar to another divine couple, Loucetius Mars and Nemetona, at Bath.[33] The dedicant's name was Peregrinus[34] and his instructions to the *scriptor*[35] were clear: in the double-name given to the male deity, the non-Roman name was to be mentioned first. We saw this with Sulis Minerva at the same sanctuary. And Loucetius Mars's consort had a significant name, the Gallo-British epithet 'Nemetona', which derives from the word *nemeton*, meaning 'sacred place' or 'sacred grove'.[36] Both deities had their roots in the Rhine region and travelled to Bath in Britannia with their devotee. Peregrinus is a prime example of someone who chose his gods to reflect his origins and brought them with him from

his homeland, as well as signing up
as a follower of the British goddess
Sulis. But he did not entirely turn
from *romanitas*, for Loucetius was
given 'Mars' as a 'surname'. And
maybe this Mars, worshipped at
a British healing spa shrine, was
nothing to do with war but was the
Treveran version, like Mars Lenus,
who presided over important sanctuaries at Trier and its environs[37] as
a healer-deity, a fighter not against
people but against disease.

And so comes the final example
of 'twinning' or conflation in action:
that of Mercury and Rosmerta, the
male having an entirely Roman
name, his partner an unequivocally
Gallo-British or 'Celtic' one. An

Altar to Loucetius Mars
and Nemetona, dedicated
by Peregrinus at Bath.
Ht 76 cm (30 in.).

important dedication to the pair comes from a temple at Niederemmel
near Neumagen, in the same tribal territory from which Peregrinus's
family originated. The significance of this Treveran inscription lies in the
identity of the dedicants: two brothers – Doccius Aprossus and Doccius
Acceptus – who jointly held the post of *seviri Augustales*.[38] This was a
college of priests associated with the Imperial Cult, and, as its second
name implies, it was founded in the reign of the first emperor, Augustus.
What is particularly special about this priesthood is that it was open not
only to high-ranking free citizens (those of the equestrian middle class)
but also to freedmen.[39] This priesthood appears to have originated in
the south of France, at Narbonne in Gallia Narbonensis. In AD 11/12, an
inscribed altar was set up by the town's citizens dedicated to the divine
spirit of the emperor Augustus, to celebrate his birthday. The inscription
carries a lot of detail, not least concerning the establishment of the *seviri
Augustales*, decreeing that there should be six of them, three recruited

from the *equites*, and three from the ranks of freedmen. These priests had the 'privilege' of paying for the festival on the emperor's birthday and on other sacred occasions, each providing a sacrificial animal and footing the bill for the incense and wine.[40]

Narbo was a very Roman town, capital of Gallia Narbonensis, dubbed 'The Province' because of its early foundation and its 'special relationship' with Rome. One would expect its *seviri Augustales* to be steeped in Roman ways, especially in religious matters, so the Treveran Doccius brothers' dedication to Mercury and Rosmerta is of especial interest. Mercury is straightforward enough, but Rosmerta seems to have been a Gallic invention of an indigenous consort, perhaps to leaven *romanitas*, to impose an *interpretatio gallica* on this most popular of gods. Rosmerta's name is a Gaulish word meaning 'the good provider'. On certain continental altars, Mercury and Rosmerta are represented both by images and epigraphic dedications, thus allowing confidence in identification in instances where only sculptures of the pair are present.[41]

This is the case in Britannia, which had its share of worshippers but where devotion was expressed through iconography rather than epigraphy. At least one major focus of their cult here was the Roman colonial city of Glevum (Gloucester), where several stone images were set up, perhaps by the same person, group or guild.[42] I will concentrate on just one: the relief-carving from Shakespeare Inn.[43] Here is a richly interwoven tapestry of *romanitas* and Gallo-Britishness. Not surprisingly, Mercury has the most overt Classical symbolism: he carries his purse, symbol of commercial success, and he rests

Mercury and Rosmerta, from Shakespeare Inn, Gloucester. Ht 57 cm (22½ in.).

his right hand on a cockerel and *caduceus* (herald's staff) positioned by his right leg. He is presented in his usual semi-nude state, his *chlamys* (short cloak) over his left shoulder. But what interests me is his head for on it, thrusting through his curls, is a pair of pointed objects where his *petasos* (winged hat) should be but which look much more like horns. The Classical Mercury possessed a range of emblems associated with his mythology and function that help identify his images: the cockerel, *caduceus* and wings[44] are all tied in to his primary role, that of the herald of the gods. But in some British portrayals,[45] including this one from Gloucester, the British predilection for horned deities[46] (see pp. 142–44) has crept into the Mercury-repertoire, as if appropriating the Roman deity for British taste. The god's female companion is almost certainly Rosmerta: she is clad in an ankle-length robe and carries in her left hand a curious long-shafted object ending in a pelta-shaped terminal, probably a sceptre of authority. In her right hand is a ladle, and by her right ankle a stave-bound wooden bucket. This last is significant, for it characterizes several Rosmerta images from the region, including one from Bath, and the vessel is distinctively British, harking back – perhaps – to the ale-buckets buried with high-status Britons from southeast England in the century before the Roman conquest.[47] The images of Mercury and Rosmerta exemplified by the Shakespeare Inn sculpture indicate a subtle blend of *romanitas* and *britannitas*. Whoever was responsible for commissioning the piece (and its execution) wanted to establish himself or herself as someone who wished to present an intercultural balance.

Observing syncretism: Roman Britain in context

"'Syncretism" is a contentious term, often taken to imply "inauthenticity" or "contamination", the infiltration of a supposedly "pure" tradition by symbols and meanings seen as belonging to other, incompatible traditions.'[48]

Is it appropriate to apply the term 'syncretism' to the way in which different religious beliefs and ritual practices manifested themselves in Roman

Britain? I would say not, at least not in the somewhat negative sense of the quoted passage. In my opinion, what happened in Britain under Roman occupation was a complicated but dynamic set of negotiations, manipulations, understandings, misunderstandings, hostility and tolerances, the whole package laced with invention and reinvention of deities and faiths. Many scholars of modern comparative religions[49] regard syncretism as superficially equal in the coming together of multiple religious systems, but in fact always skewed towards the dominant partner, for example the colonial occupier of other peoples' lands. To determine to what extent this was true of Roman Britain (setting aside, if that is possible, the issue of 'new technologies of worship'[50] discussed earlier in this chapter), I turn to a 'modern' colonial model of syncretism from the New World, in the Bahia region of eastern coastal Brazil, which demonstrates just how complex and multidirectional colonial interrelationships can be, including those associated with religious beliefs. In the early 16th century, Portuguese colonists, hungry for mineral wealth, landed at Bahia, bringing their Roman Catholicism with them. But a strong indigenous Amerindian religious tradition already existed, and proved resistant to submersion by foreign Christianity. But a third strand of religion is present in the Bahian mix: the Yoruba cults that came with West African slaves to the Portuguese at the time of European colonization of Brazil. Each of the three belief-systems has been so modified by the other two that, even today, it is hard to identify which – if any – has dominance. The healing rituals contributed by the indigenous Amerindians have melded seamlessly into the curative properties perceived as a fundamental element in the powers wielded by the Virgin Mary and the other saints within the Roman Catholic Church. Many of these saints have, in turn, become fused with the spirits (called *orixás*) of the Yoruba people.[51]

So to what extent did people living and working in Roman Britain worship together? We have seen that hostility and intolerance existed; some believers felt it incumbent upon themselves to wreak destruction on the outward manifestations of faith that they found inimical. But this trend appears to have been far outweighed by its opposite. Temples housed the images and dedications of many gods and presumably welcomed

Schematized sculpture of Mercury, with horns instead of his winged hat, from a Roman well at Emberton, Buckinghamshire. Ht 33 cm (13 in.).

their diverse adherents to pay homage there. Individuals and groups – whether military or civilian – showed their devotion to more than one deity on a single inscribed altar. The gods themselves went into partnership with those of different cultural backgrounds; one and the same deity might have both a Roman and a Gallic or British name; and some were presented in imagery that spoke of both Romanness and Britishness. Soldiers stationed on Hadrian's Wall or other military installations may have invented new gods, with British names, whom they thought it important to propitiate while on foreign ground. And we must never forget that so many army recruits were not ethnic Romans but came from Gaul, the Rhineland and beyond and, like the Spaniard Maximus in the film *Gladiator*, set up shrines to their local divine protectors wherever they went. The Bahian model is, I think, not that far away from what existed in Roman Britain. With certain notable exceptions – Druids and sometimes the Imperial Cult, for instance – the archaeological evidence at least appears to present a rich tapestry of religious cults and worship whose interaction, negotiation and mutual appropriation resulted in a series of new religious movements on the western edge of the Roman Empire.

Closing the Curtain
Reflecting on things past

The *Star Wars* films frequently make reference to the 'Outer Rim' of the Galaxy, where planets and their inhabitants are at their most bizarre. Edges and fringes are where strange things happen; hovering on the periphery, they are unstable and unpredictable – containing elements of both 'inside' and 'outside', the known and the enigmatic. They are, therefore, potentially threatening to the ordered core or centre. To the Romans, Britannia represented the outer rim of the civilized world and, at least until the Claudian invasion, it was regarded by many as even beyond that edge. It was a place of myth and legend, and for some Greeks and Romans, the very *humanitas* of its occupants was open to question.[1]

John Wyndham's chilling 1950s sci-fi novel *The Chrysalids* is set in the frighteningly unstable world of post-apocalyptic Labrador, some kind of global catastrophe having rendered most of Earth uninhabitable. The surviving Labrador communities are beset with gestational mutations, giving rise to defects in human babies and animals and causing the growth of mutant crops. 'Breeding true' has become an obsession with 'norms'. Any creature not conforming to the prescribed model of perfection must be cast out into the 'Fringes' (the twilight zone between normal communities and the badlands) or destroyed.[2] To the Romans, at any rate before Caesar's two expeditions, the island of Britannia was, like Wyndham's Fringes, 'off the map', beyond Ocean, the great river believed by the Romans to border the world, where the quirky and the wild were the norm.[3]

The geographical 'edginess' that caused Britannia to be regarded with such fascination, and not a little fear, by the Mediterranean world allowed the island to maintain a unique measure of distinctiveness and psychological independence even after its absorption into the Roman Empire. It should not be forgotten that parts of the island – much of Wales and Scotland – were never fully annexed to Rome and remained outside the province. In the early 2nd century AD, Hadrian built a wall across northern Britain that effectively set a physical and symbolic boundary between the Empire and what lay beyond, even though the Wall itself attracted so much *romanitas* because of its massive Roman army presence. Thus the Roman province of Britannia butted up against the lands of ungovernable inhabitants beyond the frontier who, nonetheless, shared its island space.

Religion and beliefs (or their absence) provide insight into the character and conventions of a people. It has been said of the modern Western world that those without faith and belief in a higher being are more likely to fill the resultant void with secular values and allegiances, whether those consist of wealth, power, sport, celebrity or whatever else is in vogue in the world of social media. To G.K. Chesterton is attributed the comment 'a man who won't believe in God will believe in anything'.[4] The imperial Romans had a huge range of deities, one for each event and every activity, as well as the high gods of the State pantheon. Yet their relationship with the spirit world included a vein of superstition and magic. Following the correct rituals was necessary in order to the keep the gods on side. Contracts were forged between people and deities, who were perceived as receptive to a kind of religious bribery, wherein the promise of a thank-offering was deemed the most likely way to achieve happy outcome to prayers.

Worship of the Roman gods was bolstered by a vivid mythology that personalized the divine world, making it seem familiarly human. The 'Cloud of Unknowing'[5] with which Christians have wrestled since the time of Christ seems not to have troubled the average Roman, although philosophers like Seneca, Lucretius and Cicero struggled with the nature of the gods and the universe. However, none of this serves to deny the religiousness of the Roman world. While one might point to the apparent cynicism that characterized the 'contractual' relationship between people living in the Roman Empire and their gods, there is no doubt about the devoutness of many. It is necessary only to read some of the touching memorials written on tombstones by the bereaved to realize that many Roman citizens had a deep sense of spirituality.

The focus of *Sacred Britannia* is the manner in which the juxtaposition of two cultures, each very different from the other in terms of political and social development, played out in the arena of religion and ritual. The religious profiles of Roman provinces varied not only in terms of their Roman elements but also in their particular pre-Roman identities. Archaeological evidence demonstrates the presence of a rich spiritual tapestry in the fabric of Britannia, whose woven complexities expressed a uniqueness derived from three factors: the province's physical position on the western periphery of the Empire; its Iron Age heritage; and the hybrid nature of Romano-British traditions. The continuing Roman military presence in frontier Britain acted as a magnet for the veneration of foreign deities, imported by the army. And it is perhaps because of Britannia's relative isolation that early Christianity thrived here; even as early as Constantine's reign, a Christian *ecclesia* (church) was able to establish itself and furnish its sacred building with the magnificent silver church plate found at Water Newton. And we should not forget the textual evidence for the presence of three British bishops at an international Christian council in AD 314.

Despite the heavy hand of *romanitas*, the retention of British identity throughout the four hundred years of Roman rule is striking. Perhaps some (or all) of the British elements that contributed so much to the vibrancy of religion were newly begotten during – and indeed triggered by – the Roman occupation. What matters is that Roman Britons never lost their sense of local identity. The presence of so many British god-names in the epigraphic record and the persistent 'surrealism' employed by artists to create sacred images – the exaggerated heads, the triplism and the horns, for instance – suggest an intentionality of Britishness that marched alongside acceptance of the Roman ways of expressing belief. Notwithstanding the new technologies of worship introduced as part of the Roman material package, indeed perhaps because of them, British religion flourished in this most remote of the Roman provinces. I am reminded of Lewis Hyde's 'trickster',[6] a character in many cultures and mythologies, whose job is to cross boundaries and push edges in order to disrupt the comfort of 'norm'. Perhaps edgy Britannia served as the 'trickster' to mainstream Roman religion, and maybe the experimentation with nature in which some Romano-British sculptors were engaged was an expression of such boundary-crossing.

The archaeological record provides striking testament to the percolation of religious beliefs and ritual through all echelons of Romano-British society, from the highest-ranking army officers to subsistence farmers and even to slaves. The relationships between people and their gods took many forms: from the most Roman, the Imperial Cult, to quasi-magical practices that embodied the grey area between religion and superstition, like ritual curses and the symbolic beheading of corpses. Despite their demotion from sacral authority after its absorption into the Empire, it is highly likely that the Druids continued to orchestrate Roman Britannia's religious vigour and spiritual independence. Ancient Britannia was indeed a most sacred isle, as culturally diverse then as it is today but, arguably, with a stronger spiritual pulse in its Romano-British past.

Notes

PROLOGUE

1   *History* 3: 14.67; trans. Whittaker 1969: 359
2   See Braund 1996: 77–80
3   Salway 1993: 291–312
4   Aldhouse-Green 2006a: 106, 132, 139; Dio Cassius *Roman History* 70, 6–7
5   Webster 2016
6   2000: 89–94
7   Hill *et al.* 2004: 1–22.
8   Smith 2001: 40–44; King and Soffe 1994
9   Creighton 2000: 192–93.
10 Mattingly 2006: 100
11 Tomlin 2014: 54

CHAPTER ONE

1   *Natural History* 30.13; after de la Bédoyère 2002: 63
2   For instance, the author Minucius Felix (*Octavius* viii. 3-xii. 6) spoke, in the earlier 3rd century AD, against early Christians, accusing them of cannibalism. Athenagoras (*Plea for the Christians* ii. 7, 9; iii, 12–13) was a Christian who defended the new faith and, in his pro-Christian letter to the emperor Marcus Aurelius and his son Commodus, written in AD 177, he denounced those who spread stories of cannibalistic rites. Lewis and Reinhold (eds) 1966: 584–86
3   *De Bello Gallico* 6.16; trans. Wiseman and Wiseman 1980: 123
4   Cunliffe 1986: 161, fig. 90
5   Aldhouse-Green 2001a: 59
6   Stead *et al.* 1986; Aldhouse-Green 2015a: *passim* (see *Index*)
7   Niblett 1999: 83–88, 319–20, 414; Mays and Steele 1996: 155–61
8   *Natural History* 16.95; trans. Rackham 1945: 549–51
9   *Annals* 14.30; trans. Grant 1956: 317
10 Macdonald 2007, *passim*
11 Farley and Hunter 2015: 32, 104
12 See, for example, Bradley 1990
13 Strabo *Geography* 4.1.13
14 Aldhouse-Green and Howell 2017: 35
15 Christopher Williams pers. comm.
16 Lavelle 1993
17 Fermor 1966; 2013
18 Aldhouse-Green 2015a: 190–91; Green 1996: 153
19 *Panegyricus Latinus* 8.11.2; after Braund 1996: 22
20 Aldhouse-Green 1999
21 Aldhouse-Green 2010: 146–68.
22 Aldhouse-Green 2015b: 166–67

23 Parfitt 1995: frontispiece and 18–20, fig. 3.
24 British Museum 1964. 62
25 Aldhouse-Green and Aldhouse-Green 2005: 132–33
26 Parfitt 1995: 105–6; fig. 46
27 See Aldhouse-Green 2010, 162–64 for a fuller explanation of this practice
28 *De Divinatione* 1.90; trans. Chadwick 1997: 104
29 Caesar *De Bello Gallico*: 1.31
30 *De Bello Gallico* 6: 13–18.
31 Caesar *De Bello Gallico* 5.6; trans. Wiseman and Wiseman 1980: 90
32 *Natural History* 30.4; after Chadwick 1997
33 *De Bello Gallico* 6.13; trans Wiseman and Wiseman 1980: 121
34 Pliny the Elder *Natural History* 30.4, after Chadwick 1997: 15
35 See opening quote for this chapter
36 Lucan *Pharsalia* 1, 422–65; trans. Graves 1956: 38
37 *Loc. Cit.*: trans Graves 1956: 38
38 Tacitus *Annals* 12.36
39 Tacitus *Histories* 3.45
40 *Annals* 14.30
41 Tacitus *Agricola* 14
42 *Aurelianus* 44.4–5; retranslated by the author (adapted from Magie 1932: 283)
43 Chadwick 1997: 81 (where the problems concerning the *Histories* are explained); the quote is after Rand 1939: 598
44 There are similar references to the accession of the emperors Numerian, Severus Alexander and Diocletian: see Green 1997: 97
45 Tacitus *Annals* 14.30; trans. Grant 1956: 317
46 *Natural History* 30.4
47 *Claudius* 25: 'Augustus had been content to prohibit any Roman citizen in Gaul from taking part in the savage and terrible Druidic cult; Claudius abolished it altogether': trans. Graves 1962: 177
48 Gordon, Joly and Van Andringa 2010; Joly, Van Andringa and Willerval 2010; Simón 2012
49 *De Bello Gallico* 6.13; trans. Wiseman and Wiseman 1980: 121
50 Sherratt 1991
51 Creighton 1995: 295
52 Holl 2002: 9
53 Crummy 2007: 394–99
54 *De Bello Gallico* 8.38
55 Chadwick 1997: 38–39; Aldhouse-Green 2010: 52–53, fig. 16

56 Chadwick 1997: 82
57 *De Bello Gallico* 6.14; trans. Wiseman and Wiseman 1980: 121
58 Tomlinson 1976: 64–71
59 So graphically described by Julius Caesar (*De Bello Gallico* 6.16) and other Roman authors.
60 Gregory 1992; Aldhouse-Green 2006a: 160–64; Johns and Potter 1983.
61 From an Irish Penitential, 7th century AD; after Green 1997: 134
62 Guest 1927: 268; Owen 1962: 203
63 Aldhouse-Green 2015b: 110
64 Aldhouse-Green 2015b: 197–99

CHAPTER TWO

1   Act 1, Scene 3; Withers ed. Undated, 11
2   This lost triumphal arch once stood at the heart of Rome. It was erected by the emperor Claudius in about AD 50; Barrett 1991: 12
3   Saunders and Gray 1996: 804
4   Braund 1996: fig. 28; Aldhouse-Green 2006a: 44–48
5   Ferris 2000: 55
6   King and Soffe 1994; Smith 2018
7   Hughes 1996
8   Macdonald 2007; Aldhouse-Green 2012: 38–39
9   Coles 1990; 1998
10 Juvenal *Satire* 13; trans. Creekmore 1963: 200
11 Hart 2016; *R.I.B.* 108, 109
12 Henig 1984: 88–89; de la Bédoyère 2002: 144–46
13 See Duncan Fishwick's discussion of the ambiguity involved in emperor-worship in the western Empire: Fishwick 1991
14 The 1st-century author Diodorus Siculus mentions that Gaulish warriors stiffened their blond hair like this in order to make themselves appear taller and more intimidating; *Library of History* 5.28
15 Images of *lituus*-like objects appear on late pre-Roman Iron Age coinage minted by the southern tribal leader Verica at the early temple on Hayling Island, Hampshire; some of the coins struck by the Catuvellaunian king Cunobelin also carry this curved staff. These coins were minted *c.* AD 20–40: Creighton 2000: 192–23, 205; 2006: 23
16 Tacitus *Annals* 14.31; trans. Grant 1956: 318

17 Armit 2012; see also this volume Chapter 7

18 Armit 2012

19 Dio Cassius *Roman History* 62.1; trans. Ireland 1996: 63

20 Excavations near the Bank of England in London in May/June 2016 revealed startling new evidence for Roman London's early prosperity as a financial centre. The material discovered consists of wooden writing tablets, preserved because of the anaerobic and watery conditions in which they were found, in the river Walbrook. Malvern 2016: 3

21 Tacitus *Annals* 14.32

22 Financial misdemeanours in today's British Parliament, not least the MPs' 'expenses scandal' of 2009, spring to mind as broad parallels to Seneca's nefarious monetary dealings.

23 Dio Cassius *Roman History* 62.2

24 *Annals* 14.30; trans. Grant 1956: 317–18

25 For the full story of the Boudican episode see Aldhouse-Green 2006a: 172–208

26 *Roman History* 62, 6–7

27 Aldhouse-Green 2010: 220–22.

28 Tacitus *Annals* 14.38; trans. Grant 1956: 321

29 Grasby and Tomlin 2002: 46

30 Tacitus *Annals* 3.42

31 Tomlin 2015: 384–86; Hayward, Henig and Tomlin 2017: 76–83

32 Henig 1993a: 30, no. 89, pl. 25

33 Neal and Cosh 2010: mosaic 421.45

34 Henig 1993a: 32, no. 93, pl. 26

35 Dio Cassius *Roman History* 60.20; trans. Ireland 1996: 45–46; Mattingly 2006: 98

36 Creighton 2000: 32

37 Juvenal *Satires* 8; trans. Creekmore 1963: 142

38 Thomson 2016

39 Genders 2016

40 Aldhouse-Green 2003: 39; Webster 1995; 1997

41 *R.I.B.* 91

42 I have argued elsewhere that Lindow Man's burial place, right on the route that Suetonius's army would have taken to Anglesey, might just be associated with this event. Aldhouse-Green 2006a: 157

CHAPTER THREE

1 *R.I.B.* 450

2 Various suggestions have been proposed for the identity of these two emperors: Severus and Caracalla is the most likely pair.

3 Coulston and Phillips 1988: no. 152, pl. 43

4 This trio of hooded figures enjoyed its greatest popularity in the Cotswolds, centred on the Dobunnic tribal capital Corinium (Cirencester). Their cult is considered in more detail in Chapter 7, this volume.

5 2003: 139

6 But we must be careful in making assumptions about voids in evidence. Until very recently, the same was thought to be true of Pembrokeshire, a region seemingly untouched by conquest or colonization, but here evidence is gradually accumulating, as a result of ever more technologically sophisticated methods of discovery and increased focus on archaeological investigation in West Wales. Edward Besly pers. comm.

7 Creighton 2006: 93–107

8 Stewart and Shaw (eds) 1994

9 *R.I.B.* 274

10 Collingwood and Richmond 1969: 220–21; de la Bédoyère 2003: 125

11 Aldhouse-Green 2004: 5, fig. 1.2, 122

12 *R.I.B.* 837, 838

13 Breeze 1997: 80

14 Nick Griffiths, pers. comm.; Holder 1982: 113. The 1st Cohort of Baetasians received a block grant of Roman citizenship sometime after AD 135, perhaps under the governor Lollius Urbicus during the advance of the army into Scotland, whence the Cohort came south to be stationed at Maryport in the later 2nd century, and later at Reculver in Kent.

15 Anderson 1987: 95; Watson 1987: 81

16 Ross 1967: 370–71; de la Bédoyère 2002: 147

17 *R.I.B.* 986, 987; Ross 1967: 169–71 Not in biblio?

18 Unusual silver or gilt-bronze plaques like this are known elsewhere in Britain, for instance at Stony Stratford in southeast England, which bear images of Mars and inscribed dedications to him. Green 1976: 179; *R.I.B.*

215–17. The Stony Stratford hoard of silver and bronze religious material also includes dedications to Vulcan, Jupiter and Minerva, all found concealed in a Roman pot, and probably once displayed in a shrine.

19 Mattingly 2006: 33

20 *R.I.B.* 1593; Coulston and Phillips 1988, nos 160, 161, pl. 45; Birley 1986: 77

21 *R.I.B.* 1594

22 King 1990: 170

23 Birley 1986: 77, with references

24 *R.I.B.* 309

25 *R.I.B.* 310

26 Wightman 1970: 211–14

27 Green 1976: 174; Henig 1993a: 42, no. 126, pl. 32

28 *R.I.B.* 317

29 *R.I.B.* 323

30 *R.I.B.* 445

31 Tacitus *Annals* 14.32

32 Manning 2001: col. pl. 5

33 Manning 2001: 92

34 What Jane Webster (2016) has termed 'new technologies of worship'.

35 *R.I.B.* 1598

36 *R.I.B.* 1692

37 For example at Housesteads: Coulston and Phillips 1988: nos 164–80

38 For a detailed discussion of the Rhenish mother-goddesses, sometimes called the *Aufaniae*, see Green 1989: 194–98. One altar to the goddesses was dedicated by a *quaestor* (a financial officer) from Cologne. The Germanic iconography of the *Matronae* is singular: a young girl, with long flowing hair, is flanked by two austere older women with spectacularly large circular hats. Unlike the Cotswolds *Matres* (see Chapter 5), the Germanic goddesses do not appear with babies or children but only with baskets of produce.

39 *R.I.B.* 1480

40 *R.I.B.* 1481

41 This tradition goes back to the late Iron Age in Celtiberia, as demonstrated by the presence of brooches, sceptres and stone images from sites like Numantia. Lorrio 1997: pls 3, 4; Martínez 1999: 7; Aldhouse-Green 2004: 141–42

42 *R.I.B.* 827–29

43 Jane Laskey, Senhouse Museum, Maryport pers. comm.; Wilson 1997

44 For a discussion of the different forms of Epona's image see Green 1989

45 *R.I.B.* 2177; soldiers at other military establishments in the north worshipped Epona too: a lost altar to the goddess is recorded at Carvoran. *R.I.B.* 1777; Coulston and Phillips 1988: no. 151; pl. 42

46 Green 1989: 16–17, Map 4; Linduff 1979

47 Epona with a key is depicted at Grand and at Allier in Gaul (Green 1989: 18). The bronze figure from southern England is from an unprovenanced site in Wiltshire: Johns 1971–72

48 Green 1976: 208 and frontispiece

49 Where naturalism is subordinate to stylization and apparent simplicity of line. This is a Gallo-British iconographic tradition where realism was less important than the message conveyed.

50 Green 1976: 167, pl. IIIa. These samples – from Peterborough and Margidunum – are just two of a number of images depicting divine cavalrymen.

51 Wilkinson and Wilkinson (eds) 1952: 275

52 de la Bédoyère 2002: 151, fig. 98; Phillips 1977: 81–83, nos 230–32, pls 60, 61; *R.I.B* 1327–29

53 Phillips 1977: 83

54 de la Bédoyère 2002: 151; Ross 1967: 163–64

55 2016. Webster argues that the absence of evidence for these British divinities in pre-Roman contexts might mean that Roman soldiers were deliberately inventing local gods, being careful to ascribe to them British names, in order to ensure their well-being in an alien and hostile environment. Personally, I find this argument suspect simply because the absence of an epigraphic tradition in the British Iron Age means that, even if these gods existed then, there could be no record of their worship. Another counter-argument to Webster's interpretation is the firm assertion made by the Roman author Cicero (*de Legibus* 2.8) that

it was forbidden to create new gods: see Chapter 4, p. 78.

56 *R.I.B.* 2091

57 Henig 1984, 103

58 *R.I.B.* 1131

59 Ferguson 1970: 216

CHAPTER FOUR

1 Pliny's *Letters* no. 39; trans. Radice 1963: 258

2 Cicero *De Legibus* 2.8; trans. Keyes 1928: 393

3 *Pharsalia III* 417–23

4 *Annals* 14.30

5 *Roman History* 62.6–7

6 Pliny the Younger's uncle, who died in the Vesuvian disaster of AD 79: *Natural History* 16.95

7 Aldhouse-Green 1999, *passim* but see particularly 61–63, 111–13 and Gray, in Aldhouse-Green 1999: 101–10

8 Examples include the temple of Claudius at Colchester and the late shrine to Nodens at Lydney.

9 For the seminal discussion of the Romano-Celtic temple form see Lewis 1966

10 2006: 70–92

11 Niblett 2001: 29–31

12 The women were of different ages: one was between 20 and 30, the second between 35 and 45 and the third between 30 and 50 years old. Niblett 1999: 20, 394 and frontispiece (for reconstruction painting of the chieftain's burial)

13 Mays and Steele in Niblett 1999: 314–21

14 Creighton 2006: 80

15 Henig 1993a: nos 103, 166; Holbrook 1998: 225, fig. 154

16 Holbrook 2016

17 Henig 1993a: nos 96, 116, 117, 120; *R.I.B.* 105

18 2016

19 Henig 1993a: no. 81

20 Henig 1993a: nos 63–65, 68–71.

21 Bauchhenss 1976; Bauchhenss & Noelke 1981

22 *R.I.B.* 103

23 Mattingly 2006: 227–29, fig. 9. The provinces were named Britannia Prima, Maxima Caesariensis, Flavia Caesariensis and Britannia Secunda.

24 Henig 1993a: nos 137, 138

25 Medlycott 2011: xiii, 14

26 Roman towns in Britain were allowed walls only after their inhabitants' loyalty to Rome was beyond question. Towns

such as Great Chesterford, on sensitive tribal boundaries and close to the principal region in which the Boudican revolt took place, were rarely granted walls until comparatively late, for reasons of security – there was always a fear that a town might fortify itself against the Roman government.

27 Medlycott 2011: 75

28 Caesar *De Bello Gallico* 6.13

29 Medlycott 2011: 75–94

30 Medlycott 2011: 82

31 Bauchhenss 1976

32 Medlycott, 2011: 92, fig. 92

33 Phrase from a speech delivered by Thomas Kielinger OBE at the conferment upon him on an Honorary Fellowship of Cardiff University, 14 July 2016

34 Wedlake 1982

35 de la Bédoyère 2002: 110

36 Wedlake 1982: 1–111; altar: 53, and pl. XXXIV

37 Wedlake 1982: frontispiece and fig. 61

38 Tomlinson 1976: 96–101; Ferguson 1970: 110

39 Anne Ross is convinced that pins as offerings were closely associated with childbirth. That may be so but the evidence is not proven. Ross 1967: 176

40 Cheesman 1994: 31–32

41 O'Connell and Bird 1994: 100–5

42 For a discussion of the Gallo-British solar cult see Green 1991

43 Bird in O'Connell 1994: 97

44 *R.I.B.* no. 306

45 Aldhouse-Green 2015b: 64–67

46 Mees 2009. For a discussion of curse tablets from Bath see Chapter 6, this volume

47 Such as the 4th-century temple within Maiden Castle, Dorset.

48 One of the Lydney model picks was a pick-head, with a hole for a separate shaft: Wheeler and Wheeler 1932: 92; the second is unpublished, and was a complete miniature implement, with integral head and handle (information from Lydney Park Estate).

49 Green 1975: 54–70

50 *R.I.B.* 305, 307

51 Wheeler and Wheeler 1932: pl. XXVI (the group of dog-images), pl. XXV (the deerhound)

52 Wheeler and Wheeler 1932: 90–91, pls XXX, XXVII

NOTES

53 For an explanation of the Severn
Bore phenomenon see Smith
2006: 68–69
54 Henig 1984: 135–36
55 Wheeler and Wheeler 1932: pl.
XXVI, no. 119
56 Vitebsky 1995; Aldhouse-Green
and Aldhouse-Green 2005
57 *R.I.B.* 305, 307

CHAPTER FIVE
1 Pliny the Elder *Natural History*
16.95; adapted by author from
trans. Rackham 1945: 549–51
2 In Roman religion colour was
important in terms of the
selection of sacrificial animals.
For instance, black beasts were
deemed appropriate as offerings
to Proserpina, goddess of the
underworld: 'Before anything else,
you must give the body proper
burial and make sacrifice of black
sheep…Aeneas sacrificed a black-
fleeced lamb to Night, the mother
of the Furies, and her great sister
Earth, and a barren heifer to
Proserpina'. Virgil *Aeneid* 6, lines
152–54, 248–50; trans. Day Lewis,
in Chisholm and Ferguson (eds)
1981: 225–47
3 The earliest find, made in 1826,
was a highly decorated copper-
alloy shield facing, the most
striking ornament being the
outline of an attenuated figure of
a wild boar that has been riveted
onto the shield's surface. Megaw
and Megaw 1989: 198
4 The timbers were not seasoned
after the trees were cut down,
which indicates only a small
margin of time between the
tree-felling and their erection:
Field and Parker Pearson 2003:
xi; Chamberlain 2003: 136–37.
Lunar eclipses are regular events
and so possible to predict with
a fair degree of accuracy from
observation rather than requiring
detailed astronomical
calculation.
5 Field and Parker Pearson 2003:
45–46; 158–59
6 Field and Parker Pearson 2003:
125–26, fig. 7.2
7 Fitzpatrick 1996
8 Aldhouse-Green 2010: 109, fig. 31
9 *De Bello Gallico* 6.18
10 Information from Mark Lodwick,
National Museum Wales, who also
provided the picture. Analysis of

the metal indicates its antiquity.
It has a superficial resemblance
to two figurines found many
years ago at Aust on the Severn in
Gloucestershire: British Museum
1925: 148, fig. 173; but these
have – probably correctly – been
identified as Iberian imports: *op.
cit.* fig. 73. While the crescent
headdress is common to the
images from Culver and from
Aust, the treatment of the face
and body on the Welsh statuette
are markedly different from those
from Aust.
11 Cunliffe 1995: 56–58, fig. 43
12 Cunliffe (ed) 1988: 6–7, fig. 4.1
13 *Pharsalia* 1, lines 445–46; trans
Duff 1977: 35–37
14 From the text of an early
medieval Swiss commentator
on Lucan's poem: Zwicker 1934:
50; trans. Marilynne Raybould
for the author: Aldhouse-Green
2001a: 85
15 See Aldhouse-Green 2010: 68
for details, with references.
Esus is unknown in Britannia
but Teutates's name appears
on a sprinkling of Romano-
British inscribed dedications,
including one of a bronze plaque
to 'Mars Toutatis' at Barkway
(Hertfordshire): Toynbee 1964:
328–30; Green 1976: 209 and
another scratched on a sherd
of pottery at Kelvedon (Essex).
It has been suggested that this
sherd might have come from the
same pot as the one depicting the
mounted warrior: information
from Paul Sealey, Castle Museum,
Colchester.
16 *R.I.B.* 452. Green 1982: pl. 1a
17 From Hispania Tarraconensis.
A *princeps* of a legion was a
centurion second in seniority
after the *primus pilus* (the highest
centurion in a legion); there were
five centurial ranks in each legion.
Green 1982: 38
18 Susini 1973: 39–42
19 Green 1984a; 1991
20 British Museum 1964: 60;
Gilbert 1978
21 As at Obernburg in Bavaria: Green
1984a: 338, fig. 1 and Meaux
(Seine-et-Marne) in France:
Green 1984a: 336, fig. 23
22 Green 1979: 350, pl. LXXXII,
fig. 64; Goodchild 1938. The
figure with the hammer may

represent the Gaulish hammer-
god Sucellus: Green 1989: 46–54.
He is rarely present in Britain but
a silver ring from York is inscribed
with his name: Royal Commission
on Historical Monuments:
Roman York 1962: no. 140, pl.
65; a relief from East Stoke,
Nottinghamshire depicts a divine
couple possibly identifiable as
Sucellus and his Gallic consort
Nantosuelta: Green 1989: 53;
Toynbee 1964: 176. Sucellus's
name means 'the good striker';
Nantosuelta may be translated
as a 'winding brook', though this
is uncertain.
23 Alföldi 1949; Green 1979: figs.
61–62
24 Green 1976: pl. 15e
25 The emphasis on the human head
is discussed in Chapter 7.
26 Wright and Phillips 1975: 73,
no. 196
27 Aldhouse-Green 2001b
28 See Aldhouse-Green 2015b for a
concise overview of Irish myths
29 Green 1989: 50, figs 19, 20
30 Green 1989: 58, fig. 22; Henig
1993a: no. 78, pl. 22
31 *R.I.B.* 140
32 Thevenot 1968: 46–71
33 Koch 2007, Map 15.5; Ross 1967:
37. For discussion of linguistic
evidence for ancient place-names
(for examples in Ptolemy's
Geography), see Koch 2007: 20–22
34 Cunliffe and Fulford 1982: no. 38
35 A thyroid condition caused by
iodine deficiency.
36 *R.I.B.* 105, 106
37 *R.I.B.* 151
38 Henig 1993a: nos 116, 118 (from
Ashcroft and the Leauses)
39 Henig 1993a: no. 117
40 The sculpture was found at
Lemington but is almost certainly
from Chedworth originally:
Henig 1993a: no. 94
41 Given the assumption that, as at
present, 90 per cent of people are
right-handed.
42 *Geography* 4.1.13; trans. Tierney
1959–60: 262
43 Aldhouse-Green 2015b: 162;
Mac Cana 1983: 32
44 O'Faoláin 1986: 132
45 Toynbee 1962: no. 29, pl. 35
46 Toynbee 1964: 86–87, pl. XIX
47 Ross 1967: 217, pl. 68a
48 Koch 2007: map 15.4
49 Koch 2007: map 15.6

50 Stead 1985 (Battersea Shield); Garrow 2008: 18, fig. 2.1 (Waterloo Helmet)

51 Bradley 1990: 180–81; Isserlin 1997: 91–100; Aldhouse-Green 2001a: 105

52 Solinus *Collectanea rerum memorabilium*; trans. after Cunliffe 1995: 16, adapted by the present author

53 Such as the 2nd-century AD geographer Ptolemy. For a concise history of Roman Bath see Cunliffe 1995: 16–29

54 Cunliffe 1995: 20, fig. 6

55 This came to me as I was preparing a talk on fire rituals to the 'Great Fire 350' event in the City of London, September 2016, at which a scale model of 17th-century London was ceremoniously set on fire.

56 A handful of coins: Sellwood 1988: 279–80

57 Cunliffe and Fulford 1982: no. 26, pl. 7

58 *R.I.B.* 143–50

59 Tomlin 1988: no. 94

60 Cunliffe and Fulford 1982: no. 25, pl. 7

61 The gorgoneion was a device to deflect evil.

62 Cunliffe and Fulford 1982: no. 38, pl. 11

63 An interesting local twist on the Minerva-cult in Britain is provided by the site of Baldock, Hertfordshire, where a cache of nineteen votive plaques and a silver figurine depict Minerva in traditional Classical form but the epigraphy names the goddess by the British name Senuna. David Mattingly (2006: 484) cites this as an example of the adoption of Roman physical imagery by a local British deity. If the three little female figures on the schist plaque at Bath do represent Sulis Minerva, the reverse seems to be occurring, with local iconography replacing Classical representational custom.

64 Lydney and its presiding deity Nodens were discussed in Chapter 4, present volume. Gaul possessed a large number of these sanctuaries: perhaps the most noteworthy, because of the wealth of images and artefacts that have survived, are Fontes Sequanae in Burgundy (Deyts 1983; 1994)

and Chamalières near Clermont-Ferrand in the Auvergne (Romeuf 2000).

65 As suggested by Martin Henig (1988: 5)

66 Allason-Jones 1989: 156

67 For detail of the offerings see Henig *et al.* 1988: 5–53

68 Cunliffe 1995: 100

69 Cunliffe 1995: 101

70 *R.I.B.* 1524, 1526

71 For the comprehensive study of Coventina's Well see Allason-Jones and McKay 1985

72 *R.I.B.* 1531

73 Allason-Jones and McKay 1985: stones 4 and 1 (pls VI and V), respectively

CHAPTER SIX

1 From the Biblical New Testament *Gospel according to Saint Luke* 13: vv10–11

2 Vitebsky 1995: 98–103

3 See Beith 1995: 45–75 for a discussion of medieval physicians and traditional medicine in the highlands and islands of Scotland

4 Crummy *et al.* 2007: 1

5 Crummy *et al.* 2007: 201–53

6 Jackson in Crummy *et al.* 2007: 236–52

7 Dr Alison Brookes pers. comm.; British Museum 1922: 34

8 Wiltshire 2007

9 Beith 1995: 229, 251; Wiltshire 2007: 397–98

10 Schultes *et al.* 1992: 98

11 *R.I.B.* 1530; Allason-Jones and McKay 1985: no. 142

12 Sherratt 1991; Aldhouse-Green and Aldhouse-Green 2005: 122–26

13 A game of some antiquity. Jane Austen was a keen player: https://www.janeausten.co.uk/spillikins

14 Crummy *et al.*2007: 209, fig. 105

15 Crummy *et al.* 2007: 224–26

16 *Germania* 10

17 Crummy *et al.* 2007: 209

18 Crummy *et al.* 2007: 186

19 Crummy 2007: 352, 357. See also Schädler 2007: 359–75

20 Schädler 2007: 375

21 Davies 2007: 86

22 Cunliffe 1995: 37

23 *R.I.B.* 155

24 For the significance of dreams, portents and omens see Wildfang and Isager (eds) 2000, and in particular Hansen's essay: Hansen 2000: 57–66

25 Wheeler and Wheeler 1932: 44–57

26 Diodorus Siculus *Library of History* 5.31; trans Tierney 1959–60: 251

27 Entitled *The Dreamwalker* BBC Radio 3, 21 August 2016. Keenan began his talk by quoting the words of a 13th-century Sufi mystic, who – contrary to some mainstream Islamic doctrine – proclaimed music as being 'the perfume breath of God'. Sufism is a branch of Islam, and it has attracted particular attention by its whirling dances, 'dervish dances' that occur when the souls of followers are intoxicated by their suffusion with spirit energy and express their joy at liberation from selfhood by their dancing: Chittick 2000: 89–96

28 Raftery 1994: pl. 58

29 Macdonald 2007: no. 31, colour pl. 1b

30 Steven Birch pers. comm.

31 Aldhouse-Green 2010: 195–98, with refs

32 Henig 1993a: no. 103, pl. 27

33 Pentikäinen 1998: 26–48

34 Pentikäinen 1998: 39

35 For an in-depth discussion of shamanism in ancient Europe see Aldhouse-Green and Aldhouse-Green 2005

36 Tomlin 1988: 166, no. 45

37 Bath: Cunliffe 1995: 107; Lydney: Wheeler and Wheeler 1932: 102, fig. 28

38 The Lydney stamp is interesting: the inscription gives instructions as to how the healing drug *collyrium* was to be administered: 'in drops, as an ointment mixed with honey, to be applied as a tincture with a brush'. Wheeler and Wheeler 1932: 102

39 Aldhouse-Green 1999: 37–40; Deyts 1983; 1994

40 *R.I.B.* 153

41 Tomlin 1988: 118, no. 8

42 Green 1975; 1981

43 The author noted these votive items on a visit to the museum at Epidaurus in the 1990s.

44 1988: 152; Aristides *Hieroi Logoi* II, 7. Aelius Aristides was born in AD 118, and spent some years living at the Pergamum shrine.

45 Johns 1982: 57–59, pl. on 58; Potter 1985; Gosden 2003: 168–69

46 1982: 59

47 Aldhouse-Green 2001c

48 Henig 1984: 153, fig. 75. As well as the model gold eyes, dozens of eye-shaped pieces of Roman wall-plaster have been found at Wroxeter, an indication of the one-time presence there of a shrine to a divine healer of eyes. www.english-heritage.org.uk/learn/story-of-england/romans/votive-body-parts

49 Badger 1838: 286–87

50 Rędzioch 1996

51 Tacitus *Annals* 2. 68: trans. Grant 1956: 109

52 Gager (ed.) 1992; Mees 2009

53 Tomlin 1993

54 Henig 1993b: 131–33. Note the presence of full-size weapons from the shrine as well as miniature ones.

55 Tomlin 1988: 114, no. 5

56 Tomlin 1988: 163, no. 44

57 Hamilton 2016

CHAPTER SEVEN

1 *The Acts of the Apostles* 8:27

2 MacGregor 2010: 225

3 Diodorus Siculus 5.29, 4–5; trans. Tierney 1959–60: 250

4 The Saluvii were a powerful tribe in the Lower Rhône Valley (see Armit 2012)

5 Armit 2006

6 For full discussion of the 'head habit' see Armit 2012. For references earlier in this volume see Chapter 2

7 Aldhouse-Green 2012; Boon 1976

8 Aldhouse-Green 2012: fig. 1

9 Yew is a highly poisonous evergreen, its blood-red berries appearing in winter, so it may be that the symbols are indicative of death and rebirth.

10 Brewer 1986: 13, no. 14

11 It is tempting to interpret this scenario as that in which the Christian householder allowed one of his staff, perhaps a bailiff or slave, to retain his/her pagan identity, as signified by the carved head, as long as it was kept out of sight.

12 Virgil *Aeneid* Book 6; trans. C. Day Lewis, in Chisholm and Ferguson (eds) 1981: 226–27

13 From the *Fourth Branch of the Mabinogi*; trans. (from the Welsh) Jones and Jones 1976: 61

14 'At that time Math son of Mathonwy might not live save while his two feet were in the fold of a maiden's lap, unless the turmoil of war prevented him': from the *Fourth Branch*; trans. Jones and Jones 1976: 55

15 Aldhouse-Green 2015b: 110–12

16 Ross 1967: 127–67

17 Henig 1993a: no. 93, pl. 26. Henig reads the motifs by the snakes' mouths as rosettes but, based on analogy with Gaulish sculptures, I think that their interpretation as open bags makes more sense.

18 Aldhouse-Green 2000: 82, fig. 7.2

19 Espérandieu 1911: no. 3133

20 Kaul 1991: 21, pl. 15; Aldhouse-Green 2004: 154, fig. 6.2

21 Aldhouse-Green 2004: 157, fig. 6.6

22 Aldhouse-Green 2000: 86, fig. 7.8

23 Stokes 1897: 384

24 Boon 1984; Aldhouse-Green 2004: 172, fig. 6.13

25 Aldhouse-Green 2015b: 48–57

26 Religious practitioners who might have had shamanic powers are discussed in Chapter 6, this volume.

27 From the *Táin Bó Cúailnge*; trans. Kinsella 1970: 60

28 For detailed discussions of shamans and animal-personae see Price (ed.) 2001; Aldhouse-Green and Aldhouse-Green 2005; Vitebsky 1995; Willis (ed.) 1994

29 Stead 1971: 260

30 A technique in which sheets of metal were placed on a firm but giving surface, such as pitch, and decorative motifs moulded into the inner side of the bronze in negative impressions, to produce positive decoration on the outer surface.

31 Green 1996: 40 and colour plate opposite; Aldhouse-Green 2004: 166, fig. 6.9

32 Arnold 2001

33 Bewley 1994: 38–40; Smith 1992: fig. 7.4

34 Aldhouse-Green 2000: 85, 87, fig. 7.9

35 From *The Destruction of Da Derga's Hostel*; trans. Gantz 1981: 65–66

36 Aldhouse-Green and Aldhouse-Green 2005: 195–96; the tale of Mog Ruith appears in a medieval mythic tale *The Siege of Druim Damgaire*: Smyth 1995; Sjoestedt 1926; Sjöblom 1996

37 Cunliffe 1986: 155–71; 1993: 100–12

38 Woodward and Woodward 2004

39 Serjeantson and Morris 2011: 88, 98–99

40 Ratcliffe 1997: 10; Wilmore 1977: 148

41 Hunter 2015: 86; Megaw 1970: no. 211

42 Green 1989: 104–5, fig. 45; Deyts 1976: no. 160. The image from Moux brings to mind the Norse god Odin, whose ravens, Huginn ('Thought') and Munin ('Memory') spied for him and brought him daily news-bulletins about happenings in the world. Faulkes 1987: 138

43 From *The Destruction of Da Derga's Hostel*; trans. Gantz 1981: 68–70

44 Green 1996: 66, 124

45 Triplistic imagery is equally prominent in Roman Gaul and the Rhineland.

46 White and Barker 1998: 9

47 White and Barker 1998: 96–97, fig. 50

48 Aldhouse-Green 2004: 208, fig. 7.15

49 Raftery 1994: 185–86, pl. 73

50 Raftery 1994: 186

51 Henig 1993a: no. 131, pl. 33. We know that weird things happened to Mars in Roman Gloucestershire: take the gabled relief dedicated to the British god Mars Olloudius from Custom Scrubs, near Bisley, depicting a strange figure with a tiny head and wardrobe-like body, with the distinctly non-warlike emblems of cornucopiae and offering-plate: Henig 1993: no. 40; pl. 13

52 Henig 1993a: no. 120, pl. 31

53 Henig 1998b

54 Aldhouse-Green 2016

55 Aldhouse-Green 2004: 208, fig. 7.16

56 Deyts 1976: no. 171; Green 1989: 192

57 Vitebsky 1995: 15

58 After the 'type-site' of La Tène in Switzerland where vast amounts of decorated metalwork were ritually cast into Lake Neuchâtel in the later first millennium BC: Megaw 1970; Garrow et al. (eds) 2008; Green 1996

59 Gombrich 1960: 331; 1972: 471–75. The term 'surrealism' was first used in 1924 to describe the desire for young artists to 'create something more real than reality itself, something of greater significance, that is, than a mere copy of what we see': Gombrich 1972: 471

60 Aldhouse-Green 2004: 194
61 Henig 1993a: no. 96; Aldhouse-Green 2004: 198–99, fig. 7.11
62 www.100swallows.wordpress.com/2008/04/27/michelangelo's-very-last-statue. It is known as the Rondanini Pietà, and is housed in the Sforza Castle in Milan.
63 The term 'robust tranquillity' was used in a recent conversation on BBC Radio 4's *Saturday Live*, 24 September 2016.

CHAPTER EIGHT
1 *Satire* 2; trans. Creekmore 1963: 48. The Orontes was the name of the principal river flowing through Syria.
2 *Satire* 3; trans. Creekmore 1963: 41
3 Malvern 2016
4 Whipple 2016
5 For example, Pliny the Elder *Natural History* 23.79; Seneca the Younger *Declamations* vol. 1 and Pomponius Mela *De Chorographia* 3.5
6 The final verse of Kipling's poem *A Song to Mithras*; Wilkinson and Wilkinson (eds) 1952: 131
7 Curtis 1993: 11–14
8 Jerome *Letters* 107; after de la Bédoyère 2002: 176
9 Dalmatia was a Roman province in what is now Croatia.
10 *R.I.B.* 1544; Coulston and Phillips 1988: 47, no. 121, pl. 31
11 de la Bédoyère 2002: 175
12 Grimes 1968: 98–117
13 Grimes 1968: 109
14 Grimes 1968: 115; Toynbee 1963; 1964: 315–17
15 2002: 176
16 Ferguson 1970: 54
17 Coulston and Phillips 1988: 47, no. 122, pl. 32
18 Hunter *et al.* 2016
19 Arnold and Davies 2000: 129–32
20 *R.I.B.* 322
21 Lewis 2016
22 Henig 1993c: 147, fig. 122
23 Lewis 2016
24 *Octavius* 6, 23. 1–4; after Lewis and Reinhold 1966: 574
25 Early Christians came under fire from pagans who wilfully interpreted the 'Body and Blood of Christ' Communion in which bread and wine were/are consumed as involving the actual consumption of human flesh and blood. See Rives 1995
26 Ferguson 1970: 14

27 Green 1976: 55–57 (with references); James 1958
28 Ovid *Fasti* 4. 183–87; after Henig 1984: 110
29 *R.I.B.* 1791
30 Ovid *Fasti* 2 refers to Augustus's imposition of a new moral code on Rome: Chisholm and Ferguson 1981: 88
31 Green 2003: 20–23; Ferguson 1970: 26–30
32 Lewis and Reinhold 1966: 579
33 Ferguson 1970: 28
34 Birley 1986: 78–79
35 *R.I.B.* 1135; Phillips 1977: 21, no. 58, pl. 17
36 Phillips 1977: 16, no. 48, pl. 12
37 Green 1976: 222; Tillyard 1917
38 Francis 1926; Green 1976: 222; Harris and Harris 1965: 109–12; Henig 1984: 110–11, fig. 44
39 Beard *et al.* 1998: 296
40 De La Bédoyère 2002: 146–47
41 It is worth noting that the site chosen for the main sanctuary in Rome itself was on the Aventine Hill, probably in acknowledgment of the god's Syrian home on Mount Commagene.
42 *R.I.B.* 992
43 *R.I.B.* 1131; Phillips 1977: 17–20, nos 51–54
44 Phillips 1977: 21, no. 57
45 A series of silver and sheet-bronze plaques depicting Dolichenus balancing on a bull come from Heddernheim in Germany: Merlat 1954: 177ff. A stone image of Dolichenus on his bull is in the Capitoline Museum in Rome: Ferguson 1970: pl. 13
46 *R.I.B.* 320
47 *R.I.B.* 2098
48 Harris and Harris 1965: 73; Green 2003: 27, pl. 12
49 *Metamorphoses I* (otherwise known as *The Golden Ass*) 11. 5–6; after Beard *et al.* 1998: 298–99
50 Graves 1950: 9–21
51 Suetonius *Life of Domitian* 1
52 Roberts 2013: 262–63
53 Henig 1984: 113
54 Beard *et al.* 1998: 299–300
55 1984: 115–16
56 British Museum 1922: 89
57 Green 1976: 222, pl. XXIIe
58 The altar was reused as a foundation-stone for a late Roman wall at Blackfriars: Henig 1984: 114; Hassall 1980: 196–98, no. 2
59 Known as a *favissa*.
60 Ferguson 1970: 37

61 Grimes 1968: 108, pl. 48
62 *R.I.B.* 658; de la Bédoyère 2002: 173, fig. 116
CHAPTER NINE
1 Tomlin 1988: 232, no. 98
2 *Adversus Judaeos*; Thomas 1981: 43
3 *De Excidio Britanniae* 10; Thomas 1981: 48
4 Thomas 1981: 48
5 *A History of the English Church and People* 1.7; trans. Sherley-Price 1955: 47
6 Bede 1.7; trans. Sherley-Price 1955: 44–45
7 Bede 1.7; trans. Sherley-Price 1955: 47
8 Salway 1981: 718, 721; Breeze 2016: 35. Breeze argues that there is a case for reinterpreting the original texts of Gildas and Bede, where they call the place of their martyrdom as *Legionum Urbs* (Caerleon), and suggests that this may be a corruption of *Legorum Urbs*, Roman Leicester.
9 *Theodosian Code* 9.16, 2; AD 319; Lewis and Reinhold 1966: 607
10 Salway 1993: 223–24
11 For a full discussion of these ancient writers' reportage, see Thomas 1981: 87
12 Ferguson 1970: 55–56
13 See Thomas 1981: 88, fig. 4 for examples/variations of the chi-rho symbol
14 Ferguson 1970: 56
15 1970: 56
16 Bede 1.8; trans. Sherley-Price 1955: 47–48
17 *Ecclesiastical History* 10.7; after Lewis and Reinhold 1966: 605
18 The Eucharist – the sharing of blessed bread and wine, as Christ did at the Last Supper.
19 Boon 1961; Brewer 2006: 23
20 Boon 1976: 173, argues that the Orpheus-and-Seasons mosaic 'could well be taken as an index of the proprietor's Christianity'
21 Brewer 2006: 23
22 See Painter 1976: 385–86
23 Painter 1977; Thomas 1981: 113–21
24 For a full discussion of later Romano-British Christian silver plate, for example the late 4th-century 'Corbridge Lanx' and the bullion from Traprain Law in Scotland see Thomas 1981: 113, 102
25 Designed to be suspended from a beam or niche.
26 Painter 1976: 385

27 The *alpha* and *omega*, the first
and last letters of the Greek
alphabet, referring to Christ's
words 'I am the alpha and
omega, the beginning and
the end'.
28 Toynbee 1978; Green 1976: pl.
XVIb; London Museum 1930: 47,
pl. XX
29 *R.I.B.* 215–17; Henig 1984: 147
30 Other, later 4th-century hoards
of silver, containing Christian
pieces, are recorded from Britain,
including the Mildenhall Treasure
from Suffolk, which has a
wonderful mixture of pagan
and Christian imagery, including
a superb head of Oceanus, who
may have been reinterpreted
as that of God: Painter 1977. At
the other end of Britannia, a
hoard of 110 pieces, of Gaulish
manufacture, of which 6 were
marked with Christian symbols,
comes from Traprain Law in East
Lothian, Scotland. Most of these
pieces had been hammered flat,
as bullion for distribution as loot,
perhaps in the early 5th century
AD, so their Christian symbolism
did not protect them from being
recycled as plunder: Thomas
1981: 102
31 Thomas 1981: 105–6, pl. 5;
Toynbee 1964: 447
32 Thomas 1981: 106
33 Toynbee 1964: 250, fn. 4
34 Toynbee 1964: 251
35 Meates 1955; Fulford 2005;
http://www.english-heritage.
org.uk/daysout/properties/
lullingstone-roman-villa
36 It is only at Dura Europos on
the Euphrates that similarly
early wall-paintings have
been recorded.
37 See Meates 1955: 131, fig. 11 for
reconstruction of the pagan and
Christian rooms.
38 Toynbee 1964: 222–23; Thomas
1981: 94; fig. 9
39 Toynbee argues for this
interpretation, based on the
painting of a curtain behind the
figure, reminiscent of portrayals
of the dead in Roman funerary
imagery: 1964: 223
40 *First Apology* 61; after Lewis and
Reinhold 1966: 589–90
41 Not unique in Roman Britain:
for discussion of such tanks see
Thomas 1981: 122

42 British Museum 1964: 62–63, fig.
30.3; Thomas 1981: 175; Henig
1984: 226
43 Goodburn 1979: 24
44 A good comparable example is
at Lydney on the Severn (see
Chapter 6), where a late temple to
the Romano-British god Nodens
was erected on the site of an Iron
Age hillfort and iron mine.
45 Mercury was the herald of the
gods and the cockerel was an
appropriate animal companion
because it heralds the dawn. Goats
and sheep were associated with
his role as god of fertility and
prosperity.
46 Woodward and Leach 1993; de la
Bédoyère 2002: 224–25
47 Thomas 1981: 237–38; Sparey
Green 1989
48 *Apologia* 37.4; after Lewis and
Reinhold 1966: 584
49 *Acta Concilia Arelatensis*;
Thomas 1981: 44, 197; Eusebius
Ecclesiastical History 10.5.21–24;
Munier 1963: 14–22
50 Brewer 2006: 45–46, 22, 15

CHAPTER TEN
1 *Aeneid* Book 6: lines 236–43;
trans. Day Lewis 1966; after
Chisholm and Ferguson 1981: 231
2 Saunders 2017.
3 This was true not just for Rome
but for all Roman cities. The
law banning intra-mural burial
stemmed from a blend of ritual
and practical considerations, not
least the danger of disease and
pollution.
4 Suetonius *Nero* 48; Hope 2000:
111
5 Bodel 2000
6 *Aeneid* 6: lines 149–56; Chisholm
and Ferguson 1981: 229
7 *Pharsalia* I, lines 441 following;
trans. Graves 1956: 38. Lucan
came from Spain, where he was
born in AD 39. He is chiefly known
for his epic poem the *Pharsalia*,
which chronicled the civil war
between Pompey and Caesar in
the mid-1st century BC.
8 *Library of History* 5.28; trans.
Tierney 1959–60: 250. Diodorus
Siculus was a contemporary
of Julius Caesar and Augustus,
and wrote his *LH* as a definitive
history of Rome. Pythagoras was
a Greek philosopher from Samos,
who taught in southern Italy in

the 6th century BC. The much
later Roman Stoic philosopher
Seneca, who became minister to
the emperor Nero, examined this
doctrine in his *Epistolae Morales*
(*Letters from a Stoic*), no. 108,
written in the AD 60s. The core
of Pythagorean teaching was the
transmigration of souls between
bodies.
9 *Geography* 4.4.4. Strabo was a
near-contemporary of Diodorus.
10 Cunliffe 1986: 155–71
11 Aelian *De Natura Animalium* 2: 22;
Silius Italicus *Punica* 3: 342–48
12 Hill 2001. This is not the first
female chariot-burial to have
been discovered at Wetwang. Two
other high-status woman's tomb
contained chariots, personal items
and pig-bones: Dent 1985: 85–92;
Green 1986: 124–26
13 At time of writing, a new
Yorkshire Iron Age chariot-
burial had just been discovered
at Pocklington. The chariot was
found – and this is a very rare
occurrence – together with the
two horses that had drawn it,
buried facing each other. *The
Times*, 31 March 2017: 23
14 Taylor 1993
15 Booth 2012: 337
16 Note that this chapter is entirely
focused on pagan Romano-British
mortuary rituals. The early
Christian tradition was entirely
different, and is discussed in
Chapter 9.
17 Matthews 1981
18 Matthews 1981: 7, 9 and *passim*
19 Macdonald 1979: 415–24
20 Philpott 1991: 77–89
21 Sophocles *Antigone*; trans. Fagles
1984
22 Aldhouse-Green 2015a, *passim*
23 See Aldhouse-Green 2015a for
in-depth discussion of the ritual
and meaning behind the bog-body
phenomenon.
24 This suggestion was made to me
in April 2017 by a member of the
audience at a lecture I gave in
Wigton to the West Cumberland
Archaeological Society. I only wish
it had been my idea!
25 From the opening of a curse, or
duscelinata ('evil death song'),
written on lead in the 1st century
AD and found in a Roman
cemetery at Larzac in southern
France: Mees 2009: 57, 196

26 Mees 2009: 50–69
27 Chapman 2000–2001
28 *De Bello Gallico* 6.18
29 Fitzpatrick 1996; Zavaroni 2007
30 Belonging to the tribe of the Cantiaci: Parfitt and Green 1987
31 *R.I.B.* 155, 162, 163
32 Pagan Romano-British burial rites were very different from those of early Christians, for whom both age and the need for elaborate tombstones or funeral goods were unimportant (see Chapter 9).
33 The most famous example was Julius Caesar's adoption of Octavian, the young man who would progress to being the first emperor of Rome.
34 *R.I.B.* 1065. The tombstone of Barathes himself was set up in Corbridge, nearby. He died at age 68, and his profession described as that of 'flag-bearer', presumably a military position.
35 Henig 1984: 194. Sadly, this table is now lost. Other burials equipped with pipes are noted by Henig 1984: 195; he comments that some tombs were furnished with lamps so that the dead person should not have to endure utter darkness.
36 Liversidge 1968: pls 3, 25a, 26c
37 Liversidge 1968: pl. 1
38 Henig 1993a: nos 137, 138, pl. 35
39 Brewer 1986: no. 29, pl. 12
40 Toynbee 1964: 112–14; pl. XXIXa, b
41 JENNINGS 1992: 70
42 St John's Gospel chapter 11, vv 1–45

CHAPTER ELEVEN

1 McDermid 2014: 302
2 *R.I.B.* 152
3 *R.I.B.* 140
4 *R.I.B.* 151
5 Cunliffe and Fulford 1982: no. 26; Cunliffe 1995: col. pl. 1 and black-and-white fig. 5: if you look closely at the right cheek, you can see faint striations from a narrow sharp-bladed instrument.
6 Tacitus *Annals* 14.31; trans. Grant 1956: 318
7 See later this chapter for an account of how this priesthood came into being. The thought occurs to me that what happened at Colchester is not unlike President Trump's plan to build a wall to keep the Mexicans

out of the US, paid for with Mexican money.
8 Webster 2016
9 Webster 2016
10 Strict Islamic law
11 MQPhil 2008
12 Ross 1967: 169
13 *R.I.B.* 986, 987
14 *R.I.B.* 988 (Felicessimus), 989 (Peltrasius)
15 Sauer 2003: 24
16 Upper Germany (*Germania Superior*) was the name given to the Rhenish province closest to Rome, as opposed to *Germania Inferior* (Lower Germany), which was to the north.
17 Sauer 2003: 26–30
18 An amusing modern take on prudery and censorship has recently occurred on the social media site Facebook which in 2016, citing ground of its indecency, took down a picture of the recently-discovered nude image of a god found this century at the Roman fort of Papcastle, near Cockermouth in Cumbria: Apperley 2016: 34
19 Aldhouse-Green 2016
20 Henig 1993a: 11, no. 24, pl. 9
21 Islam eschews holy images as being sacrilegious, and some fundamentalist Muslims see even those of the remote past as being blasphemous and ripe for destruction in the name of Allah and The Prophet Mohammed.
22 See Croxford 2003
23 Aldhouse-Green 2016
24 Woodward and Leach 1993
25 Henig 1993d: 88–94
26 Caesar *De Bello Gallico* 6: 17; trans. Wiseman and Wiseman 1980: 123
27 Tacitus *Germania* 43. He describes the Naharvali's worship of twin gods whom they called 'Alci', 'but according to the Roman Interpretation the gods so recorded are Castor and Pollux': after Henig 1984: 36
28 Webster 2016
29 Sellwood 1988
30 Green 1989: 36-54
31 Espérandieu 1915, no. 4566
32 Toynbee 1962, no. 79, pl. 78; 1964: 176
33 *R.I.B.* 140
34 Peregrinus means 'foreigner', and it is interesting that one dedication from a temple at Trier

refers to 'Mercury Peregrinorum', divine patron of foreigners and trade: Wightman 1970: 215
35 See Susini 1973: 14–20 for discussion of stonemasons and the production of inscriptions
36 Ross 1967: 36
37 Wightman 1970: 211–14
38 Wightman 1970: 209
39 These were ex-slaves who had been freed, or manumitted, by their owners but who often retained a close connection with their former owners and their families.
40 *C.I.L.* (*Corpus Inscriptionum Latinarum*) XII, no. 4333; after Lewis and Reinhold 1966: 62–63. Reference is made to the *seviri Augustales* at Colchester in Britannia early on in this chapter, their forced patronage of the Imperial Cult being a particular source of grievance to the newly conquered Trinovantes in the AD 40s and 50s.
41 As at Eisenberg in Germany and Metz in France: Green 1989: 54, with references
42 Henig 1993a: nos 78–82
43 Henig 1993a: 26–27, no. 78, pl. 22
44 Generally on his head but sometimes on his ankles.
45 A good example is the highly schematic image of Mercury found at the bottom of a well at Emberton in Buckinghamshire: Henig 1993a: 26, no. 77, pl. 22, which clearly show the god wearing horns, as does the even more abstract and perfunctory carving from Great Chesters on Hadrian's Wall, identifiable as Mercury only by his scratched-on *caduceus* and money-bag: Coulston and Phillips 1988: no. 81, pl. 22. Both these depictions show British schematism at its zenith; no attempt has been made to give 'human' reality to the body or its accompanying symbols.
46 See Ross 1967: 127–67
47 Bath: Cunliffe and Fulford 1982: no. 39, pl. 11; for an example of a late Iron Age bucket burial, at Aylesford in Kent, see Aldhouse-Green 2004: 165–68
48 Shaw and Stewart 1994: 1
49 For both sides of the debate – positive and negative – see

the individual contributions to
Stewart and Shaw (eds)
50 Webster 2016
51 Williams 1979; Green 1998: 18–19

EPILOGUE
1 I use the term *humanitas* in
the way it was employed in the
Classical world, to refer to people
perceived as so different from

Greeks and Romans as to be
outside 'civilization'.
2 Wyndham 1955
3 Aldhouse-Green 2010: 20–38;
Bradley 2007: 1–10
4 Cammaerts 1937
5 *The Cloud of Unknowing* is an
anonymous 14th-century British
Christian text (Backhouse (ed.)
2009), either written by someone

associated with the Carthusian
monastic order or by a person
outside the monastic system
altogether. I am grateful to Dr
Rowan Williams for the latter
observation.
6 Hyde 2008

Bibliography

Aldhouse-Green, M.J. *Pilgrims in Stone. Stone Images from the Gallo-Roman Sanctuary of* Fontes Sequanae. Oxford: British Archaeological Reports International Series No. 754, 1999.

Aldhouse-Green, M.J. 'Animal Iconographies: Metaphor, Meaning and Identity', in Davies, G., Gardner, A. and Lockyear, K. (eds) *TRAC 2000. Proceedings of the Tenth Annual Theoretical Roman Archaeology Conference London 2000.* Oxford: Oxbow, 2000: 80–93.

Aldhouse-Green, M.J. *Dying for the Gods. Human Sacrifice in Iron Age and Roman Europe.* Stroud: Tempus, 2001a.

Aldhouse-Green, M.J. 'Pagan Celtic Iconography and the Concept of Sacral Kingship', *Zeitschrift für celtische Philologie* 52, 2001b: 102–17.

Aldhouse-Green, M.J. 'Devotion and Transcendence: Discrepant Function in Sacred Space', in Smith, A.T. and Brookes, A. *Holy Ground: Theoretical Issues Relating to the Landscape and Material Culture of Ritual Space. Papers from a session held at the Theoretical Archaeology Group conference, Cardiff 1999.* Oxford: British Archaeological Reports International Series No. 956, 2001c: 61–72.

Aldhouse-Green, M.J. 'Alternative Iconographies. Metaphors of Resistance in Romano-British Cult-Imagery', in Noelke, P. ed. *Romanisation und Resistenz.* Mainz: Verlag Philipp Von Zabern 2003: 39–48.

Aldhouse-Green, M.J. *An Archaeology of Images.* London: Routledge, 2004.

Aldhouse-Green, M.J. *Boudica Britannia. Rebel, War-Leader and Queen.* London: Pearson Longman, 2006a.

Aldhouse-Green, M.J. 'Metaphors, meaning and money: contextualising some symbols on Iron Age coins', in De Jersey, P. ed. *Celtic Coinage: New Discoveries, New Discussion.* Oxford: British Archaeological Reports International Series No. 1532, 2006b: 29–40.

Aldhouse-Green, M.J. *Caesar's Druids. Story of an Ancient Priesthood.* Yale: Yale University Press, 2010.

Aldhouse-Green, M.J. '"Singing Stones": Contexting Body-Language in Romano-British Iconography', *Britannia* 43, 2012: 115–34.

Aldhouse-Green, M.J. *Bog Bodies Uncovered: Solving Europe's Ancient Mystery.* London and New York: Thames & Hudson, 2015a.

Aldhouse-Green, M.J. *The Celtic Myths. A Guide to the Ancient Gods and Legends.* London and New York: Thames & Hudson, 2015b.

Aldhouse-Green, M.J. '"Prayers to Broken Stone". Fragmentation, iconoclasm and divinduation in Romano-British religious sculpture'. Paper delivered at a conference, entitled *Stories in Stone. The Religious, Iconographic and Epigraphic Significance of Romano-British Sculpture from the Cotswolds,* held at Corinium Museum, Cirencester and organized by the Roman Society, 14 May 2016.

Aldhouse-Green, M.J. and Howell, R. *Celtic Wales.* Cardiff: University of Wales Press, 2017 (2nd edn).

Aldhouse-Green, M.J. 'Twinning and Pairing. Rethinking Number in the Roman Provincial Religious Imagery of Gallia and Britannia', in Patton, K.C. ed. *Gemini and the Sacred. Twins and Twinship in Religion and Myth.* New Jersey: Tauris Inc., 2018, in press.

Aldhouse-Green, M.J. and Aldhouse-Green, S. *The Quest for the Shaman. Shape-Shifters, Sorcerers and Spirit-Healers of Ancient Europe.* London: Thames & Hudson, 2005.

Alföldi, A. 'The bronze mace from Willingham Fen, Cambridgeshire', *Journal of Roman Studies* 39, 1949: 19–22.

Allason-Jones, L. *Women in Roman Britain.* London: British Museum Publications, 1989.

Allason-Jones, L. 'The Women of Roman Maryport', in Hill ed. 1997: 105–11.

Allason-Jones, L. and McKay, B. *Coventina's Well.* Chesters: The Trustees of the Clayton Collection, Chesters Museum, 1985.

Anderson, A. Scott 'The Imperial Army', in Wacher, J. ed. *The Roman World. Vol. II*, 1987: 89–106.

Apperley, E. *Roman Papcastle (Derventio).* Cockermouth: Grampus Heritage and Training Ltd., 2016.

Armit, I. 'Inside Kurtz's Compound: Headhunting and the Human body in Prehistoric Europe', in Bonogofsky, M. ed. *Skull Collection, Modification and Decoration.* Oxford: British Archaeological Reports International Series 1539, 2006: 1–14.

BIBLIOGRAPHY

Armit, I. *Headhunting and the Body in Iron Age Europe*. Cambridge: Cambridge University Press, 2012.

Arnold, B. 'Power Drinking in Iron Age Europe', *British Archaeology* 57, February 2001: 14–19.

Arnold, C.J. and Davies, J.L. *Roman and Early Medieval Wales*. Stroud: Sutton, 2000.

Backhouse, H. ed. 2009. *The Cloud of Unknowing*. London: Hodder & Stoughton, 2009.

Badger, G.P. *Description of Malta and Gozo*. Malta: Muir, 1838.

Barrett, A.A. 'Claudius' British Victory Arch in Rome', *Britannia* 22, 1991: 1–19.

Bauchhenss, G. *Jupitergigantensäulen*. Stuttgart: Württembergisches Landesmuseums, 1976.

Bauchhenss, G. and Noelke, P. *Die Iupitersäulen in den germanischen Provinzen*. Köln/Bonn: Rheinland-Verlag, 1981.

Beard, M., North, J. and Price, S. *Religions of Rome: Volume 2: A Sourcebook*. Cambridge: Cambridge University Press, 1998.

Beith, M. *Healing Threads. Traditional Medicines of the Highlands and Islands*. Edinburgh: Polygon, 1995. Bewley, B. *Prehistoric Settlements*. London: English Heritage, 1994.

Birch, S. 'Steps into the Underworld: Excavations at High Pasture Cave, Skye'. Cardiff: Cardiff University Archaeology Research Seminar, 29.11.2007.

Bird, J. 'Other finds excluding pottery', in O'Connell and Bird 1994: 93–132.

Birley, E. 'The Deities of Roman Britain', in Temporini, H. and Haase, W. (eds) *Aufstieg und Niedergang der Römischen Welt. II Principat*: 6–112, 1986.

Bodel, J. 'Dealing with the dead: undertakers, executioners and potter's fields in ancient Rome', in Hope and Marshall (eds) 2000, 128–51.

Bogaers, J.E. 'King Cogidubnus in Chichester: another reading of *RIB* 91', *Britannia* 10, 1979, 243–54.

Boon, G.C. 'A trace of Romano-British Christianity at Caerwent', *Monmouthshire Antiquary* 1, part 1, 1961: 8.

Boon, G.C. 'The shrine of the head, Caerwent', in Boon, G.C. and Lewis, J.M. *Welsh Antiquity*. Cardiff: National Museum of Wales, 1976: 163–75.

Boon, G.C. 'Potters, Oculists and Eye-Troubles', *Britannia* 14, 1983: 1–12.

Boon, G.C. *Laterarum Iscanum: The Antefixes, Bricks and Tile Stamps of the Second Augustan Legion*. Cardiff: National Museum of Wales, 1984.

Booth, P. 'Roman Britain in 2011: South-Western Counties', *Britannia* 43, 2012: 337–41.

Bradley, R. *The Passage of Arms. An archaeological analysis of prehistoric hoards and votive deposits*. Cambridge: Cambridge University Press, 1990.

Bradley, R. *The Prehistory of Britain and Ireland*. Cambridge: Cambridge University Press, 2007.

Braund, D. *Ruling Roman Britain. Kings, Queens, Governors and Emperors from Julius Caesar to Agricola*. London: Routledge, 1996.

Breeze, A. '*Legionum Urbs* and the British Martyrs Aaron and Julius', *ВОПРОСЫ ОНОМАСТИКИ* 2016, T. 13, No. 1.C.: 30–42.

Breeze, D. 'The regiments stationed at Maryport and their commanders', in Hill ed. 1997: 67–89.

Brewer, R. *Caerwent Roman Town*. Cardiff: Cadw, 1986.

British Museum *Guide to the Antiquities of Roman Britain*. London: British Museum, 1922.

British Museum *Guide to Early Iron Age Antiquities*. London: British Museum, 1925.

British Museum *Guide to the Antiquities of Roman Britain*. London: British Museum, 1964.

Cammaerts, E. *The Laughing Prophet. The seven virtues and G.K. Chesterton*. London: Methuen, 1937.

Chadwick, N. *The Druids*. Cardiff: University of Wales Press, 1997.

Chamberlain, A.T. 'Lunar Eclipses, Saros Cycles and the Construction of the Causeway', in Field and Parker Pearson 2003: 136–48.

Chapman, A. 'Excavation of an Iron Age Settlement and a Middle Saxon Cemetery at Great Houghton, Northampton, 1996', *Northamptonshire Archaeology* 29, 2000–1: 1–41.

Cheesman, C. 'The coins', in O'Connell and Bird 1994: 31–92.

Chisholm, K. and Ferguson, J. (eds) *Rome. The Augustan Age*. Oxford: Oxford University Press, 1981.

Chittick, W.C. *Sufism: a short introduction*. Oxford: One World, 2000.

Collingwood, R.G. and Richmond, I. *The Archaeology of Roman Britain*. London: Methuen, 1969 (rev. edn).

Coulston, J.C.N. 'The stone sculptures', in Hill ed. 1997: 112–31.

Coulston, J.C. and Phillips, E.J. *Corpus Signorum Imperii Romani. Corpus of Sculpture of the Roman World. Great Britain. Vol. I, Fascicule 6. Hadrian's Wall West of the North Tyne, and Carlisle*. London/Oxford: British Academy/Oxford University Press, 1988.

Creekmore, H. trans. *The Satires of Juvenal*. New York: Mentor, 1963.

Creighton, J. 'Visions of power: imagery and symbols in late Iron Age Britain', *Britannia* 26, 1995: 285–301.

Creighton, J. *Coins and Power in Late Iron Age Britain*. Cambridge: Cambridge University Press, 2000.

Creighton, J. *Britannia. The creation of a Roman province*. London: Routledge, 2006.

Croxford, B. 'Iconoclasm in Roman Britain?', *Britannia* 34, 2003: 81–95.

Crummy, P., Benfield, S., Crummy, N., Rigby, V. and Shimmin, D. *Stanway: An Élite Burial Site at Camulodunum*, London: *Britannia* Monograph Series No. 24, 2007.

Cunliffe, B. *Danebury: Anatomy of an Iron Age Hillfort*. London: Batsford, 1986.

Cunliffe, B. ed. *The Temple of Sulis Minerva at Bath. Vol. 2. The Finds from the Sacred Spring*. Oxford: Oxford University Committee for Archaeology Monograph No. 16, 1988.

Cunliffe, B. *Danebury*. London: English Heritage, 1993.

Cunliffe, B. *Roman Bath*. London: Batsford/English Heritage, 1995.

Cunliffe, B. and Fulford, M.G. *Corpus Signorum Imperii Romani. Corpus of Sculpture of the Roman World. Great Britain. Vol. 1, Fasc. 2 Bath and the Rest of Wessex*. London/Oxford: The British Academy/Oxford University Press, 1982.

Curtis, V.S. *Persian Myths*. London: British Museum Press, 1993.

Davies, S. trans. *The Mabinogion*. Oxford: Oxford University Press, 2007.

De la Bédoyère, G. *Gods with Thunderbolts. Religion in Roman Britain*. Stroud: Tempus, 2002.

De la Bédoyère, G. *Eagles over Britannia. The Roman Army in Britain*. Stroud: Tempus, 2003.

Dent, J. 'Three Cart Burials from Wetwang, Yorkshire', *Antiquity* 59, 1985: 85–92.

Deyts, S. *Dijon, Musée Archéologique: sculptures gallo-romaines mythologiques et religieuses*. Paris: Éditions de la Réunion des Musées Nationaux, 1976.

Deyts, S. *Les Bois Sculpté des Sources de la Seine*. Paris: XLIIe supplement à *Gallia*, 1983.

Deyts, S. *Un Peuple de Pèlerins. Offrandes de Pierre et de Bronze des Sources de la Seine*. Dijon: *Révue Archéologique de l'Est et du Centre-Est*. Treizième Supplément, 1994.

Duff, J.D. trans. *Lucan. The Civil War*. London: Heinemann (Loeb Edition), 1977.

Egger, R. 'Bescheidene Ex-votos', *Bonner Jahrbücher* 158, 1954: 73–80, Taf. 30.

Espérandieu, E. *Recueil Général des Bas-Reliefs de la Gaule Romaine et Pré-Romaine* vol. 4, Paris: Ernest Leroux, 1911.

Espérandieu, E. *Recueil Général des Bas-Reliefs de la Gaule Romaine et Pré-Romaine* vol. 5, Paris: Ernest Leroux, 1913.

Espérandieu, E. *Recueil Général des Bas-Reliefs de la Gaule Romaine et Pré-Romaine* vol. 6, Paris: Ernest Leroux, 1915.

Fagles, R. *Sophocles. The Three Theban Plays: Antigone, Oedipus The King, Oedipus at Colonus*. Harmondsworth: Penguin, 1984.

Farley, J. and Hunter, F. (eds) *Celts. Art and Identity*. London/Edinburgh: British Museum/National Museums Scotland, 2015.

Faulkes, A. trans./ed. *Edda. Snorri Sturluson*. London: Dent, 1987.

Ferguson, J. *The Religions of the Roman Empire*. London: Thames & Hudson, 1970.

Fermor, P.L. *Roumeli*. London: John Murray, 1966.

Fermor, P.L. *The Broken Road*. London: John Murray, 2013.

Ferris, I. *Enemies of Rome. Barbarians Through Roman Eyes*. Stroud: Alan Sutton, 2000.

Field, N. and Parker Pearson, M. *Fiskerton. An Iron Age Timber Causeway with Iron Age and Roman Votive Offerings*. Oxford: Oxbow, 2003.

Fishwick, D. 'Seneca and the Temple of Divus Claudius', *Britannia* 22, 1991: 137–41.

Fitzpatrick, A.P. 'Night and Day: the symbolism of astral signs on later Iron Age short swords', *Proceedings of the Prehistoric Society* 62, 1996: 273–98.

Francis, A.G. 'On a Romano-British Castration-Clamp used in the Rites of Cybele', *Proceedings of the Royal Society of Medicine* 19, 1926: 19ff.

Fulford, M.G. *Lullingstone Roman Villa*. London: English Heritage, 2005.

Gager, J.G. ed. *Curse Tablets and Binding Spells from the Ancient World*. Oxford: Oxford University Press, 1992.

Gantz, J. *Early Irish Myths and Sagas*. London: Penguin, 1981.

Garrow, D. 'The time and place of Celtic Art: interrogating the 'Technologies of Enchantment' database', in Garrow, D., Gosden, C. and Hill, J.D. (eds) *Rethinking Celtic Art*. Oxford: Oxbow, 2008: 15–39.

Genders, Rev. N. 'Faith in Schools', letter to *The Times*, 26 May 2016: 28.

Gilbert, H. 'The Felmingham Hall Hoard, Norfolk', *Bulletin of the Board of Celtic Studies* 28, part 1, 1978: 159–87.

Gombrich, E. *Art and Illusion. A study in the psychology of pictorial representation*. London: Phaidon, 1960.

Gombrich, E. *The Story of Art*. London: Phaidon, 1972.

Goodburn, R. *The Roman Villa Chedworth*. London: National Trust, 1979.

Goodchild, R.G. 'A priest's sceptre from the Romano-Celtic temple at Farley Heath, Surrey', *Antiquaries Journal* 18, 1938: 391–96.

Gordon, R., Joly, D. and Van Andringa, W. 'A prayer for blessings on three ritual objects discovered at Chartres-*Autricum* (France, Eure-et-Loir)', in Gordon, R. and Simón, F. Marco (eds) *Magical Practice in the Latin West. Papers from the International Conference held at the University of Zaragoza 2005*. Leiden: Brill, 2010: 487–518.

Gosden, C. 'Object lessons and Wellcome's Archaeology', in Arnold, K. and Olsen, D. (eds) *Medicine Man. The Forgotten Museum of Henry Wellcome*. London: Wellcome Trust/British Museum Publications, 2003: 161–70.

Grant, M. trans. *Tacitus. The Annals of Imperial Rome*. Harmondsworth: Penguin, 1956.

Grasby, R.D. and Tomlin, R.S.O. 'The sepulchral monument of C. Julius Classicianus', *Britannia* 33, 2002: 43–76.

Graves, R. trans. *Apuleius. The Golden Ass*. Harmondsworth: Penguin, 1950.

Graves, R. trans. *Lucan Pharsalia*. Harmondsworth: Penguin, 1956.

Graves, R. *The Twelve Caesars*. London: Cassell, 1962.

Gray, M. 'Pilgrimage: a comparative perspective', in Aldhouse-Green 1999: 101–10.

Green, M.J. 'Romano-British Non-Ceramic Model Objects from South-east Britain', *The Archaeological Journal* 132, 1975: 54–70.

Green, M.J. *The Religions of Civilian Roman Britain*. Oxford: British Archaeological Reports No. 24, 1976.

Green, M.J. 'The Worship of the Romano-Celtic Wheel-God in Britain seen in relation to Gaulish Evidence', *Collections Latomus*, vol. 38, fasc. 2, 1979: 345–67.

Green, M.J. 'Model Objects from Military Areas of Roman Britain', *Britannia* 12, 1981: 253–69.

Green, M.J. 'Tanarus, Taranis and the Chester Altar', *Journal of the Chester Archaeological Society* 65, 1982: 37–44.

Green, M.J. *The Wheel as a Cult-Symbol in the Romano-Celtic World*. Brussels: Latomus, 1984a.

Green, M.J. 'Mother and Sun in Romano-Celtic Religion', *Antiquaries Journal* 64, part I: 25–33, 1984b.

Green, M.J. *The Gods of the Celts*. Stroud: Alan Sutton, 1986.

Green, M.J. *Symbol and Image in Celtic Religious Art*. London: Routledge, 1989.

Green, M.J. *Sun Gods and Symbols of Ancient Europe*. London: Batsford, 1991.

Green, M.J. *Animals in Celtic Life and Myth*. London: Routledge, 1992.

Green, M.J. *Celtic Goddesses*. London: British Museum Press, 1995.

Green, M.J. *Celtic Art. Reading the Messages*. London: Weidenfeld & Nicolson, 1996.

Green, M.J. *Exploring the World of the Druids*. London and New York: Thames & Hudson, 1997.

Green, M.J. 'God in man's image: thoughts on the genesis and affiliations of some Romano-British cult-imagery', *Britannia* 29, 1998: 17–30.

Green, M.J. *The Gods of Roman Britain*. Princes Risborough: Shire Publications, 2003.

Gregory, A.K. *Excavations at Thetford 1980–82, Fison Way*. Norwich: East Anglian Archaeological Report 53, 1992.

Grimes, W.F. *The Excavation of Roman and Mediaeval London*. London: Routledge and Kegan Paul, 1968.

Guest, Lady Charlotte *The Mabinogion*. London: Dent, 1927.

Hamilton, F. 'Imam 'beaten to death in attack by Isis', *The Times* 24 August 2016.

Hansen, H.L. '"The Truth without nonsense": Remarks on Artemidorus' *Interpretation of Dreams*', in Wildfang and Isager (eds) 2000: 57–66.

Harris E. and Harris, J.R. *The Oriental Cults in Roman Britain*. Leiden: Brill, 1965.

Hart, A. 'Corinium Tombstones', paper delivered at a conference entitled *Stories in Stone*, sponsored by the Roman Society, at Corinium Museum 14 May 2016.

Hassall, M.W.C. 'The Inscribed Altars', in Hill, C., Millett, M. and Blagg, T. *The Roman Riverside Wall and Monumental Arch in London*. London and Middlesex Archaeological Society Occasional Paper No. 3, 1980: 195–98.

Hayward, K.M.J., Henig, M. and Tomlin, R.S.O. 'The Tombstone', in Holbrook, N., Wright, J., McSloy, E.R. and Geber, J. *The Western Cemetery of Roman Cirencester. Excavations at the former Bridges Garage, Tetbury Road, Cirencester, 2011–2015*. Cirencester: Cotswold Archaeology Excavations Vol. VII (2017), 76–83.

Henig, M. *Religion in Roman Britain*. London: Batsford, 1984.

Henig, M. et al. 'Objects from the Sacred Spring', in Cunliffe 1988: 5–6.

Henig, M. *Roman Sculpture from the Cotswold Region*. Oxford: *Corpus Signorum Imperii Romani* Vol. 1, Fascicule 7, 1993a.

Henig, M. 'Votive objects: weapons, miniatures, tokens, and fired clay accessories', in Woodward and Leach 1993b: 131–48.

Henig, M. 'Ceramic "altar", in Woodward and Leach 1993c: 146–47.

Henig, M. 'Sculpture in stone', in Woodward and Leach 1993d: 88–95.

Henig, M. 'Togidubnus and the Roman Liberation', *British Archaeology* 38, 1998a: 8–9.

Henig, M. 'A Relief of a Mater and Three Genii from Stratton', *Transactions of the Bristol and Gloucestershire Archaeological Society* 1998b, 116: 186–89.

Hill, J.D. 'A New Cart/Chariot Burial from Wetwang, East Yorkshire, *PAST* no. 38, August 2001: 2–3.

Hill, J.D., La Niece, A.J. and Worrell, S. 'The Winchester Hoard: a find of unique Iron Age gold jewellery from Southern England', *Antiquaries Journal* 84, 2004: 1–22.

Hill, P.R. 'The Maryport altars: some first thoughts', in Hill ed. 1997: 92–104.

Holbrook, N. 'Shops V6 and V7 in the western corner of *Insula* V. Excavations and Observations at Price's Row 1972–3', in Holbrook, N. ed. *Cirencester V. Cirencester, The Roman Town Defences, Public Buildings and Shops*. Cirencester: Cotswold Archaeological Trust, 1998: 217–45.

Holbrook, N. 'The Archaeological Context of Sculptural Finds', paper delivered at a conference entitled *Stories in Stone*, sponsored by the Roman Society, at Corinium Museum 14 May 2016.

Holder, P.A. *The Roman Army in Britain*. London: Batsford, 1982.

Holl, J. 'An investigation into three Romano-British religious sites in Surrey'. Bristol: unpublished dissertation, 2002.

Hope, V.M. 'Contempt and respect: the treatment of the corpse in ancient Rome', in Hope and Marshall (eds), 2000: 104–27.

Hope, V.M. and Marshall, E. (eds) *Death and Disease in the Roman City*. London: Routledge, 2000.

Hughes, G. *The Excavation of a Late Prehistoric and Romano-British Settlement at Thornwell Farm, Chepstow*. Oxford: British Archaeological Reports British Series No. 244, 1996.

Hunter, F. 'Powerful Objects: the Uses of Art in the Iron Age', in Farley and Hunter (eds), 2015: 81–105.

Hunter, F., Henig, M., Sauer, E. and Gooder, J. 'Mithras in Scotland: A Mithraeum at Inveresk (East Lothian)', *Britannia* 47, 2016: 119–68.

Hyde, L. *The Trickster. How Disruptive Imagination Creates Culture*. London: Canongate, 2008.

Ireland, S. *Roman Britain. A Source Book*. London: Routledge, 1996 (2nd edn).

Isserlin, R.M.J. 'Thinking the Unthinkable: Human Sacrifice in Roman Britain', *Proceedings of the Sixth Annual Theoretical Roman Archaeology Conference (TRAC)*. Oxford: Oxbow, 1997: 91–100.

Jackson, R. *Doctors and Diseases in the Roman Empire*. London: British Museum Publications, 1988.

Jackson, R. 'The surgical instruments', in Crummy *et al.* 2007: 236–52.

James, E.O. *Myth and Ritual in the Ancient Near East*. London: Thames & Hudson, 1958.

Jennings, E. *Selected Poems*. Manchester: Carcenet Press, 1992: Poem no. 72.

Johns, C.M. 'A Roman bronze statuette of Epona', *British Museum Quarterly* vol. 36, 1971–72: 37–41.

Johns, C.M. *Sex or Symbol. Erotic Images of Greece and Rome*. London: British Museum Publications, 1982.

Johns, C.M. and Potter, T. *The Thetford Treasure*. London: British Museum Publications, 1983.

BIBLIOGRAPHY

Joly, D., Van Andringa, W. and Willerval, S. 'L'attiralil d'un magician range dans un cave de Chartres (*Autricum*). *Gallia* 67.2, 2010: 125–208.

Jones, G. and Jones, T. trans. *The Mabinogion*. London: Dent, 1976.

Kaul, F. *Gundestrupkedlen*. Copenhagen: National Museum of Denmark, 1991.

Keyes, C.W. *Cicero De Re Publica, De Legibus*. London: Heinemann, 1928.

King, A. *Roman Gaul and Germany*. London: British Museum Press, 1990.

King, A. and Soffe, G. 'The Iron Age and Roman temple at Hayling Island, Hampshire', in Fitzpatrick, A. and Morris, P. (eds) *The Iron Age in Wessex: Recent work*. Salisbury: Trust for Wessex Archaeology, 1994: 114–16.

Kinsella, T. *The Táin. From the Irish epic Táin Bó Cuailnge*. Oxford: Oxford University Press, 1970.

Koch, J. *An Atlas for Celtic Studies. Archaeology and Names in Ancient Europe and Early Medieval Ireland, Britain and Brittany*. Oxford: Oxbow, 2007.

Lavelle, D. *The Skellig Story*. Dublin: O'Brien Press, 1993.

Lewis, M. 'Shedding Light on Mithraism at Roman Isca?: Roman clay altars from Caerleon, South Wales, U.K.', unpublished draft paper, 2016.

Lewis, M., Clarke, S. and Bray, J. 'Roman Clay Altars from Caerleon', *The Monmouthshire Antiquary* 24, 2008: 31–45.

Lewis, M.J.T. *Temples in Roman Britain*. Cambridge: Cambridge University Press, 1966.

Lewis, N. and Reinhold, M. (eds) *Roman Civilization: Sourcebook II. The Empire*. New York: Harper & Row, 1966.

Linduff, K. 'Epona: a Celt among the Romans', *Collections Latomus* vol. 38, fasc. 4, 1979: 817–37.

Liversidge, J. *Britain in the Roman Empire*. London: Routledge and Kegan Paul, 1968.

London Museum, *London in Roman Times. London Museum Catalogues No. 3*. London: London Museum, 1930.

Lorrio, A. *Los Celtíberos*. Madrid/ Alicante: Universidad Complutense/ Universidad de Alicante, 1997.

Lurker, M. *The Gods and Symbols of Ancient Egypt*. London and New York: Thames & Hudson, 1974.

Mac Cana, P. *Celtic Mythology*. London: Newnes, 1983.

Macdonald, J.L. 'Religion', in Clarke, G. *The Roman Cemetery at Lankhills*. Oxford: Winchester Studies 3. Pre-Roman and Roman Winchester: 403–33, 1979.

Macdonald, P. *Llyn Cerrig Bach. A Study of the Copper Alloy Artefacts from the Insular La Tène Assemblage*. Cardiff: University of Wales Press, 2007.

MacGregor, N. 'Head of Augustus', in MacGregor, N. *A History of the World in 100 Objects*. London: Allen Lane/ Penguin, 2010: 221–26

Magie, D. trans. *The Scriptores Historiae Augustae III*. London: Heinemann (Loeb Edition), 1932.

Malvern, J. 'London: wild west of Roman empire', *The Times* 2 June 2016: 3.

Mann, J.C. 'A note on the Maryport altars', in Hill ed. 1997: 90–91.

Manning, W.H. *Roman Wales. A Pocket Guide*. Cardiff: University of Wales Press, 2001.

Martínez, A.J. 'Religión y Ritual Funerario Celtibéricos', *Revista de Soria* No. 25: 5–18, 1999.

Matthews, C.L. 'A Romano-British Inhumation Cemetery at Dunstable, Durocobrivae', *Bedfordshire Archaeology Journal* 15, 1981: 1–79.

Mattingly, D. *An Imperial Possession. Britain in the Roman Empire*. London: Penguin/Allen Lane, 2006.

Mays, S. and Steele, J. 'A mutilated human skull from Roman Saint Albans, Herts., England', *Antiquity* 70, 155–61, 1996.

Mays, S.A. and Steele, J. 'The Human Bone', in Niblett 1999: 307–23.

McDermid, V. *The Skeleton Road*. London: Little Brown, 2014.

Meates, G.W. *Lullingstone Roman Villa*. London: Heinemann, 1955.

Medlycott, M. *The Roman Town of Great Chesterford*. Chelmsford: Essex County Council/East Anglian Archaeology Report No. 137, 2011.

Mees, B. *Celtic Curses*. Cambridge: Boydell Press, 2009.

Megaw, J.V.S. *Art of the European Iron Age*. London: Hart Davis, 1970.

Megaw, R. and Megaw, V. *Celtic Art. From its Beginnings to the Book of Kells*. London: Thames & Hudson, 1989.

Merlat, P. 'Notes Dolichéniennes', *Revue Archéologique* 43, 1954: 177ff.

MQPhil. https://mqphil.wordpress. com/2008/02/16/moral-relativism-and-the-case-of-sharia.

Munier, C. *Concilia Galliae a. 314-a.506*. Turnhout: Brepols, 1963.

Neal, D.S. and Cosh, S.R. *The Roman Mosaics of Britain, Vol. IV Western Britain, including Wales*. London: ASPROM (The Association for the Study and Preservation of Roman Mosaics)/Society of Antiquaries of London, 2010.

Niblett, R. *The Excavation of a Ceremonial Site at Folly Lane, Verulamium*. London: Britannia Monograph Series No. 14, 1999.

Niblett, R. *Verulamium. The Roman City of St Albans*. Stroud: Tempus, 2001.

O'Connell, M.G. and Bird, J. *The Roman Temple at Wanborough*. Guildford: The Surrey Archaeological Society (*Surrey Archaeological Collections* Vol. 82), 1994.

O'Faoláin, E. *Irish Sagas and Folk Tales*. Dublin: Poolbeg Press, 1986.

Owen, A.L. *The Famous Druids. A Survey of Three Centuries of English Literature on the Druids*. Oxford: Clarendon Press, 1962.

Painter, K.S. in Wright, R.P., Hassall, M.W.C. and Tomlin, R.S.O. 'Roman Britain in 1975: II Inscriptions', *Britannia* 7, 1976: 385–87.

Painter, K.S. *The Water Newton Early Christian Silver*. London: British Museum Press, 1977.

Parfitt, K. *Iron Age Burials from Mill Hill, Deal*. London: British Museum Press, 1995.

Parfitt, K. and Green, M. 'A Chalk Figurine from Upper Deal, Kent', *Britannia* 18, 1987: 295–98.

Pentikäinen, J. *Shamanism and Culture*. Helsinki: Etnika, 1998.

Phillips, E.J. *Corpus Signorum Imperii Romani. Corpus of Sculpture of the Romane World. Great Britain, Volume 1, Fasc. 1: Corbridge. Hadrian's Wall East of the North Tyne*. London/Oxford: British Academy/Oxford University Press, 1977.

Philpott, R. *Burial Practices in Roman Britain: A survey of grave treatment and furnishing AD43–410*. Oxford: British Archaeological Reports British Series No. 219, 1991.

Potter, T.W. 'A Republican healing sanctuary at Ponte di Nona near Rome and the Classical tradition of votive medicine', *Journal of the British Archaeological Association* 138, 1985: 23–47.

Price, N. ed. *The Archaeology of Shamanism*. London: Routledge, 2001.

Rackham, H. trans. *Pliny Natural History*. Cambridge (Mass): Harvard University Press (Loeb Edition), 1945.

Radice, B. trans. *The Letters of the Younger Pliny*. Harmondsworth: Penguin, 1963.

Raftery, B. *Pagan Celtic Ireland*. London: Thames & Hudson, 1994.

Rand, E.K. *The Cambridge Ancient History*, vol. 12. Cambridge: Cambridge University Press, 1939.

Ratcliffe, D. *The Raven*. London: Poyser, 1997.

Rędzioch, W. *Our Lady of Fatima*. Narni: Case Editrice Plurigraf, 1996.

Rives, J. 'Human Sacrifice among Pagans and Christians', *Journal of Roman Studies* 85, 1995: 65–85.

R.I.B. Collingwood, R.G. and Wright, R.P. *The Roman Inscriptions of Britain*. Oxford: Oxford University Press, 1965.

Roberts, P. *Life and Death in Pompeii and Herculaneum*. London: The British Museum, 2013.

Romeuf, A.-M. *Les Ex-Voto Gallo-Romains de Chamalières (Puy de Dôme)*. Paris: Éditions de la Maison des Sciences de l'Homme, 2000.

Ross, A. *Pagan Celtic Britain*. London: Routledge and Kegan Paul, 1967.

Royal Commission on Historical Monuments. *Eburacum. Roman York*. R.C.H.M. London: H.M.S.O, 1962.

Salway, P. *Roman Britain*. Oxford: Oxford University Press, 1981.

Salway, P. *The Oxford Illustrated History of Roman Britain*. Oxford: Oxford University Press, 1993.

Sauer, E. *The Archaeology of Religious Hatred*. Stroud: Tempus, 2003.

Saunders, G. *Lincoln in the Bardo*. London: Bloomsbury Press, 2017.

Saunders, N.J. 'Tezcatlipoca. Jaguar Metaphors and the Aztec Mirror of Nature', in Willis, R. ed. *Signifying Animals: Human Meaning in the Natural World*. London: Routledge, 1994: 159–77.

Saunders, N.J. and Gray, D. 'Zémis, trees and symbolic Landscape: Three Taíno Carvings from Jamaica', *Antiquity* 70, 1996: 801–12.

Schädler, U. 'The Doctor's game – new light on the history of ancient board games', in Crummy et al. 2007: 359–75.

Schultes, R.E., Hofmann, A. and Rätsch, C. *Plants of the Gods. Their Sacred, Healing and Hallucinogenic Powers*. Rochester Vermont: Healing Arts Press, 1992.

Sellwood, L. 'The Celtic Coins', in Cunliffe (ed.) 1988: 279–80.

Serjeantson D. and Morris, J. 'Ravens and crows in Iron Age and Roman Europe', *Oxford Journal of Archaeology* 30 (1), 2011: 85–107.

Shaw, R. and Stewart, C. 'Introduction: problematizing syncretism', in Stewart and Shaw (eds) 1994: 1–26.

Sherley-Price, L. trans. *Bede. A History of the English Church and People*. Harmondsworth: Penguin, 1955.

Sherratt, A. 'Sacred and profane substances: the ritual use of narcotics in later Neolithic Europe', in Garwood, P., Jennings, D., Skeates, R. and Toms, J. (eds) *Sacred and Profane: Proceedings of a Conference on Archaeology, Ritual and Religion, Oxford 1989*. Oxford: Oxford University Committee for Archaeology No. 32, 1991: 50–64.

Simón, F. Marco 'Discrepant Behaviour: on magical activities in Hispania and Gallia, in King, T., Schoerner, G., Simón, F. Marco and Haeussler, R. (eds) *Religion in the Roman Empire: The Dynamics of Individualisation*. Oxford: Oxbow, 2012.

Sjöblom, T. 'Advice from a Birdman: Ritual Injunctions and Royal Instructions in TBDD', in Ahlqvist, A., Banks, G.W., Latvio, R. and Nyberg, H. (eds) *Celtica Helsingiensia. Commentationes Humanorum*

Litterarum 107. Helsinki: Societas Scientarum Fennica, 1996: 233–51.

Sjoestedt, M.-L. 'Forbuis Droma Damhghaire. Le Siège de Druim Damhghaire', *Revue Celtique* 43, 1926: 1–123.

Smith, A. *The Differential Use of Constructed Sacred Space in Southern Britain, from the Late Iron Age to the 4th Century* AD. Oxford: British Archaeological Reports British Series No. 318, 2001.

Smith, A. 'Religion and the rural population', in Smith, A., Allen, M., Brindle, T., Fulford, M., Lodwick, L. and Rohnbognor, A. *New Visions of the Countryside of Roman Britain Vol. 3: Life and Death in the Countryside of Roman Britain*. London: Britannia Monograph Series, 2018, in press.

Smith, C. *Late Stone Age Hunters of the British Isles*. London: Routledge: 1992.

Smith, K. *Guides, Guards and Gifts to the Gods: Domesticated Dogs in the Art and Archaeology of Iron Age and Roman Britain*. Oxford: British Archaeological Reports British Series No. 422, 2006.

Smyth, M. 'The Earliest Written Evidence for an Irish View of the World', in Edel, D. ed., *Cultural Identity and Cultural Integration. Ireland and Europe*. Dublin: Four Courts Press, 1995: 23–44.

Sparey Green, C. 'The early Christian Cemetery at Poundbury', Rome: *Publications de l'École Française de Rome. Actes du XIe Congrès International d'Archélogie Chrétienne* Vol. 123, 1989: 2073–75.

Stead, I.M. 'The Reconstruction of Iron Age Buckets from Aylesford and Baldock', in Sieveking, G. de G. ed. *Prehistoric and Roman Studies*. London: British Museum, 1971: 250–82.

Stead, I.M. *The Battersea Shield*. London: British Museum Publications, 1985.

Stead, I.M., Bourke, J.B. and Brothwell, D. (eds) *Lindow Man. The Body in the Bog*. London: British Museum Publications, 1986.

Stewart, C. and Shaw, R. (eds) *Syncretism/Anti-Syncretism. The Politics of Religious Synthesis*. London: Routledge, 1994.

Stokes, W. *Cóir Anmann*. Leipzig: Irische Texte, 1897.

Susini, G. *The Roman Stonecutter. An Introduction to Latin Epigraphy.* Oxford: Basil Blackwell, 1973.

Taylor, A. 'A Roman Lead Coffin with Pipeclay Figurines from Arrington, Cambridgeshire', *Britannia* 24, 1993: 191–225.

The Times 'Dig reveals Iron Age horses and chariot', *The Times* Friday 31 March 2017: 23.

Thevenot, É. *Divinités et sanctuaires de la Gaule.* Paris: Fayard, 1968.

Thomas, C. *Christianity in Roman Britain.* London: Batsford, 1981.

Thomson, A. 'Faith schools need to stamp out prejudice', *The Times* 25 May 2016: 25.

Tierney, J.J. 'The Celtic Ethnography of Posidonius', *Proceedings of the Royal Irish Academy* 60, 1959–60: 247–75.

Tillyard, E.M.W. 'A Cybele Altar in London', *Journal of the Roman Society* 7, 1917: 284–88.

Tomlin, R.S.O. 'The Curse Tablets', in Cunliffe ed. 1988: 59–277.

Tomlin, R.S.O. 'The inscribed lead tablets: an interim report', in Woodward and Leach, 1993: 113–30.

Tomlin, R.S.O. *Roman London's First Voices. Writing Tablets from the Bloomberg Excavations 2010–2014.* London: Museum of London Monograph No. 72, 2014.

Tomlin, R.S.O. 'Roman Britain in 2014: III Inscriptions', *Britannia* 46, 2015, 382–420.

Tomlinson, R.A. *Greek Sanctuaries.* London: Book Club Associates, 1976.

Toynbee, J.M.C. *Art in Roman Britain.* London: Phaidon, 1962.

Toynbee, J.M.C. *A Silver Casket and Strainer from the Walbrook Mithraeum in the City of London.* Leiden: Études préliminaires aux religions orientales dans l'empire romain 4, 1963.

Toynbee, J.M.C. *Art in Britain under the Romans.* Oxford: Clarendon Press, 1964.

Toynbee, J.M.C. 'A Londinium Votive Leaf or Feather and its fellows', in Bird, J., Chapman, H. and Clark, J. *Collectanea Londinensia. Studies in London Archaeology and History Presented to Ralph Merrifield.* London and Middlesex Archaeological Society, Special Paper No. 2, 1978: 128–47.

Untermeyer, L. ed. *Collins Albatross Book of Verse. English and American Poetry from the Thirteenth Century to the Present Day.* London & Glasgow: Collins, 1960.

Vitebsky, P. *The Shaman. Voyages of the Soul: Trance, Ecstasy and Healing from Siberia to the Amazon.* London: Macmillan, 1995.

Watson, G.R. 'The Army of the Republic', in Wacher, J. ed. *The Roman World. Vol. I*, 1987: 75–88.

Webster, J. 'Roman word-power and the Celtic Gods', *Britannia* 26, 1995: 153–61.

Webster, J. 'Necessary comparisons: a post-colonial approach to religious syncretism in the Roman provinces', *World Archaeology* 28 (3), 1997: 324–38.

Webster, J. 'The divine diaspora: problematizing Celtic deities on Hadrian's Wall', paper delivered at the *4th Annual Colloquium on Thinking about Celtic Mythology in the 21st Century, with special reference to archaeology.* Edinburgh: School of Celtic and Scottish Studies, 19–20 November 2016.

Wedlake, W.J. *The Excavation of the Shrine of Apollo at Nettleton, Wiltshire, 1956–1971.* London: Society of Antiquaries of London, 1982.

Wheeler, R.E.M. and Wheeler, T.V. *Report on the Excavation of the Prehistoric, Roman, and Post-Roman Site in Lydney Park, Gloucestershire.* Oxford: Oxford University Press (for the Society of Antiquaries), 1932.

Whipple, T. 'Chinese bones rewrite Roman history', *The Times* Friday 23 September 2016: 21.

White, R. and Barker, Philip. *Wroxeter: Life and Death of a Roman City.* Stroud: Tempus, 1998.

Whittaker, C.R. trans. *Herodian.* London: Heinemann (Loeb), 1969.

Wightman, E.M. *Roman Trier and the Treveri.* London: Hart Davis, 1970.

Wildfang, R.L. and Isager, J. (eds) *Divination and Portents in the Roman World.* Odense: Odense University Press, 2000.

Wilkinson, W.A.C. and Wilkinson, N.H. (eds) *The Dragon Book of Verse.* Oxford: Clarendon Press, 1952.

Williams, D. 'Green Lane, Wanborough: excavations at the Roman religious site 1999', *Surrey Archaeological Collections* vol. 93, 2007: 149–265.

Williams, P.V.A. *Primitive Religion and Healing.* Cambridge: Cambridge University Press, 1979.

Wilmore, S.B. *Crows, Jays, Ravens and their Relatives.* Newton Abbot: David and Charles, 1977.

Wilson, R.J.A. ed. *Roman Maryport and its Setting.* Cumberland & Westmoreland Archaeological Society, 1997.

Wiltshire, P. 'Palynological Analysis of the Organic Material Lodged in the Spout of the Strainer Bowl [from Stanway]', in Crummy et al. 2007: 394–98.

Wiseman, A. and Wiseman, P. *Julius Caesar. The Battle for Gaul (a new translation).* London: Chatto and Windus, 1980.

Withers, H.L. *The Merchant of Venice.* London & Glasgow: Blackie & Son, undated.

Woodward, A. and Leach, P. *The Uley Shrines. Excavation of a ritual complex on West Hill, Uley, Gloucestershire: 1977–9.* London: English Heritage, 1993.

Woodward, P. and Woodward, A. 'Dedicating the Town: urban foundation deposits in Roman Britain', *World Archaeology* 36, 2004: 68–86.

Wright, R.P. and Phillips, E.J. *Roman Inscribed and Sculptured Stones in Carlisle Museum.* Carlisle: Tullie House Museum, 1975.

Wyndham, J. *The Chrysalids.* Harmondsworth: Penguin, 1955.

Zavaroni, A. *On the Structure and Terminology of the Gaulish Calendar.* Oxford: British Archaeological Reports International Series No. 1609, 2007.

Zwicker, I. *Fontes Historiae Religionis Celticae.* Berlin: Walter de Gruyter, 1934.

Acknowledgments

I would like to express my gratitude to a whole range of individuals and institutions that have helped enable this book to come to fruition. First, may I thank the staff at Thames & Hudson, particularly Colin Ridler, Jen Moore, Pauline Hubner, Celia Falconer and Sam Clark for their enthusiasm and support for the project and for their unfailing courtesy and good humour. I am also indebted to the two external reviewers of the text, who made constructive and helpful comments that have served to improve the book. I am grateful to a number of museums, particularly the National Museum Wales, Senhouse Museum, Maryport and Corinium Museum. Steven Birch, leader of the High Pasture Cave Project, has been very generous in sharing unpublished material, as have Dr Mark Lewis and Mark Lodwick of the National Museum Wales. Val McDermid kindly allowed me to use a quote from her book *The Skeleton Road*. Paul Jenkins and Nick Griffiths have permitted my use of their illustrations. My thanks go too to Dr Rowan Williams, who kindly read the text in draft. To you all, and others who have contributed to *Sacred Britannia*, a huge thank you.

Picture Credits

Index

INDEX